The Shadow of Totalitarianism

SUNY series, Intersections: Philosophy and Critical Theory
Rodolphe Gasché, editor

The Shadow of Totalitarianism

Action, Judgment, and Evil in Politics

Javier Burdman

Cover: Jacques Bedel, *Aproximación al mal*, reference Number: R0836 P07, owned by Banco Central De La República Argentina [Central Bank Of Argentina]. Used by permission.

Published by State University of New York Press, Albany

© 2022 State University of New York

All rights reserved

Printed in the United States of America

No part of this book may be used or reproduced in any manner whatsoever without written permission. No part of this book may be stored in a retrieval system or transmitted in any form or by any means including electronic, electrostatic, magnetic tape, mechanical, photocopying, recording, or otherwise without the prior permission in writing of the publisher.

For information, contact State University of New York Press, Albany, NY
www.sunypress.edu

Library of Congress Cataloging-in-Publication Data

Name: Burdman, Javier, 1983– author.
Title: The shadow of totalitarianism : action, judgment, and evil in politics / Javier Burdman.
Description: Albany : State University of New York Press, [2022] | Series: SUNY series, intersections : philosophy and critical theory | Includes bibliographical references and index.
Identifiers: LCCN 2022005751 | ISBN 9781438489995 (hardcover : alk. paper) | ISBN 9781438490014 (ebook) | ISBN 9781438490007 (pbk. : alk. paper)
Subjects: LCSH: Kant, Immanuel, 1724–1804. | Arendt, Hannah, 1906–1975. | Lyotard, Jean-François, 1924–1998. | Totalitarianism. | Good and evil. | Act (Philosophy) | Judgment (Logic) | Political science—Philosophy.
Classification: LCC JC480 .B865 2022 | DDC 320.53—dc23/eng/20220427
LC record available at https://lccn.loc.gov/2022005751

10 9 8 7 6 5 4 3 2 1

Mais, au-delà de l'apparence, dans le cœur de Mlle Vinteuil, le mal, au début du moins, ne fut sans doute pas sans mélange. Une sadique comme elle est l'artiste du mal, ce qu'une créature entièrement mauvaise ne pourrait être car le mal ne lui serait pas extérieur, il lui semblerait tout naturel, ne se distinguerait même pas d'elle; et la vertu, la mémoire des morts, la tendresse filiale, comme elle n'en aurait pas le culte, elle ne trouverait pas un plaisir sacrilège à les profaner.

—Marcel Proust

To María Teresa and José, for the curiosity

Contents

Acknowledgments — xi

Introduction: Totalitarianism and the Problem of Evil in Politics — 1

Part 1: Action

Chapter 1 Arendt's Reassessment of Responsibility — 33

Chapter 2 Kant on the Deceptiveness of Evil — 63

Part 2: Judgment

Chapter 3 Kant on the Sublime and the Judgment of Action — 93

Chapter 4 Lyotard on Good and Evil in Postmodernity — 127

Conclusion: Extreme Evil as a Response to Political Uncertainty — 153

Notes — 173

Bibliography — 195

Index — 205

Acknowledgments

This being my first book, it is indebted to many people and institutions who contributed to my intellectual trajectory until this point. Given that the project started during my graduate studies, I will begin there. I thank, first of all, those who encouraged and supported my first steps in academic research in Argentina: Emilio de Ipola, Ernesto Laclau, Gerardo Aboy Carlés, and Marcos Novaro. The University of Buenos Aires supported my first research project through an "Estímulo" research grant for senior students, and the Argentine National Research Council (CONICET) supported part of my graduate studies in Argentina with a doctoral fellowship.

The two years I spent as a graduate student in the Comparative Literature program at the State University of New York at Buffalo were intellectually decisive. Tyler Williams was not only an acute intellectual partner, but also a great friend and office mate who helped me navigate life in the United States during my first days there. Among the faculty, Joan Copjec and Rodolphe Gasché were especially influential in my way of thinking and supportive of my projects. If Rodolphe had not taken a moment to tell me "I think you have something there" after reading my seminar paper on Kant's notion of radical evil in connection to Arendt's *Eichmann in Jerusalem*, this book would probably not have been written. I am thankful to SUNY Buffalo for the financial support to my graduate studies between 2009 and 2011.

I developed most of the research for this book throughout my PhD studies in political science at Northwestern University. I am thankful to Sara Monoson, James Farr, and Bonnie Honig for discussing with me different parts of the project at the early stages. I am also thankful to my colleagues at Northwestern for the intellectual and personal support:

Boris Litvin, Tristan Bradshaw, Emre Gercek, Desiree Weber, Chris Sardo, Giuseppe Cumella, Lucy Cane, Gent Carrabregu, Arda Güçler, Anna Terwiel, Jennifer Forestal, Hye-Yun Kang, Kevin Levay, Sean Lee, Erin Lockwood, Rodrigo Barrenechea, and Isabel Castillo. I read Lyotard for the first time in the "Deleuze Reading Group" at Northwestern, and this ended up having a crucial impact on the project that led to this book. I am thankful to David Johnson, Jonathan Agins, and Guy Elgat for the thorough discussion of Lyotard's *The Differend* in 2013. The members of my dissertation committee were of course closely involved in helping me develop and refine my ideas, so this book is deeply indebted to Mary Dietz, who was a generous and supportive adviser throughout my time at Northwestern, as well as to Lars Toender, Peter Fenves, Samuel Weber, and Christoph Menke.

I am thankful to Northwestern University for its financial support to my graduate studies. Within Northwestern, the Holocaust Educational Foundation and the Paris Program in Critical Theory supported part of my research. I am thankful to Marc Crépon and to the École Normale Supérieure for hosting my research between 2014 and 2015, as part of an exchange program. My colleague and friend Agnès Grivaux helped me learn the workings of the French academy during that time. The Deutscher Akademischer Austauschdienst (DAAD) supported a one-year research stay at the Goethe University Frankfurt between 2015 and 2016. I am thankful to the Goethe University and to Christoph Menke for hosting me during that time.

I developed significant parts of this book after the conclusion of my PhD in 2018. The Research Center "Normative Orders" at the Goethe University Frankfurt supported my research between 2018 and 2019, with a postdoctoral fellowship. I am thankful to Frieder Vogelmann, Kristina Lepold, Linda Monsees, Franziska Fay, Jason Mast, Alexis Galán, Tobias Wille, and Jonas Heller for their friendship and intellectual support during this time. The European Commission supported my research between 2020 and 2021, through a Marie Skłodowska-Curie Individual Fellowship to develop my research at the University of Strasbourg. I am thankful to Franck Fischbach and to the Department of Philosophy at Strasbourg for hosting and supporting my research there. During this time, Carmen Lea Dege became a friend and an intellectual partner who was enormously helpful in improving the ideas in this book. I am especially thankful to Carmen and to Frieder Vogelmann for their comments on the last version of the manuscript.

The trajectory that led to this book involved multiple moves across countries and languages. In order to face this challenge, it was crucial to have the support of my family and friends. My lifelong friends from Argentina always encouraged and supported my projects. For that, I am deeply thankful to Alejandro Flombaum, Juan Pablo Beltrán, Lionel Skliar, Martín Menashed, and Julián Tolchinsky. I am also enormously thankful to Tomás Bril Mascarenhas and Gonzalo Miri for their unyielding company from the distance and the wise advices throughout the years. Maïté Marciano, Sabrina Jaromin, and Fyodor Sakhnovski became close friends toward the end of my graduate studies in Chicago and gave me invaluable support in difficult times. My four years in Frankfurt were much more fun and less lonely thanks to my friends Lucio Mamone, Daniel Dodds, Eduardo Chia, and Dafni Tokas. Throughout the years, ever since I arrived to Buffalo in 2009, Lena Taub's company and intellectual support has been a crucial part of my life. I am deeply thankful to Lena for helping me in the worst moments and for celebrating with me in the good ones.

I owe to my family a passion for intellectual inquiry and a desire for new challenges. My parents, María Teresa and José, and my sister Luciana, supported me at every step of my intellectual development, even when it led me far away from them. The concern of my parents and my sister for my happiness and well-being above everything else was a constant reminder that no difficulty was the end of the world. Their unconditional company was essential for persevering in an often lonely, yearslong project. Despite the distance, my parents and my sister remained close, and the moments we spent reconvening in different cities and countries have been among the happiest of my life.

Parts of chapters 1 and 2 were published in the article "Between Banality and Radicality: Arendt and Kant on Evil and Responsibility," *European Journal of Political Theory* 18, no. 2 (2019). Parts of chapter 4 were published in "Universality without Consensus: Jean-François Lyotard on Politics in Postmodernity," *Philosophy and Social Criticism* 46, no. 3 (2020). Parts of this book were developed within the Marie Skłodowska-Curie Action "Universality, Conflict, and Social Critique," funded through the European Union's Horizon 2020 research and innovation program under grant agreement no. 841825.

Introduction

Totalitarianism and the Problem of Evil in Politics

In her 1954 essay "Understanding and Politics," commenting on the recent emergence of "the popular use of the word 'totalitarianism' for the purpose of denouncing some supreme political evil," Hannah Arendt claims,

> Yet while popular language thus recognizes a new event by accepting a new word, it invariably uses such concepts as synonyms for others signifying old and familiar evils—aggression and lust for conquest in the case of imperialism, terror and lust for power in the case of totalitarianism. . . . It is as though with the first step, finding a new name for the new force which will determine our political destinies, we orient ourselves toward new and specific conditions, whereas with a second step (and, as it were, on second thought) we regret our boldness and console ourselves that nothing worse or less familiar will take place than general human sinfulness.[1]

Ever since the end of World War II, we have been aware that "totalitarianism" represents a new form of evil, which is why a new word has appeared to designate it. Yet the acknowledgment of this novelty does not necessarily mean that we have come to terms with it, that we have overcome the temptation to go back to familiar ground by interpreting the new under the light of older, long-established concepts. In order to fully accept the novelty of a phenomenon, it is necessary to have the boldness to move and remain beyond our familiar conceptions about the conditions in which we live. This is what Arendt calls "understanding": the judgment of that which has ruined our standards for judgment, so that by our own initiative we become capable of finding new meaning in a world that has seemingly lost it.[2] The very appearance of the word *totalitarianism* shows that a new form of political evil emerged in the middle of the twentieth century, but the work of understanding this novelty is indefinitely open: "if we want to be at home on this earth, even at the price of being at home in this century, we must try to take part in the interminable dialogue with the essence of totalitarianism."[3]

Although Arendt wrote these remarks in the years following the discovery of the camps, the impact of totalitarianism on politics and political theory is very much present today. Together with other events of around the middle of the twentieth century, such as total war and anticolonial struggles, totalitarianism constitutes a foundational experience for contemporary political theory. It marks the end of the Enlightenment's confidence in reason and historical progress as a ground for political action, and the transition to an intellectual context that has been repeatedly characterized as "postmetaphysical," "postfoundational" and "postmodern." The fact that terror and systematic mass murder could happen along, and not against, the forces of progress and modernization, showed to what extent the whole conceptual framework of modern political thought needed to be revised.[4] Today, as political phenomena that resemble central aspects of totalitarianism, such as ethno-nationalism, authoritarianism, detention camps, and widespread lying in the public sphere, become once again prominent features of Western politics, the need to revisit many of the questions connected to the emergence of totalitarianism becomes pressing.

This book is concerned with one of the central challenges that, according to Arendt, totalitarianism presented to the modern world, namely, understanding a new form of evil. I argue, following a series of remarks by Arendt, that our understanding of evil is imbedded in our conception of action and judgment. Departing from a series of previous studies that focus exclusively on Arendt's and Kant's notions of evil, I examine how the problem of understanding the emergence of a new form of evil contributes to shape notions of action and judgment in moral and political philosophy. I explore this issue in Kant, Arendt, and Lyotard, because the three thinkers develop their notions of action and judgment to a large extent in response to their views on evil. Following their perspectives, one central goal of my inquiry is to show that the problem of evil is not an independent, isolated concern for political theory, but rather essential in the development of some of the central categories of the field. Specifically, my claim is that in order to understand the kind of evil displayed by totalitarianism, we need an understanding of action and judgment that accounts for it. This approach is indebted to Susan Neiman's study of the centrality of the problem of evil in the development of modern philosophy.[5] However, while Neiman focuses on the importance of the problem of evil for questions of knowledge, I focus on its impact on questions of moral and political action and judgment.

In order to arrive at a conception of action and judgment that responds to the kind of evil displayed by totalitarianism, I develop an interpretative and a theoretical argument. The interpretative argument is that the concern with the emergence of a new form of evil in modernity can be traced back to Kant's moral philosophy, and that this concern contributes to shape the concepts of action and judgment in Kant as well as in two post-Kantian political thinkers influenced by the experience of totalitarianism, namely, Arendt and Lyotard. Going back to Kant for an understanding of totalitarian evil may seem counterintuitive, given Arendt's claim that it represents a new kind of evil. However, this claim does not mean, as Arendt shows in *The Origins of Totalitarianism*, that the multiple trends that would culminate in totalitarianism had not been unfolding in the decades and even centuries before it. Kant knew nothing of totalitarianism as a political movement or regime, but he did observe the incipient development of new forms of evil that contained the seeds of the totalitarian mentality. Richard J. Bernstein has noted the originality of Kant's conception of evil in his late writings, which break with the long-standing philosophical view of evil as deficiency.[6] Building on Bernstein's thesis, I will argue in chapters 2 and 3 that Kant's concern with a new kind of evil plays a central role in his conception of action and judgment.

The relevance of Kant's practical philosophy for an understanding of totalitarianism becomes clear if we read it in dialogue with Arendt and Lyotard, whose work is deeply influenced by it. Both authors are concerned with the novelty of totalitarian evil, and develop their notions of action and judgment in response to it. In so doing, they continue Kant's insight into the nature of action and judgment in modernity, while explicitly unpacking its political implications. This does not mean that they follow every aspect of Kant's thought, or that the three authors have identical views. However, as I will show throughout the chapters, they pursue a similar conceptual framework stemming in part from the acknowledgment of the emergence of a new form of evil in modernity. By reconstructing this conceptual framework running through Kant, Arendt, and Lyotard, my interpretative argument will stress the importance of the problem of evil for our understanding of action and judgment in modern politics.

The interpretative argument that will orient my inquiry leads to a theoretical argument regarding the nature of evil in modern politics. On the basis of my readings of Kant, Arendt, and Lyotard, I will argue that the kind of evil displayed by totalitarianism consists in the refusal of a fundamental uncertainty involved in action and judgment. I will show that, for the three authors, action and judgment involve an experience of uncertainty in the following two senses: the actor does not know the meaning or the outcome of her action when it takes place, and the person who judges lacks an unquestionable rule that guarantees that her judgment is valid. By contrast to the long-standing view of evil as failure to comply with a law, principle, or procedure, I will claim that evil, or at least the kind of evil characteristic of those who become complicit in totalitarian regimes, stems from a decision to refuse the fundamental uncertainty involved in action and judgment. This experience of uncertainty, I will hold, constitutes a basis for a nonfoundationalist political ethics that, instead of grounding moral action and judgment on a rule, affirms the exposure to uncertainty that is inherent to them. According to this political ethics, the good (which, as we will see, should be understood as "the lesser evil") consists in accepting the fundamental uncertainty involved in acting and judging, while evil consists in refusing this uncertainty and striving to eliminate it.

The Problem: A "New" Form of Evil

The point of departure of my inquiry is Arendt's claim that totalitarianism constitutes a new form of evil. It is therefore necessary to specify what exactly she means by this. Arendt explains the novelty of totalitarianism in her essay "Social Science Techniques and the Study of Concentration Camps." The camps, she claims, represent a "stumbling-block on the road toward the proper understanding of contemporary politics and society," which must lead social scientists "to reconsider their hitherto unquestioned fundamental preconceptions regarding the course of the world and human behavior."[7] The main perplexity that the camps present to our conception of human behavior is that they have no utility, that is, they serve no evident purpose that could be explained in terms of self-interest. Given the usual idea that evil deeds stem from serving some sort of self-interest, the existence of the camps appears to be completely senseless: "If we assume that most of our actions are of a utilitarian nature and that our evil deeds spring from some 'exaggeration' of self-interest, then we are forced to conclude that this particular institution of totalitarianism is beyond human understanding."[8] The systematic extermination of entire populations, according to Arendt, was not only useless for the war efforts, but even detrimental to them, to the point that "it was as though Nazis were convinced that it was of greater importance to run extermination factories than to win the war."[9] It is this anti-utilitarian nature of totalitarian crimes that renders them "unprecedented." While mass murder for the sake of economic gains or power has been frequent throughout human history, the extermination of entire populations against any visible self-interest is new: "The extraordinary difficulty which we have in attempting to understand the institution of the concentration camp and to fit it into the record of human history is precisely the absence of such utilitarian criteria."[10]

Totalitarian evil is then "new" because it lacks the utilitarian motivations that we usually associate with evil deeds, which makes difficult to understand in what sense it is "evil" at all. But if this nonutilitarian evil is new, how does it differ from "old" kinds of evil? We find a partial response to this question in *The Origins of Totalitarianism*, where Arendt claims that "it is inherent in our entire philosophical tradition that we cannot conceive of a 'radical evil,'" which she describes as an evil beyond recognizable evil motives such as self-interest, greed, covetousness, resentment, lust for power, and cowardice.[11] Arendt does not explain why philosophers have not conceived of an evil beyond these motivations. In a later essay, however, she claims: "that evil is a mere privation, negation, or exception from the rule is the nearly unanimous opinion of all philosophers."[12] From the viewpoint of philosophy, evil is never done willingly, but only as the effect of a failure to do good. If I kill an innocent person, it must be because of some sort of self-interest that prevents me from doing good, and not because killing an innocent person is an end in itself. Therefore, according to this conception, evil must always be explained in terms of a utilitarian motive that prevents us from doing good, as opposed to a willful choice. In the case of totalitarianism, this framework does not work, because systematic mass murder produces no evident benefit. How, then, are we to understand the crimes that took place in the Nazi death camps?

We can further specify the contrast between the new kind of evil displayed by the camps and the traditional, pretotalitarian image of evil by turning to Jean-Luc Nancy, who analyzes the novelty of the camps for the philosophy of evil. In *The Experience of Freedom*, commenting on Thomas Mann's words from 1939, according to which "we know once again what good and evil are," Nancy claims that "the first requirement is not to understand by this the return to a 'well-known' good and evil."[13] In order to explain this "well-known" understanding of evil to which we must not return, Nancy claims that there are three lessons we must heed:

1. the closure of all theodicy or logodicy, and the affirmation that evil is strictly unjustifiable;

2. the closure of every thought of evil as the defect or perversion of a particular being, and its inscription in the being of existence: evil as positive wickedness;

3. the actual incarnation of evil in the exterminating horror of the mass grave: evil is unbearable and unpardonable.[14]

These three elements constitute what Nancy calls "the modern knowledge of evil," which is "different in nature and intensity from every prior knowledge, though it still harbors certain of its traits (essentially, in sum, the evil that was 'nothing' has become 'something' that thought cannot reduce)."[15] Before modernity, most philosophers saw evil as nothing, in the sense that it had no cause or substance on its own, but was rather the deficiency of a cause or substance. We can only know what the good is, and then proceed to know evil by subtracting something from it. This means, in turn, that nothing "produces" evil. There is no force of evil, but only a force of goodness that, for reasons that must be explained, sometimes fails to be effective. It is the attempt at an explanation of the absence of complete goodness that has led to theodicy and logodicy, that is, to the idea that evil is ultimately justifiable and therefore, at least from a certain viewpoint, forgivable. According to this conception, the only reason why someone would do evil is because of an incapacity to do good, never because of a willful choice, never as "positive wickedness."

Reading Nancy's remarks on the philosophy of evil in dialogue with Arendt's description of the nature of the camps, we see that the novelty of totalitarian evil consists in that it does not fit the long-standing philosophical association of evil with deficiency. We cannot explain the existence of the camps in Nazi Germany in terms of ignorance, irrational impulses, or exaggerated self-interest, as if Nazi criminals lacked knowledge, reason, or self-restraint. As both Arendt and Nancy point out, this idea of evil as deficiency is a consistent image in the philosophical tradition, from Plato's claim that injustice brings disharmony to the soul, through Aristotle's idea that evil stems from error regarding what is good, Plotinus's conception of evil as an imperfect imitation of the good, Augustine's and Leibniz's claims that evil is not a cause but the privation of a cause, Spinoza's view that evil stems from a failure to understand the necessity of one's own actions, to Hegel's interpretation of evil as a necessary moment in the unfolding of reason.[16] Although all these philosophers suggest at some points that evil is something more than mere absence of goodness, they all repeatedly identify evil with lack of knowledge or lack of self-mastery. The problem posed by totalitarian evil is that it does not correspond to this image and to the motivations associated with it, which is why we need a new understanding.

Although few scholars today defend the view of evil as deficiency, few studies have developed an alternative to it. Recent inquiries into the problem of evil influenced by Arendt have adopted three main approaches. One approach, developed by Charles T. Mathewes, revisits the notion of evil as deficiency in response to Arendt's views on totalitarian evil. These views, Mathewes argues, are part of what he calls an "Augustinian tradition" on evil, according to which "evil action is a kind of action which fails, in an important way, to be action at all."[17] A second approach, developed by Neiman, Richard Bernstein, and Peter Dews, traces the importance of the problem of evil in the history of philosophy, showing that it plays a more prominent role than it is usually believed.[18] A third approach, presented by María Pía Lara and Bernstein in another study, shifts the focus from evil as such to the ways in which we respond to novel experiences of evil, developing new ways to talk about it and to judge it.[19] While Mathewes remains within the paradigm of evil as deficiency, Neiman, Bernstein, Dews, and Lara refrain from developing a theory of evil, shifting the focus instead to the ways in which philosophers and ordinary people write and talk about evil. Thus, it would seem like there is no theoretically sound notion of evil that replaces the image of deficiency. Either we remain and actualize this image, as Mathewes proposes, or we leave behind the attempt to develop a theory of evil on the grounds that what we call "evil" is mutable and unpredictable, as Neiman, Bernstein, Dews, and Lara suggest in different ways.

One goal of this book is to move the discussion on evil forward by proposing a new, theoretically coherent perspective that departs from the model of deficiency and the motivations associated with it. According to my theoretical argument of evil as a refusal of uncertainty, people do not engage in the kind of evil displayed by totalitarianism because their capacity to do the right thing is overpowered by prejudice, ignorance, selfishness, or hatred. Instead, they engage in this kind of evil because they choose to act and to judge in a way that conceals the uncertainty regarding the meaning and outcome of action and the validity of judgment. As we will see in each of the chapters, action and judgment involve uncertainty because they generate relations with other actions and judgments. This uncertainty is a source of anxiety, because there is no guarantee that the meaning of our action or the validity of our judgment will remain the way we intended. In the face of this anxiety, one may choose to act and to judge in such a way that one endures the uncertainty that is inherent to the establishment of relationships, or otherwise seek to cover the anxiety under rules for action and judgment that determine their meaning. The kind of evil displayed by totalitarianism stems from this choice.

Of course, totalitarian evil is a complex and multifaceted phenomenon, and I do not intend to cover all its aspects. There are certainly people who play a role in totalitarian movements on the basis of many different motivations. However, one kind of motivation that is especially difficult to understand is that of people who seem perfectly normal and usually capable of distinguishing between right and wrong, yet adapt and become functional to widespread crimes. This kind of complicity is perhaps the least spectacular, for it is characteristic of everyday functionaries rather than ideological leaders. But it is likely the most widespread under totalitarianism, for it underlies the support of millions of otherwise normal people to the regime. For the sake of conceptual simplicity, I will often use the term *evil* to refer to this specific kind of evil. I will bracket the question of how it connects to other kinds of evil—for example, that of those with long-standing ideological commitments to totalitarian ideologies, or who become complicit with them out of sheer opportunistic selfishness. The goal of this study is not to settle the problem of evil by reducing it to one of its faces, but rather to illuminate one of its most perplexing manifestations.

Uncertainty

In the context of this book, "uncertainty" refers to lack of mastery over the meaning of action and the validity of judgment by virtue of their inherent exposure to other actions and judgments. Every time we act with or on others, the action is exposed to their reactions, and every time we express a judgment to others, our judgment is exposed to other judgments. As a consequence of this exposure, the meaning of action and the validity of judgment are uncertain. An action that seems courageous, virtuous, or generous at the instant it takes place may be considered cowardly, vicious, or selfish later on. A judgment that seems justified may be later revealed as flawed, erroneous, or deceitful. This may sound like a banal fact, for it is obvious that we are limited beings who cannot achieve absolute certainty over the meaning of action and the validity of judgment. However, for the authors that are at the center of this book, uncertainty is not merely an empirical limitation to our capacity to master our actions and judgments, but rather a fundamental experience without which we would be unable to act and to judge at all. Uncertainty is not only the absence of certainty, which just happens to be out of reach for us. Instead, the lack of mastery that we experience in action and judgment is essential to them, because it is part of our capacity to establish relations with others. Uncertainty is not only an epistemic category, but also an experience—a kind of feeling that emerges out of the establishment of relations.

The experience of uncertainty that is involved in action and judgment is at the basis of different ethical stances. As we will see in chapter 1, Arendt believes that the unpredictability of action produces frustration, and thus the desire to withdraw from action altogether. Building on Arendt's views on this point, I will argue throughout the chapters that action and judgment generate a desire to withdraw from their uncertainty, in an attempt to make their meaning and validity secure. Whether we accept uncertainty or pursue the desire to overcome it is a fundamental ethical choice that determines two ways of acting and judging. If we accept the uncertainty of action and judgment, we welcome our exposure to the establishment of unpredictable relationships with others. If, by contrast, we reject uncertainty, we attempt to subordinate these relationships to fixed rules and patterns that reduce and potentially eliminate unpredictability. The kind of evil that is at the basis of complicity in totalitarianism, according to my theoretical argument, consists in an extreme form of this attempt to overcome uncertainty. In the context of this book, evil refers to an attitude by which abiding by a rule that determines that our actions are morally good, and our judgments valid, takes primacy over the uncertain outcome of acting and judging in ways that expose their meaning and validity to relationships with others.

In order to avoid misunderstandings, some preliminary clarifications (to which I will return in the conclusion) are important. First, the alternative between accepting and rejecting uncertainty is often concealed behind everyday practices and comes to the fore only in exceptional occasions. It is in situations where we face ethical decisions that uncertainty becomes an issue. Evidently, we cannot always act as if our values were questionable and mutable. There are moments, however, when we do experience the uncertainty of such values, or the fact that we do not clearly know how to act or judge on their basis. As we will see in chapter 1, this is the kind of situation produced by totalitarian regimes, which overturn long-standing values and replace them with new ones. In this kind of situation, people face the choice of whether to look for some kind of rule that conceals uncertainty and provides them with peace of mind, or accept the fact that the meaning of their actions and the validity of their judgments will be determined by the web of actions and judgments in which they insert themselves, and which they partly constitute. While the second stance does not guarantee that one will do the right thing, the first stance is at the core of the kind of evil that leads to complicity in totalitarianism. To reject uncertainty means that when confronting situations where our values become problematic, we hold on to rules or procedures that provide a sense of moral assurance. As we will see in chapters 1 and 2, this attitude undermines our sense of responsibility and makes us indifferent to the moral worth of our actions.

A second point of clarification is that accepting uncertainty does not lead to a sort of skepticism, but rather to a specific attitude toward the meaning of action and the validity of judgment. Awareness that the values on the basis of which we act and judge are ambivalent and changing does not imply that we should not really believe in them. It is perfectly possible to act on the basis of an idea, while remaining aware that whether our action or judgment adequately expresses this idea is uncertain. As it will become clear, especially in chapter 3, practical ideas, that is, the ideas that determine the worth of actions, are inherently unpresentable (there are courageous actions, but no action that corresponds to the idea of courage). We do not know what courage, justice, or goodness as such look like, even if we need these ideas to orient our actions toward others. Given that the ideas that orient the establishment of relationships with others involve uncertainty (we cannot know if our actions and judgments truly correspond to these ideas), we cannot act or judge without confronting this uncertainty. Yet precisely because this uncertainty is involved in every action and judgment, accepting uncertainty is an attitude that enables the universalistic aspirations of political action and judgment. As we will see in part 2, judgments are universal not by virtue of correctly applying a rule, but rather by virtue of expressing the experience of uncertainty that is inherently involved in every action and judgment. This is the kind of universality grounded on feeling that Kant identifies as specific to aesthetic judgments.

Finally, the distinction between accepting and refusing uncertainty does not overlap with a new straightforward distinction between good and evil. While refusing uncertainty is at the basis of the kind of evil characteristic of totalitarianism, accepting uncertainty is not equivalent to moral virtue. As I will argue in the conclusion, accepting the uncertainty of action and judgment entails replacing a politics oriented to the good with one oriented to what Lyotard calls "the lesser evil." This means that action and judgment should not be oriented to the realization of moral ideas, because we can never know whether our representation of such ideas is adequate. Instead, action and judgment should strive to counteract an evil with another evil: injustice with a lesser injustice, exclusion with a lesser exclusion, oppression with a lesser oppression. Of course, we never know what the "lesser" evil is, but this is precisely why we must be ready to face the unpredictable meaning of our actions and judgments. Unlike the politics of the good, which seeks to approximate moral ideals that are presumed to be objects of knowledge, the politics of the lesser evil acts and judges on the basis of the uncertainty of such ideas, welcoming unexpected responses that may expose their complicity with injustice, exclusion, and domination.

This last point of clarification should warn against the idea that uncertainty constitutes a new moral foundation on which we can rely to orient action and judgment, as if any attempt to limit them through predictable, durable institutions and social behaviors were complicit with evil. Evidently, this is not what Kant, Arendt, or Lyotard have in mind. Accepting uncertainty does not mean rejecting anything predictable, stable, or durable—on the contrary, it means welcoming the fragile relations between actions and judgments that are the source of predictability, stability, and durability. Accepting uncertainty means accepting that the meaning and validity of the institutions and social relations that orient action and judgment may change and call for new actions and judgments, leading to new institutions and kinds of social relations. Evil in politics, according to my thesis, is not an effect of limiting uncertainty. Instead, it is an effect of imagining and positing standards for action and judgment that are certain, in the sense that they are independent of responses by other actions and judgments. In other words, evil in politics takes place when we attempt to replace the predictability, stability, and durability that we build within relationships between actions and judgments with purportedly certain standards that stand above them.

By putting uncertainty at the center of the problem of evil, this book seeks to contribute to our understanding of political ethics in a context of growing pluralism. In the last decades, a number of political theorists have argued for an ethics based on the acknowledgment of the radical pluralism characteristic of modern societies, by contrast to the search for transcendental moral foundations for action and judgment.[20] One of the implications of pluralism is that different values are often in conflict with one another, and it is difficult, if not impossible, to find universally shared principles for action and judgment. While I agree that political ethics in contemporary societies must take pluralism as a point of departure, as opposed to subordinating it under transcendental principles, it is also the case that the uncertainty generated by this pluralism is a potential source of new forms of evil in politics. The instability and plasticity of values generates anxiety and the desire for stable, secure rules for action and judgment. Although this book is partly an attempt to understand political ethics in a way that is responsive to value pluralism and the readiness to endure uncertainty that it demands, it also brings attention to the dangerous reactions that such pluralism may generate. In my view, it is important that political theorists examine not only the foundations and orientation of political ethics, but also the reasons why political actors often disregard and even undermine ethical consideration altogether.

Given that this book is mainly concerned with the problem of evil in politics, I will devote more systematic attention to the ways in which people refuse uncertainty than to the question of how to accept uncertainty. This latter question is of course essential, and it has been the subject of multiple studies in recent decades. In examining the attitude of those who refuse uncertainty, I will touch on the issue of how action and judgment can accept uncertainty. "The politics of the lesser evil," which I briefly develop in the conclusion on the basis of my reading of Lyotard in chapter 4, hints at a possible orientation in response to the fundamental uncertainty involved in action and judgment. If I do not engage with this and other implications of the thesis of evil as a refusal of uncertainty more systematically, it is in order to keep the inquiry focused on the problem of evil in politics. Because of this focus, the question of "what not to do" will be more central throughout the book than the question of "what to do." My hope is that my account of evil, based on my readings of Kant, Arendt, and Lyotard, will inform future studies of political ethics in contemporary societies.

The Nature of Totalitarian Crimes

My inquiry takes as its point of departure a question that was a sustained concern in Arendt's late writings, as well as in historical studies of Nazi crimes: why do ordinary people, usually capable to distinguishing between right and wrong, become complicit with regimes that demand that they act in ways that are glaringly morally criminal? Arendt's famous and polemical notion of "the banality of evil" emerged to a large extent in response to this question. I will examine the implications of this notion in detail in chapter 1. But before turning to the conceptual analysis that will orient my inquiry, it is necessary to consider to what extent Arendt's reflections adequately respond to historical facts, as far as historical research has described them. While it is beyond the scope of this book to engage in historiographical debates regarding the motivations and psychological traits of ordinary people who turned into willful executioners of mass murder, it is important to stress that historical studies do not disprove, but rather support the relevance of Arendt's perspective, as well as of the focus on uncertainty that will be at the center of my inquiry.

In a recent book, historian Bettina Stangneth challenges Arendt's account of Adolf Eichmann, the man responsible for executing the "Final Solution" and exterminating all European Jews, on the grounds that it wrongly dismisses his ideological commitment to the worldview of National Socialism. After the Israeli Foreign Intelligence Service detected and seized Eichmann in Argentina, where he was living under a false identity since the end of the War, he was taken to Jerusalem, where he stood trial for crimes against the Jews in 1961. While according to Arendt, who witnessed the trial and wrote weekly reports on it for *The New Yorker*, Eichmann was above all a careerist, largely indifferent to the task that he had to perform for the sake of his personal advancement, Stangneth shows that Eichmann remained an anti-Semite well after his involvement in the Final Solution. In trying to understand Eichmann by taking his words at face value, Stangneth claims, Arendt "fell into his trap: Eichmann-in-Jerusalem was little more than a mask."[21] In other words, Arendt's description of Eichmann as a thoughtless individual, lacking ideological convictions, was nothing but a misrepresentation produced by Eichmann himself. In reality, according to Stangneth, Eichmann shared and wanted to actively pursue the cause of National Socialism.

While Stangneth's historical analysis complicates parts of Arendt's description of Eichmann, it does not remove the problem that she referred to with the notion of "the banality of evil." Stangneth believes that Eichmann's long-standing anti-Semitism shows that he was not thoughtless, but rather ideologically committed to the Final Solution. However, as we will see in chapter 1, Arendt does not see thoughtlessness and ideological commitment as contradictory or mutually exclusive. She may have neglected, due to unavailable information at the time, Eichmann's enduring anti-Semitism, but she did not deny the fact that he had been committed to the cause for which he was acting. In her report of Eichmann's trial, it is clear that Eichmann did become committed to the execution of the Final Solution, even to the point of disobeying direct orders by his superiors and putting his own well-being in danger toward the end of the war. The core of the problem involved in the notion of "the banality of evil," which concerned Arendt in her late writings, is not whether individuals believe or not in the cause for which they are acting, but rather how they believe in this cause. Arendt does not deny that Eichmann was committed to the Final Solution when he was responsible for it, but she believes that this commitment was "superficial" and "shallow," because it was detached from any thinking about the meaning of his actions. For Eichmann, subjecting himself to a cause and sacrificing his self-interest for it was an assurance that he was doing the right thing—that he was "a good citizen."

Historical debates around the nature of totalitarian crimes suggest that Arendt's reflections in *Eichmann in Jerusalem* and later writings are not empirically misguided. In this regard, it is worth considering part of the controversy that followed the publication of Daniel Goldhagen's *Hitler's Willing Executioners*. In this book, Goldhagen argues that the main reason why hundreds of thousands of Germans became complicit with mass murder is a long-standing, progressively "eliminationist" anti-Semitism characteristic of Germany. As he puts it succinctly: "antisemitism moved many thousands of 'ordinary' Germans—and would have moved millions more, had they been appropriately positioned—to slaughter Jews."[22] This anti-Semitism, Goldhagen argues, constituted a "dominant cognitive thread" that allowed people to quickly adapt to the eliminationist program developed by National Socialism.[23] Even if most people had previously never engaged in actions against the Jews, strong negative beliefs about them were so ingrained among Germans that many were predisposed to be convinced that such actions were necessary. In sum, an anti-Semite worldview explains why ordinary people became willfully complicit with the mass murder of Jews, even if they did not actively participate in the development of the extermination plan.

The responses that followed Goldhagen's book show how difficult it is to describe the actions of people who became complicit in mass murder without considering theoretical problems concerning moral agency. Leaving aside the debates around the evidence supporting Goldhagen's argument, one central point of discussion was whether his analysis adequately described the active complicity, as opposed to passive submission, of those responsible for executing criminal orders. By emphasizing anti-Semitism as a primary, and even sole, causal element determining complicity in totalitarian crimes, Goldhagen sought to stress the willfulness of the criminals, so as to dispel the idea that they were forced to act against their will. Yet Goldhagen's emphasis on anti-Semitism leads to another kind of seemingly exculpatory account: if the Germans saw the world through an anti-Semitic cognitive framework, was their will not deterministically shaped by it?[24] Is not the anti-Semitic cognitive framework, rather than any moral choice, responsible for what happened? As historian Christopher Browning pointed out, the dichotomy between doing something willfully or against one's will does not exhaust the possibilities involved in making moral decisions. Shifting the focus from "willfulness" to "choice," Browning claims that "the perpetrators not only had the capacity to choose but exercised that choice in various ways that covered the spectrum from enthusiastic participation, through dutiful, nominal, or regretful compliance, to different degrees of evasion."[25]

Browning's nuanced reflections on the motivations of complicity in totalitarian crimes capture the depth of the problem in a way that resembles Arendt's own inquiries. According to Arendt, Eichmann's actions, as well as those of other Nazi criminals, challenged long-standing ideas about moral agency and personal responsibility, because they acted as if they had made no moral choice. By describing Eichmann as "unable to think," Arendt conveyed the idea that he had performed his duty without ever considering the moral implications of doing so. Moreover, he took for granted than compliance with duty above any regard for his own interests was the only morally right thing to do. Based on an analysis of the members of the Police Battalion 101, which was deployed to Poland during the war to capture and kill Jews, Browning arrives at a fairly similar idea:

> The largest group within the battalion did whatever they were asked to do, without ever risking the onus of confronting authority or appearing weak, but they did not volunteer for or celebrate the killing. Increasingly numb and brutalized, they felt more pity for themselves because of the "unpleasant" work they had been assigned than they did for their dehumanized victims. For the most part, they did not think what they were doing was wrong or immoral, because the killing was sanctioned by legitimate authority. Indeed, for the most part they did not try to think, period.[26]

Like Arendt, Browning identifies a kind of engagement in glaringly criminal actions (killing hundreds of innocent people) that lacks the traditional marks of evil, such as selfishness, cruelty, or hatred. Moreover, these actions have an element in common with moral virtue, namely, the fulfillment of one's duty even against one's own wishes. The problem posed by the complicity of otherwise ordinary people in totalitarian crimes is to understand the kind of moral agency that is involved in them. In chapter 1, I will argue that it is this kind of moral agency that Arendt captured with her notion of "the banality of evil," and which is ultimately rooted in a refusal to relate to others by means of action and judgment.

As Browning points out in the end of his book, the perplexing fact that ordinary people are capable of becoming willfully complicit in mass murder cannot be reduced to the deterministic effect of preexisting systems of beliefs. In order to understand the nature of totalitarian evil, at least as far as complicity by ordinary people is concerned, it is necessary to problematize the categories by which we understand moral and political action. Eichmann and the members of Police Battalion 101 did not become involved in mass murder out of a genuine belief in a murderous ideology, but rather out of a willingness to adapt to this ideology as it became dominant at the time. Their actions are perplexing because they combine a strong sense of duty and commitment to the cause with an almost complete indifference to the moral implications of the cause itself. It is as if acting for the sake of a cause was the only important thing, while the content of the cause was of no concern at all. My theoretical argument of evil as a refusal of uncertainty represents an attempt to explain this strange mentality. According to this argument, the uncertainty involved in action and judgment produces what Arendt calls "frustration," and thus the desire to subordinate them to rules and processes that regulate them. As the desire for rules for action and judgment becomes more important than what the rules are, people become indifferent to the meaning of what they do. Totalitarian ideologies foment and latch on this indifference.

Subjective Evil and Bureaucratization

My focus on the motivation that underlies complicity in totalitarianism builds on Simona Forti's recent contribution to our understanding of evil in contemporary politics on the basis of biopolitics, but also departs from it in important ways. Forti claims that while modern philosophers such as Kant, Schelling, and Nietzsche conceived of evil as a striving for absolute power, posttotalitarian thinkers such as Arendt and Foucault conceive of it in terms of what she calls (modifying Arendt's notion) "the normality of evil," which unfolds through the mechanisms of biopower. Focusing on these mechanisms, Forti identifies a posttotalitarian paradigm according to which evil does not stem from any subjective intention, but rather from the routinization and normalization of a series of practices that render individuals unconcerned with the moral implications of their actions. This represents a shift "from a purely subjective idea of evil—hence, aimed at grasping the actor's evil attitude and intentions—to a notion that we might call the 'bureaucratization of evil.'"[27] Thus, following Forti, instead of inquiring into the subjective motivations that underlie evil actions, we should focus on the mechanisms that produce the bureaucratic mentality by which individuals become tools of evil. The lesson of totalitarianism is that political evil requires more than evil intentions—it requires thoughtless individuals unwilling to question their bureaucratic duties.

Forti's analysis is crucial for our understanding of evil in politics in two ways. First, she acknowledges that totalitarianism represents a historical turning point in our understanding of evil, which requires that we reconsider our approach to political action more broadly. Second, and perhaps more significantly, she shifts the focus from evil ideologies to evil as an ordinary, almost everyday phenomenon. One of the central problems posed by totalitarianism, which has long-standing implications for the conditions that make political evil possible, is that it relies on the complicity of thousands and even millions of seemingly normal individuals. Why do people adapt so easily to practices that we usually consider to be glaringly against basic moral values? Answering this question, as Forti shows, requires more than an analysis of totalitarian ideologies. It also requires an understanding of the conditions by which people become indifferent to the moral implications of these ideologies, to the point that their moral values are radically subverted.

While this book is indebted to Forti's thesis on the historical transformation of the predominant approach to evil, as well as to her focus on ordinary complicity in evil ideologies, my interpretative and theoretical arguments depart from her perspective. According to my interpretative argument, concerns with a kind of evil that is not grandiose and absolute but rather normalized and bureaucratized did not begin with totalitarianism. Instead, as I will show in chapter 2, this concern can be traced at least back to Kant. Despite frequent misinterpretations, Kant's analysis of the subjective motivations that underlie evil actions does not imply that evil stems from a demonic intention, as a sort of mysterious determination to transgress moral principles. Instead, Kant, like some of his contemporaries and followers, observed the dangerous development of a bureaucratic mentality that makes evil deceptive and normalized. Therefore, I read his thesis of "radical evil" not as part of a pretotalitarian paradigm on evil, but rather as an important reference point to better understand the theoretical problems posed by what Arendt called "the banality of evil."

My theoretical argument, on the other hand, departs from Forti's biopolitical approach by taking what we may call a "subjective" approach to evil, that is, by focusing on the attitude of evildoers rather than on the social structures that produce it. My claim is that the mechanisms of power described by Forti can only succeed in making individuals complicit in evil if individuals decide to become complicit, and that this decision to be complicit is determined by the desire to overcome the uncertainty constitutive of action and judgment. In this sense, evil is not merely a structural, but also a subjective phenomenon. If social structures could completely eliminate the capacity of individuals to choose what to do, then their actions would cease to be evil, for the very idea of evil presupposes the capacity to make moral choices. Following Arendt, I will claim that totalitarian evil takes place when individuals choose to eliminate or efface their own capacity to choose, thus behaving like thoughtless functionaries.

Of course, the focus on individual choice does not remove the need to examine the social structures and processes that produce or facilitate evil. Kant examined this issue in his writings on history, Arendt above all in *The Origins of Totalitarianism*, and Lyotard in the sections on totalitarianism in *The Differend*. However, it is no coincidence that the concept of evil appears most insistently in the context of reflections on moral philosophy. As Arendt claims in *Eichmann in Jerusalem*, the focus on larger processes and structures characteristic of the social sciences tends to explain away personal responsibility, and there is no evil in the moral sense without personal responsibility.[28] This book focuses on the subjective dimension of evil partly in order to avoid the potential self-exculpatory mentality that stems from situating the source of evil actions in impersonal structures and processes. This does not mean, however, that this subjective dimension is unrelated to structures and processes that contribute to generate and feed from evil actions. While I will not ignore this latter aspect, I acknowledge that my engagement with it will be limited. My hope is that my analysis of the subjective basis of evil will provide a new perspective by which to consider how structures and processes (such as bureaucracy, capitalism, ideology, and colonialism, among others) are linked to evil actions performed by individuals.

Moral Foundations

My theoretical argument regarding the link between totalitarian evil and refusal of uncertainty represents a contribution to a nonfoundationalist approach to political ethics. Foundationalist approaches to political ethics, such as those developed by Jürgen Habermas and John Rawls, assume that it is possible to find a procedure that determines the distinction between good and evil, but they say little about the reasons why people choose one or the other. This is not necessarily a problem, for it may be the case that the nature of moral agency simply falls outside the scope of their inquiries. However, leaving aside the subjective dimension of morality can be a problem if it conveys the idea that people have a natural tendency to do what is good and reject what is wrong, provided that they know how to make the distinction between one and the other. As mentioned above, one of the lessons of totalitarianism is that people do not do evil only because they fail to know what is truly good or to act on the basis of it, but rather, in many cases, because they actively choose to act in a way contrary to basic moral principles. Both Habermas and Rawls acknowledge that their projects of bringing society progressively in agreement with universal moral foundations encounter a limit in those who refuse to recognize such foundations as binding.[29] However, they say little about the moral decision involved in either recognizing or otherwise ignoring such foundations. My claim is that understanding the nature of such decision is essential for political theory because prominent cases of political evil stem from it. Given the persistence of evil in politics, and thus the need to respond to it, it is important not to leave the problem of evil aside as if it were a sort of mystery inaccessible to theoretical understanding. If political actors want to make the world less evil, it is not enough that they achieve a better understanding of what is objectively good. It is also necessary that they understand why individuals and groups often choose to do what is wrong.

This point can be further specified by means of Simon Critchley's contrast between "justifying reasons" and "exciting reasons."[30] Justifying reasons refers to the practice of identifying universally valid moral foundations. Exciting reasons, by contrast, refers to the "ethical experience" of being motivated to act morally. Rawls and Habermas, according to Critchley, are concerned above all with justifying reasons. As Critchley points out, however, the point of departure for the practice of justifying reasons is a subjective ethical experience: "ethical experience furnishes an account of the motivational force to act morally, of that by virtue of which a self decides to pledge itself to some conception of the good."[31] Note that, as Critchley points out, pledging oneself to "some" conception of the good precedes the determination of what is the right conception of the good. If this is the case, the project of determining the right moral foundations for politics is dependent on a previous ethical experience that makes us care about the good to begin with. Political action, following Critchley, consists not only in persuading people of the right moral orientation, but also in motivating people to care about doing what is right. Theories of justification and public reason leave this problem aside when they take for granted that people care about doing what is right. As a consequence, they say little about the politically relevant problem that individuals and groups often refuse to act morally, whatever the true foundation of morality may be.

My interpretative and theoretical arguments regarding the nature of totalitarian evil build on Critchley's philosophical inquiry into the fundamental ethical experience. Critchley rightly traces the distinction between the rational justification of moral norms and the experience of morality back to Kant. As we will see in chapter 2, Kant's concern with the subjective experience of morality, by contrast to its rational justification, becomes especially prominent in his late writings. This concern, I will argue, is largely indebted to his reflections on the problem of evil. Theoretically, my focus on the problem of evil will show that the ethical experience described by Critchley is determined by the constitutive uncertainty involved in action, due to the unpredictability of its meaning and outcome, and judgment, due to the absence of unquestionable rules that secure its validity. This experience of uncertainty confronts us with the decision of either accepting it, with the implication that we lack mastery over our actions and judgments, or refusing it, in an attempt to achieve such mastery. This latter stance underlies the kind of evil displayed by totalitarianism.

The approach to political ethics that I pursue in this book resonates with that of theorists of democracy and post-Marxists, who also conceive of totalitarianism as stemming from the refusal of an essential uncertainty or indetermination. Political theorists like Claude Lefort, Ernesto Laclau and Chantal Mouffe, Slavoj Žižek, and Alain Badiou claim that totalitarianism stems from a desire to eliminate an uncertainty that is constitutive of the political community, pursuing the fantasy that society can become fully coherent and undisturbed.[32] By contrast to these theorists, however, I focus not on the ideology of totalitarian or proto-totalitarian movements, but rather on what I would call, reformulating Arendt's famous notion, the "everydayness of evil." Instead of asking what the source of totalitarian ideologies is, I ask why seemingly normal people, usually capable of telling the difference between good and evil, become complicit in these ideologies. This question leads me to consider the uncertainty involved in seemingly ordinary actions and judgments, by contrast to the focus on social identities and power struggles that is central to theories of democracy and post-Marxism. Therefore, the approach to political ethics that I will propose takes the experience of uncertainty that is constitutive of moral choices as imbedded in everyday political commitments. Political good and political evil can be everyday phenomena, even though they sometimes become exceptional and grandiose.

A Critical Political Theory of Evil

My interpretative and theoretical arguments contribute to the development of a theory of evil that is both critical and political. The theory is *critical* because it interrogates the meaning and applicability of a concept, as opposed to either taking its meaning for granted or simply deriving it from experience. This critical approach departs from Lara's recent claim that our understanding of evil is based on what she calls "learning from catastrophes," as well as from Bernstein's pragmatist perspective, according to which the meaning of evil is constantly redrawn in response to new experiences. I share Lara's and Bernstein's views that the meaning of the concept of evil is not fixed, but rather transformed in response to experiences of evil and through conversations around them. But our interpretations of new experiences as well as our conversations around them are framed by long-standing patterns of thinking. Therefore, without interrogating such patterns, we run the risk of interpreting and discussing new experiences in a way that overlooks their novelty and reproduces long-standing views. In order to avoid this, the critical theory of evil that I pursue is sensitive to both the new experience represented by totalitarianism and to long-standing conceptual frameworks that condition how we interpret this experience. This critical theory proceeds by examining the views of three thinkers who addressed the emergence of a new form of evil with philosophical sensitivity and conceptual rigor.

The critical theory of evil that I pursue is also *political* because it seeks to oppose the ideological manipulation of the notion of evil in public discourse. This manipulation is described by Jacques Rancière, who claims that contemporary liberal societies constantly reaffirm the idea of an undivided humanity by stressing the contrast between "the victim, the pathetic figure of a person to whom such humanity is denied, and the executioner, the monstrous figure of a person who denies humanity."[33] Following Rancière, political groups and institutions often rely on images of a "monstrous figure" who threatens an image of humanity that is constructed as universal. Bernstein has more recently criticized what he calls "the abuse of evil," namely, a political and media discourse that espouses a simplistic, clear-cut distinction between good and evil, with the aim of securing our moral certainties.[34] In agreement with this perspective, Dews has claimed that "the idea of evil, precisely because of its intense semantic charge, its mobilizing force, lends itself to exploitation in the hands of theocrats and rabble-rousers—not to mention cynical and unscrupulous politicians."[35] Rancière, Bernstein, and Dews identify what I would call an "ideology of evil," which depicts the evil of certain people, actions, or regimes as self-evident and absolutely external to our moral values. This ideology uses evil as a sort of moral relief: as long as we have a "monstrous figure" to separate ourselves from, we can be content with the superiority of our own moral values. The critical and political theory of evil that I will develop challenges this ideological manipulation by showing that, notwithstanding its changing nature, evil can be the object of rigorous conceptual analysis and understanding. This understanding can inform political practices and debates around evil in a way that resists uncritical, reflexive moralistic reactions.

Although political theorists, by contrast to moral philosophers and theologians, rarely put evil at the center of their inquiries, they do often indirectly touch upon it. It is therefore important to acknowledge the indebtedness of my inquiry to previous studies on the relationship between morality and politics that contribute to our understanding of evil. One important book in this regard is Patchen Markell's *Bound by Recognition*. Departing from the frequent attempt to find moral grounds for political action and judgment, Markell asks why people act unjustly. Specifically, Markell criticizes Axel Honneth's model of recognition as a ground for politics, because it says "little about the complementary question of the motives, investments, and experiences that sustain misrecognition."[36] Importantly, Markell stresses that the problem of injustice is not a separate issue that a politics based on recognition may disregard: "understanding the meaning and sources of injustice is part and parcel of understanding what injustice itself is and why it is objectionable; and it has important implications for the question of how best to respond to it."[37] My inquiry shares Markell's concern with considering not only the reasons why people do what is right, but also the reasons why they do wrong. However, I focus on *evil* rather than *injustice*, because the former notion is more closely connected to the kind of agency involved in the actions of those involved in totalitarianism. Beyond this discrepancy, which leads me to a different body of texts than Markell, I share his view that doing injustice stems from a desire for sovereignty, understood as mastery and invulnerability, which is (falsely) sustained at the expense of others: "social subordination . . . involves closing off some people's practical possibilities for the sake of other people's sense of mastery or invulnerability."[38]

A second and more recent antecedent to my approach to evil is Shalini Satkunanandan's *Extraordinary Responsibility*. One important contribution of this book is a conception of political action not as grounded on moral rules that can be used to determine what to do, but rather on the extraordinary experience of realizing that we bear responsibility for our actions. Satkunanandan shifts the focus away from morality as a series of objective rules, which stems from the idea that responsibility consists in fulfilling a series of specified tasks (what she calls "calculable responsibility"), to morality as a response to the call to be responsible, even if we do not know how to be responsible (what she calls "extraordinary responsibility").[39] Both calculable and incalculable responsibility, according to Satkunanandan, are essential dimensions of morality—attentiveness both to rules and to calls for responsibility that lie beyond rules. Although she does not engage with the problem of evil extensively, Satkunanandan explicitly links Arendt's notion of "the banality of evil," complemented by Simone Weil's analysis of lack of attention, to a disregard for "extraordinary responsibility": "Weil, like Arendt, believes that we can inhibit our capacity for evil by engaging in a kind of attention that is different from narrowly ethical attention" (that is, the attention characteristic of "calculable responsibility").[40] Thus, while Satkunanandan is more concerned with affirming the need to complement calculable responsibility with incalculable responsibility than with explaining the frequent absence of the latter, she hints at an account of evil that is close to the one that I will pursue throughout the chapters. In this account, evil does not stem from failure to identify or to comply with a rule that hangs over our actions and judgments. Instead, it stems from an unwillingness to be attentive to an ethical demand that is beyond rules.

Structure and Method

The three authors that are the focus of this book address the novelty of evil in modernity and its implications for the notions of action and judgment. There are certainly many other thinkers who may have been included, but there are important reasons for focusing the inquiry on these three. In responding to totalitarianism, both Arendt and Lyotard find in Kant, and especially in his late work, resources for an antitotalitarian conception of action and judgment. Although neither of them systematically engages with Kant's conception of evil (beyond Arendt's frequent but rather brief remarks on "radical evil"), this conception is one reason why Kant's practical philosophy is nevertheless, for both, essential for understanding political action and judgment in the posttotalitarian world. If we focus on the problem of evil in modernity, we can see a consistent line of inquiry unfolding throughout the three authors. One essential premise of my analysis is that a reason why Kant provides the resources for the kind of posttotalitarian political thought developed by Arendt and Lyotard is that he acknowledged the novelty of evil in modernity. By reconstructing the importance of the question of evil in Kant's practical philosophy, and reading it in dialogue with posttotalitarian thinkers such as Arendt and Lyotard, we can better understand the implications of reflecting on modern evil for political theory.

The order of the analysis is based on the structure of the problem, rather than the chronology of the authors. I take as a point of departure Arendt's inquiries into the novelty of evil with totalitarianism and her formulation of the concept of action as a response to it. I then proceed to connect these inquiries with Kant's practical philosophy, following Arendt's own remarks on Kant in connection to the problem of evil. Reading Kant through the lenses of the problem of totalitarian evil, I show that that his understanding of action and judgment in late writings contributes to clarify some of the problems contained in what Arendt called "the banality of evil." Finally, in order to grasp the implications of Kant's understanding of judgment for contemporary politics, I turn to Lyotard, who found in it a model for an antitotalitarian political judgment. Thus, rather than tracing and reconstructing the history of a concept, the book develops a framework for addressing the problem of evil after totalitarianism, as well as its implications for our understanding of action and judgment in modern politics. While at some points I identify historical elements that contribute to explain the views of the authors, as well as the intellectual connections between them, I proceed mainly by tracing the conceptual links connecting Kant, Arendt, and Lyotard. One goal of this procedure is to illuminate the implications of Kant's practical philosophy for contemporary political theory by reading it in dialogue with Arendt and Lyotard, as well as to clarify problematic aspects of Arendt's and Lyotard's political views by identifying some of its sources in Kant's philosophy.

The reading of Kant, Arendt, and Lyotard in dialogue with one another that I will develop does not assume that their perspectives are identical or even consistent with one another. My goal is not to reconstruct a full-fledged theory of evil developed by the three authors, nor do I presuppose that each author individually has a unified theory of evil. Instead, I trace shifting views evolving around the problem of understanding a new kind of evil. I focus on uncertainty because, as will become clear throughout the chapters, the link between evil and uncertainty is a shared concern in the three authors. My theoretical thesis of evil as stemming from the refusal of uncertainty is both a heuristic devise by which to interpret the thought of each author on evil, and an attempt to draw a substantive theoretical implication from their inquiries. The thesis does not exhaust or settles the views of each of the authors on evil, but condenses some consistent trends of thought that serve as a basis for moving forward discussions around evil in modern politics, and for improving our understanding of action and judgment.

By putting the problem of evil upfront, I will show that it plays a central role in shaping Kant's, Arendt's, and Lyotard's approaches to action and judgment, leading the three authors to depart from long-standing philosophical assumptions about both concepts. It is not by coincidence that Kant's central text on evil, *Religion within the Boundaries of Mere Reason*, is one of his most perplexing from a philosophical point of view, nor that Arendt's and Lyotard's concerns with totalitarianism as a new manifestation of evil led them to depart from the discourse of philosophy when reflecting on politics. While philosophy, at least as it is usually understood, is concerned above all with consistency and validity, experiences of evil often disrupt systematic ways of thinking. Scholars have noted that the experience of totalitarianism led Arendt to develop a new methodology and terminology for political thinking that departs from the philosophical focus on conceptual consistency, and I believe that this methodological and terminological shift is characteristic of Kant's and Lyotard's reflections on evil as well.[41] If evil, following my theoretical argument, stems from a refusal of uncertainty, understanding evil demands a kind of thinking and writing that welcomes and affirms uncertainty. This is why, as I will point out throughout the chapters, Kant's, Arendt's, and Lyotard's views on action and judgment in response to evil often lead to shifts and inconsistencies which, although problematic from a strictly philosophical point of view, nevertheless illuminate their constitutive uncertainty.

The inquiry will proceed through four chapters. Chapter 1 analyzes the relationship between evil, action, and thinking in Arendt's work. I argue that despite Arendt's shifts on the issue, she consistently links totalitarianism to a form of evil that destroys responsibility for action. This destruction proceeds by concealing the actor's spontaneity, or his capacity to begin, under fixed processes and rules that are given to him from without, in such a way that he cannot take responsibility for them. In response to this destruction, Arendt locates responsibility not in compliance with rules, but rather in the capacity to begin by means of action, thus disclosing an actor with a unique identity that can be forgiven or punished for what he has done. Because this disclosure depends on the presence of others, it requires the establishment of relations that render the outcome as well as the meaning of the act uncertain. This means that, counterintuitively, we are not responsible for that which we can control, which would demand a complete lack of relation with others, but rather for assuming the risk of beginning something unpredictable. A similar conception of responsibility can be found in Arendt's later analysis of thinking, in response to what she characterized as Eichmann's "inability to think." Thinking is essential for responsibility because it makes us remember what we do, thus generating a stable person behind the act. Although Arendt often describes thinking as the internal dialogue between the self and itself performed in solitude, she also suggests that this inner self with whom we speak is a representative of others. Therefore thinking, like action, depends on the establishment of relations with others, and it is this establishment of relations that makes us responsible. The refusal to establish relations by means of action and thinking entails a refusal of responsibility, which is an essential characteristic of totalitarian evil.

Chapter 2 connects Arendt's remarks on "the banality of evil" with Kant's notion of "radical evil." I show that Kant's "radical evil" emerges as a response to a concern similar to the one that led Arendt to the notion of "the banality of evil," namely, a form of evil-doing that seems to lack motivations and, consequently, responsibility. By focusing on the link between evil and responsibility in Kant, I show that the thesis of radical evil constitutes a response to an issue that remained unclear in Kant's practical philosophy until its development, namely, the ground of responsibility for evildoing. While in his main writings on practical philosophy Kant situates the source of evil in our egoistic impulses, his later text, *Religion within the Boundaries of Mere Reason*, situates it in choice, which means that evil is not external to, but rather integrated in freedom. Yet because this choice is inscrutable, we cannot know what our intentions are, and therefore whether our actions are good or evil. For Kant, there is no rule or procedure that determines whether a certain action is good or evil, which means that the moral worth of our actions cannot be judged with certainty. To objectify the distinction between good and evil behind fixed rules or procedures is already a way to conceal our responsibility for judging our actions anew. This concealment is precisely what Kant calls "radical evil," whose radicality consists in corrupting the choice of a maxim for action, and thus responsibility for it.

Chapter 3 turns to the problem of the judgment of action in Kant. I take as a point of departure Arendt's turn to Kant's analysis of the judgment of taste in response to what she characterized as Eichmann's "inability to judge." Scholars have often criticized Arendt's interpretation of the judgment of taste as a model for political judgment on the grounds that it lacks a successful account of validity, beyond the empirical agreement of one's community. The usual solution to this problem consists in grounding judgment on a universal moral foundation, that is, on the moral law. I argue that this solution does not hold within the framework of Kant's thought, according to which there is an unbridgeable gap between the moral law and phenomenal actions. In order to understand how the power of judgment can establish a relationship between the two, it is necessary to analyze how it connects the faculty whose object is phenomena, which is the imagination, with the faculty whose object is the moral law, which is reason. This connection is the object of Kant's "Analysis of the Sublime," which shows that a judgment of action is possible not by means of a rule mediating between it and the moral law, but rather by the feeling of sublimity that the act arouses in the spectator. Given that the moral law lacks any possible representation, there is no standard for determining that an action is moral. However, there are certain actions that bring the capacity to represent to its limit, thus arousing the idea of the moral law in the spectator, who experiences this arousal as a feeling of sublimity. Precisely because it stems from the idea of the law, which we share with all beings capable of action, the sublime feeling is universally communicable, beyond any empirical community or established set of norms.

Chapter 4 examines the importance of the sublime for Lyotard's understanding of the distinction between good and evil in postmodernity. Lyotard's famous diagnosis of a "postmodern condition," in which a multiplicity of discourses interact with one another without the mediation of universally shared standards, has been often interpreted as leading to political nihilism, in the sense that political judgments should refrain from any universalist aspiration. A focus on Lyotard's interpretation of Kant shows that this view is mistaken. Reading Lyotard's main political text, *The Differend*, in dialogue with his two main studies on Kant's critical philosophy, *Enthusiasm* and *Lectures on the Analytic of the Sublime*, I show that universality and disagreement are not mutually exclusive, but rather fundamentally intertwined. The reason is that it is in the attempt to make communicable what remains incommunicable within a certain disagreement that judgments that demand universal approval emerge. This demand for approval does not stem from any rule or procedure that could be showed and controlled by a concrete subject, which is the source of what Lyotard calls "terrorism." Rather, the need to communicate what remains incommunicable produces a feeling, akin to the "sublime feeling" in Kant, which is a sign of universal ideas. The political good, according to Lyotard, consists in inventing new idioms that allow heterogeneous parties to communicate with one another, without disavowing their heterogeneity. Evil, by contrast, consists is attempting to subordinate heterogeneity under the rules of a single, totalizing language.

By reading Kant, Arendt, and Lyotard in dialogue with one another around the problem of modern evil, this book challenges some common interpretations of the notions of action and judgment in the three authors. In the conclusion, I address some of the implications of the analysis for debates around the nature of political action and political judgment in contemporary political theory.

PART 1
Action

Chapter 1

Arendt's Reassessment of Responsibility

Hannah Arendt's analysis of Eichmann's trial in *Eichmann in Jerusalem*, together with her later writings on moral philosophy, showed that evil is more than a theological or purely moral problem, and that it is essential to modern politics. One question that persistently concerned Arendt is why people who seem perfectly normal, and usually capable of telling the difference between right and wrong, become complicit in ideologies that are glaringly contrary to long-standing moral standards. As we saw in the introduction, Arendt believes that the traditional image of evil as deficiency and the motivations associated with it do not accurately describe the kind of evil displayed by totalitarianism. The many people responsible for running the camps were not morally ignorant or stupid, in the sense that they lacked the capacity to distinguish between right and wrong. They were also not irrational, in the sense that some sort of impulse (egoism, hatred, lust for power) overcame their natural inclination to do what is morally right. In what sense, then, are their actions evil?

This chapter argues that the kind of evil characteristic of totalitarianism, as described by Arendt, consists in the elimination of the sense of responsibility for action, which depends on accepting a fundamental uncertainty regarding its meaning and outcome. Despite the many studies in recent years that have analyzed Arendt's views on evil, the problem of responsibility, which is central in Arendt's writings on the topic, has received scarce attention. Most studies have focused on the continuities and discontinuities in Arendt's remarks, which are rather unsystematic throughout her work. Some scholars argue that, despite Arendt's own admission that she changed her mind, her early characterization of totalitarianism as "radical evil" and her later notion of "the banality of evil" constitute two different aspects of a same phenomenon.[1] Others have stressed the discontinuities between the two notions, arguing that Arendt did indeed change her mind regarding the nature of evil in totalitarianism.[2] A third perspective seeks to find a middle ground, arguing that the two notions share some elements but are different in others.[3] While the reading that I will develop generally supports the thesis of continuity, my focus is less on the content of Arendt's notions of "radical evil" and "the banality of evil," and more on the problem that both notions address. This problem, I argue, is one of responsibility for action. Although they capture different aspects of totalitarianism, both "radical evil" and "the banality of evil" refer to an attempt to eliminate responsibility, due to the unwillingness to accept the uncertainty of the meaning of action.

Although Arendt only addresses the problem of responsibility systematically in her late writings, I will show that it constitutes a central concern in the development of the central category of her political thought, namely, action. Following Margaret Canovan's and Mary Dietz's claims that Arendt's political thought, as developed mainly in *The Human Condition*, is largely indebted to her analysis of totalitarianism, I read Arendt's notion of action as a response to the destruction of responsibility that, in her view, takes place in totalitarian regimes.[4] In order for there to be an actor who outlives the act and can consequently take responsibility for it, it is first of all necessary that the act discloses the unique identity of the actor to others. Because this disclosure requires the establishment of relations with others, whose responses and reactions the actor cannot control, action involves an unavoidable uncertainty regarding its meaning. Counterintuitively, the same condition that makes the actor responsible for her action makes it impossible for her to have full control over its meaning. This lack of control generates a feeling of frustration that is at the root of the desire to eliminate uncertainty and thus responsibility altogether, and which is essential to the kind of evil displayed by totalitarianism.

Radical Evil and the Destruction of Responsibility

In the first pages of her analysis of anti-Semitism in *Origins*, Arendt claims that "the last century has produced an abundance of ideologies that pretend to be keys to history but are actually nothing but desperate efforts to escape responsibility."[5] Although the sources and structure of modern ideologies will be a central topic toward the end of the book, Arendt never comes back to the idea that they stem from an effort to escape responsibility—and indeed that they are "nothing but" this effort. However, Arendt's frequent remarks on the absence of a sense of responsibility in Nazi criminals throughout her early writings on totalitarianism suggest that this view on ideology is not a passing thought.[6] As I will show throughout this chapter, Arendt's concern with responsibility, as well as with the "desperate efforts" to escape it, play a central and systematic role in the development of her political thought, and in her notion of action in particular. My thesis in this section is that the kind of "radical" and "absolute" evil that Arendt associates with totalitarianism in *Origins* consists in the destruction of responsibility, both of the victims and of those in charge of the camps. I will show this by reconstructing a recurrent theme connecting a number of apparently casual remarks on responsibility throughout the analysis of totalitarian regimes in the third part of the book. In the next section, I read Arendt's notion of action in *The Human Condition* as an attempt to understand and preserve responsibility against the desire to escape it.

One of Arendt's most prominent theses regarding the novelty of totalitarianism is that it represents a new form of evil that disrupts our traditional understanding of it. This idea appears toward the end of the analysis of the concentration camps in *Origins*, where she claims,

> When the impossible was made possible it became the unpunishable, unforgivable absolute evil which could no longer be understood and explained by the evil motives of self-interest, greed, covetousness, resentment, lust for power, and cowardice . . . Just as the victims in the death factories or the holes of oblivion are no longer "human" in the eyes of their executioners, so this newest species of criminals is beyond the pale even of solidarity in human sinfulness.[7]

While traditional motivations for evildoing entail some sort of fault with which we can at least identify, and consequently punish or forgive, totalitarian crimes stem from no recognizable motivation. The existence of the camps cannot be explained by any sort of utilitarian self-interest, for, as Arendt clarifies, they did not serve the war efforts and were even detrimental to it at some points: "neither military, nor economic, nor political considerations were allowed to interfere with the costly and troublesome program of mass exterminations and deportations."[8] Given the traditional conception of evil as stemming from some sort of self-interest or uncontrollable impulse, it would seem like the systematic mass murder that took place in the camps lies beyond the kinds of action that we usually consider "evil." As a consequence, Arendt claims, "we actually have nothing to fall back on in order to understand a phenomenon that nevertheless confronts us with its overpowering reality and breaks down all standards we know."[9] This lack of understanding, however, is not complete, for

> there is only one thing that seems to be discernible: we may say that radical evil has emerged in connection with a system in which all men have become equally superfluous. The manipulators of this system believe in their own superfluousness as much as in that of all others, and the totalitarian murderers are all the more dangerous because they do not care if they themselves are alive or dead, if they ever lived or never were born.[10]

Even if we cannot understand the motivation behind the camps, we do recognize their goal, namely, to make everyone, the victims as well as the perpetrators, superfluous. The key to understanding the "radical evil" of totalitarianism lies then in the production of superfluousness, not only of the victims but of the murderers themselves.

So what is superfluousness? To make human beings superfluous means to eliminate their spontaneity, that is, their capacity to act in an unpredictable way. This is a necessary condition for exercising total domination over men. According to Arendt, "totalitarianism strives not toward despotic rule over men, but toward a system in which men are superfluous." While despotic rule still presupposes that individuals are capable of spontaneous action, and consequently that it is at least possible that they deviate from what is expected from them, "total power can be achieved and safeguarded only in a world of conditioned reflexes, of marionettes without the slightest trace of spontaneity."[11] Therefore, being superfluous means that one is unable to act in any other way than the one that is determined by a series of conditioned reflexes. This entails a lack of "individuality," that is, of "anything indeed that distinguishes one man from another."¹² From the viewpoint of totalitarianism, all people are or must be nothing but the effect of a series of preexisting causes, independently of anything that can be attributed to their individual characteristics. Only this kind of individual can be the subject of total domination, in the sense that every aspect of their lives is controllable and made entirely predictable. The superfluous individual is one whose actions are determined by larger forces and cannot do anything by his or her own initiative.

While the literature on *Origins* has given extensive attention to the totalitarian production of superfluousness, scholars have rarely focused on the destruction of responsibility that is essential to this production. Some studies do note that totalitarianism destroys the responsibility of those complicit in it, but they do not examine the specific mechanisms that produce this destruction.¹³ This is an important issue because, as we will see farther down, some of Arendt's political categories, such as action and thinking, emerge to a large extent as a response to what she sees as the modern tendency to escape responsibility. I will now show that for Arendt one essential characteristic of totalitarianism is the fulfillment of this tendency by means of the systematic elimination of the sense of responsibility of the entire population. Many of the novel domination techniques developed by totalitarianism, which culminate in the institution of the concentration camps, converge around this elimination. This concern with the modern tendency to escape and even eliminate responsibility for action runs through Arendt's writings on politics and morality, as I show in the following sections. The goal of the remaining of this section is to identify the emergence of this concern in Arendt's first major account of totalitarianism.

One central thread in Arendt's analysis of totalitarianism consists in explaining how totalitarian organizations eliminate personal responsibility for action. Already in the initial stages of the totalitarian movement, its organization relies on what Arendt calls the "Leader principle," according to which the leader "claims personal responsibility for every action, deed, or misdeed, committed by any member or functionary in his official capacity."¹⁴ This organizational principle anticipates one central characteristic of the totalitarian state, namely, the fact that no one is responsible for what he or she does, because their actions are nothing but the effect of a higher law that they do not control. Given that in the totalitarian movement only the leader is responsible for what anyone does, "every functionary is not only appointed by the Leader but is his walking embodiment, and every order is supposed to emanate from this one ever-present source."[15]

Unlike even the most tyrannical regimes, the totalitarian movement lacks a hierarchical structure that distinguishes the functionaries from the leader, which means that there is no mediation between the leader's orders and those in charge of their execution. In the totalitarian movement, "nobody ever experiences a situation in which he has to be responsible for his own actions or can explain the reasons for them," given that "since the Leader has monopolized the right and possibility of explanation, he appears to the outside world as the only person who knows what he is doing."[16] Even before taking full control of the state, the totalitarian movement operates according to the principle that no one knows why they do what they do, because everyone embodies a principle that they do not understand. The members and functionaries within the movement are therefore unable to take responsibility for their actions, because they operate on the assumption that only the leader knows the reason behind them. This constitutes an incipient state of superfluousness, in which individual actions matter only as an emanation of the will of the leader, not as an expression of the reasons and motivations of a concrete individual.

The development of totalitarianism in power intensifies this elimination of responsibility for action up to its ultimate consequences. While the leader principle eliminates responsibility for any deed or misdeed by members and functionaries of the totalitarian movement, the secret police eliminates legal responsibility for any crime committed within the totalitarian state. The reason is that the secret police does not prosecute people on the basis of what they have done, but rather on the basis of what they are and could potentially do—it does not deal with "suspects," but rather with "objective enemies." The totalitarian state does not need to wait for specific actions to consider some people its enemies, because it "defined its enemies ideologically before it seized power, so that categories of the 'suspects' were not established through police information."[17] And given that new objective enemies may be "discovered" according to changing circumstances, no one in a totalitarian state is safe from becoming a criminal at any given moment, independently of what he or she has done. What matters is no longer the offense, either real or merely suspected, but rather the "possible crime": "while the suspect is arrested because he is thought to be capable of committing a crime that more or less fits his personality (or his suspected personality), the totalitarian version of the possible crime is based on the logical anticipation of objective developments."[18]

In a totalitarian state, the criminal does not deserve punishment on the basis of what he or she has done, which is a precondition of personal responsibility, but rather on the basis of objective developments. In its advanced stages, the totalitarian state disregards even the pretense that these developments have any connection to the characteristics of the "criminals," and those who are deemed "unfit to live" are chosen on the basis of sheer arbitrariness. This exposes the ultimate goal of destroying the link between deed and punishment, namely, to render deeds meaningless from a legal standpoint, so that not even opposition to the regime matters: "theoretically, the choice of opposition remains in totalitarian regimes too; but such freedom is almost invalidated if committing a voluntary act only assures a 'punishment' that everyone else may have to bear anyway."[19] While transgressing a law is still an act of freedom, which is why it may be punished, totalitarianism makes punishment arbitrary, with the consequence that the very distinction between a criminal and a noncriminal act disappears. People are no longer punished on the basis of their voluntary actions, but rather on the basis of developments that have nothing to do with what they have done. This instability, as Hanna Pitkin points out, is a means by which "totalitarianism undermines the very notion of agency—people's responsibility for deeds and the consequences of those deeds."[20]

The utter destruction of the legal and moral categories by which we adjudicate responsibility for action is essential to render people superfluous and dominate them completely. This is the goal of the camps, which constitute "a world which is complete with all sensual data of reality but lacks that structure of consequence and responsibility without which reality remains for us a mass of incomprehensible data."[21] The camps develop to its ultimate implications the destruction of the distinction between guilt and innocence, and thus of responsibility, because no one is in them as a consequence of what they have done: "the categories gathered in the camps—Jews, carriers of diseases, representatives of dying classes—have already lost their capacity for both normal or criminal action."[22] This is part of what Arendt calls the killing of "the juridical person in man," which consists in making juridical standards for action meaningless, so that one's free choices cease to matter. For the totalitarian regime, it does not matter whether one consents with it or not, for "the arbitrary arrest which chooses among innocent people destroys the validity of free consent."[23] This arbitrariness applies to the whole population, for anyone may be subject to arrest and become an inmate of a camp at any given moment. Therefore, although only the inmates are subject to the most thorough destruction of spontaneity and individuality, the mere existence of the camp-system entails that the whole population is deprived of rights: "The aim of an arbitrary system is to destroy the civil rights of the whole population, who ultimately become just as outlawed in their own country as the stateless and homeless."[24] If anyone may become an inmate of a camp at any given moment for arbitrary reasons, the legal distinction between guilt and innocence becomes meaningless.

We can see that there is a connection between the production of superfluousness, which is the defining characteristic of the "radical evil" of totalitarianism, and the impossibility to forgive or punish it. Forgiveness and punishment presuppose that one is responsible for their actions, in the sense that they stem from the person's initiative. In a totalitarian state, however, responsibility is not only ignored, but systematically eliminated. As we have seen, Arendt claims that modern ideologies, of which totalitarianism is the ultimate outcome, are "nothing but desperate efforts to escape responsibility." Ideology, according to Arendt, is the "logic of an idea," which is applied to history so as to explain all possible events in accordance with it.[25] This means that human actions, like any other natural event, stem from this logical process, and, consequently, "guilt and innocence become senseless notions; 'guilty' is he who stands in the way of the natural or historical process."[26] Both the victims and the executioners of totalitarian terror are merely the tools of an objective law, which is why they are all "subjectively innocent": "the murdered because they did nothing against the system, and the murderers because they do not really murder but execute a death sentence pronounced by some higher tribunal."[27] In a totalitarian state, the subjective conditions of action do not matter, because they are nothing but the effect of an objective law. As Canovan points out, "totalitarians, including the dictators themselves, had taken refuge from responsibility in ideologies that told them what must inevitably happen."[28] Therefore, when Arendt claims that the evil of totalitarianism is unpunishable and unforgivable, she is referring to a kind of evil performed by people who do not consider themselves responsible for what they do. Without a sense of responsibility, punishment and forgiveness are impossible.

The elimination of responsibility is a recurrent concern in *Origins*, and it is closely connected to one of the central traits of the new kind of evil represented by it, namely, the impossibility to punish it and forgive it. If the experience of totalitarianism plays a decisive role in the development of Arendt's political thought, then her concern with the elimination of responsibility must have influenced one of its central concepts, namely, action. Although Arendt only addresses responsibility systematically in her later writings, I will now argue that the development of the notion of action in *The Human Condition* represents, to some extent, an attempt to rethink our understanding of responsibility. Writing against the totalitarian effacement of responsibility under historical processes, Arendt affirms and reconsiders responsibility by linking it to the capacity to begin and to the public disclosure of the actor.

Beginning, Disclosure, Distinctness

The Human Condition has often been read as a continuation of Nietzsche's critique of the Platonic subordination of appearances to essences. In both Dana Villa's and Bonnie Honig's readings, Arendt's emphasis on the virtuosity of the act, by contrast to its moral or cognitive foundations, seeks to question the image according to which action stems from an autonomous subject that preexists the act. In this regard, according to both Villa and Honig, Arendt's notion of action resembles Nietzsche's claim that "there is no 'being' behind doing . . . the deed is everything."[29] But while it is clear that both Arendt and Nietzsche criticize the idea of the subject as a substance prior to the act, Arendt's emphasis on the revelatory character of action and on the disclosure of the actor in it suggests that, taken literally, the idea that "there is no 'being' behind the doing" and that "the deed is everything" neglects an important aspect of her conception of action. A central concern of *The Human Condition*, I show in this section, is to understand how action gives rise to a durable self who can be held responsible for it, thus becoming "forgivable" as well as "punishable." If we keep this problem in mind, we see that the shift of focus from the actor to the act only goes halfway, for it is indeed a characteristic of the totalitarian mentality that people do not care about the actor behind the deed. Together with a critique of its subordination to a preexisting subject, Arendt's notion of action constitutes an attempt to understand under what conditions action leaves behind an actor who can take responsibility for it, and under what conditions it does not.

One clear connection between Arendt's notion of action in *The Human Condition* and her earlier analysis of totalitarianism is the category of "beginning." In *Origins*, as we have seen, Arendt describes totalitarianism as a system that attempts to destroy spontaneity. The use of this term is consistent with its formulation by Kant, who defined spontaneity as "the capacity to begin a state from itself," adding that this capacity is "the real ground of imputability" for action.[30] While Arendt acknowledges the importance of Kant's understanding of free action as a beginning, she finds a problem with its detachment from the realm of appearances. In her lecture notes on the "Political Theory of Kant" from 1953, Arendt claims that Kant identifies spontaneity with activity and appearance with passivity: "Being-Appearance becomes the cleavage between Ought and Is. . . . But this in appearance only: The true cleavage is between man as a passive and an active being: Spontaneity."[31] For Kant, spontaneity belongs to the noumenal realm, which means that it does not appear. The act itself, however, does appear, which introduces a duality in the actor: "man at the same time: The beginner and subject to processes: Whenever the beginning appears, it falls into the laws of appearances: Causality, or non-freedom."[32]

There is clearly one element of Kant's notion of spontaneity that Arendt considers worth preserving, namely, the idea that people are capable of beginning, and that this capacity is the source of freedom. However, she questions the dichotomy between the spontaneous, nonappearing self and the appearing self that is not spontaneous, which leads to the dichotomy between freedom and the world of appearances: "The opposite of the Givenness of the world (Affiziertheit) is the Spontaneity of Being which so to speak is not of this world."[33] In order for the capacity to begin to be a worldly rather than a transcendent condition, it must be linked to the world of appearances. This complicates the distinction between freedom as activity and appearing as passivity, as we will see. In Arendt's view, Kant's separation between activity as freedom and passivity as necessity stems from his failure to acknowledge that there is virtue not only in what we make ourselves, but also in the endurance of what is given to us.[34]

According to Arendt, the beginning of something new through action does not entail an absolute beginning, and thus pure activity, but rather an insertion into an existing world. This insertion is an actualization of the condition of natality, that is, of the fact that we are a new beginning by virtue of being born into the world: "by speaking and acting we insert ourselves into the human world, which existed before we were born in it, and this insertion is like a second birth, in which we confirm the naked fact of our being-born [*Geborenseins*], and at the same time take upon ourselves the responsibility [*Verantwortung*] for it."[35] Evidently, we are not responsible for our own birth, yet we take responsibility for it from the moment we confirm that we are a new beginning by means of action and speech. This means that beginning is neither purely active nor purely passive: the fact of birth is given to us, yet it is on the basis of this fact that we are able to actively begin. Arendt develops this idea further in "The Crisis of Education," where she claims that "insofar as the child is not yet acquainted with the world, he must be gradually introduced to it; insofar as he is new, care must be taken that this new thing comes to fruition in relation to the world as it is."[36] Beginning is therefore not opposed to the world as it is, because one can only begin by being inserted into a preexisting world. At the same time, the existing world can only be preserved by means of its renovation, because "to preserve the world against the mortality of its creators and inhabitants it must be constantly set right anew."[37] By contrast to Kant's stark distinction between spontaneity as activity and the given as passivity, Arendt conceives of activity and passivity as interdependent: we can begin by inserting ourselves into a world that existed before us, and this insertion is essential for preserving the world as it is given.

A second, and perhaps more essential difference between Arendt's notion of beginning and Kant's notion of spontaneity concerns its connection with appearances. For Kant, spontaneity does not belong to the world of appearances, which is ruled by natural causality and necessity, but rather to the noumenal realm. For Arendt, by contrast, beginning and appearances are intertwined, because beginning is essentially appearing: "in acting and speaking, men show who they are, reveal actively their unique personal identities and thus make their appearance in the human world."[38] Just like birth represents the physical insertion of a new person into the world, action and speech represent a second insertion that reveals who this new person is, given that they "contain the answer to the question asked of every newcomer: 'Who are you?' "[39] This "who" is not a substance that preexists the act, but rather an effect of its revelatory character. By contrast to mere physical difference, which is a characteristic common to all beings, men are distinct by virtue of actively distinguishing themselves: "Human distinctness is not the same as otherness—the curious quality of *alteritas* possessed by everything that is . . . Only man can express this distinction and distinguish himself."[40] We are an actor with a unique identity because we reveal this identity through action and speech. Without this revelation, we remain physically different from other people and things, but we do not have a distinct identity. Thus beginning, appearing, and distinctness are intertwined: "appearance, as distinguished from mere bodily existence, rests on initiative, but it is an initiative from which no human being can refrain and still be human."[41] To refrain from beginning means not to appear to others as a distinct agent, thus losing one's humanity. If, as Arendt claims, it is by means of beginning that we take responsibility for our own birth, refusal to begin entails a refusal of responsibility altogether—just like those in charge of the camps, indifferent to their own actions, do not care about whether or not they should have been born.

Because we can only begin by appearing to others, responsibility for action presupposes a degree of uncertainty and unpredictability. Arendt claims that "this revelatory quality of speech and action comes to the fore where people are *with* others and neither for nor against them—that is, in sheer human togetherness," and therefore "although nobody knows whom he reveals when he discloses himself in deed or word, he must be willing to risk the disclosure."[42] We do not know who we are before the act takes place, because the "who" will be determined by the way it appears to others. Arendt compares this "who" with the Greek *daimon*, which "accompanies each man throughout his life, always looking over his shoulder from behind and thus visible only to those he encounters."[43] This incapacity to know who we are before the act is seen by others is linked to its unpredictability. The meaning of the act is not something we possess before we perform it, but rather an effect of the process that is set in motion by it: "the light that illuminates processes of action, and therefore all historical processes, appears only at their end, frequently when all participants are dead."[44] This process constitutes a story, which can only be told by someone witnessing its entire development. The actor does not make the story, in the sense of having its final product in mind from the moment he acts. Rather, it is the storyteller who discloses the meaning of the actions that make up the story: "What the storyteller narrates must necessarily be hidden from the actor himself, at least as long as he is in the act or caught in its consequences, because to him the meaningfulness of his act is not in the story that follows."[45] It is in this sense that the actor must "risk his disclosure," for "one discloses one's self without ever either knowing himself or being able to calculate beforehand whom he reveals."[46] Action reveals who we are, but only insofar as it starts an unpredictable process that retroactively illuminates the meaning of the act.

The fact that the outcome as well as the meaning of an action are unpredictable would seem to imply that the actor is not responsible for it, but Arendt's goal is precisely to question the assumption that we are only responsible for what we can control. This assumption underlies Kant's claim that the ground of imputability for action is its "absolute spontaneity," that is, its quality of being a beginning completely undetermined by anything external to it, and thus purely active. As we have seen, Arendt preserves the idea that we are responsible insofar as we begin. However, she questions the idea that this beginning is absolute, for two reasons. On the one hand, every beginning is an insertion into a world that preexists it. On the other, each beginning establishes relations with other beginnings, which means that we can never control the consequences of what we do. Action, Arendt claims, "acts into a medium where every reaction becomes a chain reaction and where every process is the cause of new processes."[47] Due to the unpredictability of the chain reaction, we do not know who will have been revealed by the act before it has taken place. Yet it is only by virtue of beginning something new that we take responsibility for what we have begun, thus becoming unique.

In order for the actor to acquire a distinct identity, such identity must endure uncertainty. Arendt compares the state of having a unique personal identity to the Greek *eudaimmia*, which, she claims, refers to "the well-being of the *daimon* who accompanies each man throughout life, who is his distinct identity, but appears and is visible only to others."[48] To have a unique personal identity thus depends on appearing to others, facing uncertainty regarding what this identity consists in: "This unchangeable identity of the person, though disclosing itself intangibly in act and speech, becomes tangible only in the story of the actor's and speaker's life; but as such it can be known . . . only after it has come to its end."[49] Without appearing to others, our identity would not be uncertain, but by the same token it would cease to be: "whatever lacks this appearance comes and passes away like a dream, intimately and exclusively our own but without reality."[50]

It is important to note that, for Arendt, the unpredictability of the outcome of action is linked to the unpredictability of its meaning and of the identity of the actor. The idea of unpredictability refers not only to an empirical, but also to an existential condition: action is unpredictable not only because of the impossibility of controlling what will happen, but also because of the impossibility of knowing what it will have meant and who the actor will have been as a consequence of it. In acting, we put our very being into question, and we cannot act without risking our identity by establishing unpredictable relationships with others. Arendt's point is that this existential uncertainty is not a limitation to our capacity to act, which we could hypothetically overcome by increasing our capacity to control the outcome of action, but rather a constitutive aspect of action. Our willingness to act depends on our willingness accept our limitation in our capacity to control the meaning of what we do and who we are as a consequence of it. Enduring uncertainty, or what Arendt calls "the burden of unpredictability," is a precondition for having a distinct identity that can assume responsibility for action. Unwillingness to endure uncertainty is at the basis of the desire to escape responsibility that, Arendt believes, underlies modern ideologies and totalitarianism.

Forgiveness and the Burden of Unpredictability

The implications of Arendt's conception of personal identity in connection to the uncertainty of action for our understanding of responsibility become clear in Arendt's analysis of forgiveness. It follows from Arendt's attempt to detach responsibility from mastery over the meaning of action that forgiveness is also independent from such mastery. Moreover, Arendt believes that the absence of such mastery is the precondition for the actor to be subject to forgiveness. Given that action begins a process that the actor is unable to control, either by predicting or reversing its outcome, it places a burden on him. This burden stems from the fact that the actor "never quite knows what he is doing," and "always becomes 'guilty' of consequences he never intended or even foresaw."[51] For Arendt, it is by virtue of distinguishing the actor and giving him an identity that outlasts the act that the latter places a burden on him, rendering him guilty for a process which, although set in motion by him, he cannot control. This lack of control is precisely the reason why others have the power to forgive him.

On this point, Arendt finds a model of forgiveness in Jesus's teachings, and specifically in the idea that the reason why we must forgive is that "they know not what they do."[52] Given that we do not know the consequences of our actions, they produce what Jesus calls "trespassing," which, according to Arendt's interpretation, means "to miss" or "fail and go astray," rather than "to sin." Trespassing has nothing to do with the psychological state of the actor, but is rather an effect of the inherently relational nature of the act: "Trespassing is an everyday occurrence which is in the very nature of action's constant establishment of new relationships within the web of relations, and it needs forgiving, dismissing, in order to make it possible for life to go on by constantly releasing men from what they have done unknowingly."[53] Forgiveness thus releases the agent from his action "going astray," allowing him to begin again, and this releasement is only possible on the assumption that trespassing is an effect of the action "going astray" by virtue of its unpredictability.

Arendt's remarks on forgiveness show that, in her view, responsibility is inherently limited and relational. On the one hand, the act discloses a unique agent who remains responsible for the process that he or she has begun. On the other hand, because this process is inherently beyond his control, his responsibility is limited by the presence of others to whom he discloses himself and with whom he establishes relationships. As Garrath Williams points out, responsibility presupposes the establishment of relationships with others, even at the expense of our capacity to control the outcome of our actions.[54] Just like the act would have no underlying agent if it did not appear to others, the agent could not be forgiven if the outcome and the meaning of this appearing were completely under his control. In the public realm, where every action entails the establishment of relationships with others, responsibility implies a certain irresponsibility. Arendt claims that one of the aporias of action consists in "the impossibility to make the individual responsible for what occurs," as a consequence of which "it has always been a great temptation, for men of action no less that for men of thought, to find a substitute for action in the hope that the realm of human affairs may escape the haphazardness and moral irresponsibility inherent in a plurality of agents."[55] For Arendt, morality concerns the relationship between the self and itself, as opposed to its relationship with others. Alone with myself, I can control what I do, and thus remain absolutely responsible for the outcome. But as soon as my action appears to others,

I lose control and become dependent on their views and their reactions. Therefore, action in public makes the actor partly irresponsible for what he or she has done—but only "partly," because it is by virtue of acting in public that the actor acquires a unique identity that outlives the individual act, and that can consequently be forgiven for it. Without disclosing a "who" to others, there would be no durable actor behind the act that could be the subject of forgiveness: "the fact that the same *who*, revealed in action and speech, remains also the subject of forgiving is the deepest reason why nobody can forgive himself; here, as in action and speech generally, we are dependent upon others, to whom we appear in a distinctness which we ourselves are unable to perceive."[56]

It is precisely because responsibility depends on relationship with others, and is therefore never absolute, that it produces the desire to escape from plurality and the realm of human affairs. Given that every action begins a process that escapes our control, as soon as we act we are burdened with a guilt that exceeds our capacity to assume responsibility for it, and "this is reason enough to turn away with despair from the realm of human affairs and to hold in contempt the human capacity for freedom, which, by producing the web of human relationships, seems to entangle its producer to such an extent that he appears much more the victim and the sufferer than the author and doer of what he has done."[57] The only salvation from this entanglement, Arendt claims, "seems to lie in non-acting, in abstention from the whole realm of human affairs as the only means to safeguard one's sovereignty and integrity as a person," which leads to the identification of freedom with sovereignty, "the ideal of uncompromising self-sufficiency and mastership," which "is contradictory to the very condition of plurality."[58] The identification of freedom with absolute self-sufficiency is an effect of the desire to escape the burden of guilt that action imposes on us by virtue of starting a process that we do not control. Evidently, this identification has disastrous implications for the public realm, given that it implies that the existence of others is a limitation, rather than a precondition for freedom. If, however, we become responsible agents by means of beginning, this identification of freedom with self-sufficiency cannot but eliminate responsibility. An individual who does not appear to others remains master of his or her deeds, but by the same token lacks a unique identity, that is, a "who" that outlives his or her actions and is therefore subject to forgiveness.

We can see now that Arendt's account of forgiveness connects her notion of action in *The Human Condition* and her analysis of superfluousness and the elimination of responsibility in *Origins*. Superfluousness, as we have seen, is an effect of the destruction of all the standards by which we can be held responsible for our actions, in such a way that we cease to be individuals and become mere executors of an objective process. This process, unlike the processes begun by action, is not conformed by a web of relationships with multiple beginnings, but rather by a single logical development in which multiple people behave as if they were parts of "One Man." Under these conditions, there is no personal responsibility, because there are no beginnings aside from that of the process itself. To make oneself superfluous is to make oneself unforgivable, because we can only forgive those who begin, and thus we can only accept responsibility for the uncontrollable process that we set in motion. As Williams puts it, "a person can only answer for her deeds to the extent that her conduct is not hidden but seen by others, and is acknowledged as owing to her own initiative."[59] Given that it is intertwined with disclosure, beginning reveals a distinct, enduring actor that is the "who" underlying his act. Without this "who," there is no durable identity that can be held responsible for the act and thus be released from its consequences. And given that we can only become a "who" by risking our disclosure in the establishment of unpredictable relationships with others, willingness to endure uncertainty regarding the meaning of actions is a precondition for responsibility for action altogether.

Evil and Responsibility after Eichmann

The previous sections have shown that Arendt's notion of action in *The Human Condition* represents a reconsideration of the source of our sense of responsibility in response to the totalitarian attempt to eliminate it, and that this source is the uncertainty experienced in the establishment of relationships with others. Now I turn to Arendt's more explicit engagement with responsibility in her later writings, in connection to what she called "the banality of evil." I will show that, despite a shift of focus, Arendt's notion of "the banality of evil" is consistent with her characterization of totalitarianism as "radical evil" in one aspect: both notions refer to a kind of evil that consists in the elimination of responsibility for action. Arendt describes "radical evil" as stemming from a motivation that is beyond human comprehension, and "the banality of evil" as stemming from a lack of motivations altogether. However, a focus on the problem of responsibility in connection to "the banality of evil" will show that it also stems from a decision to escape one's own responsibility. This does not mean that both notions are identical. My claim is that they represent two different angles by which Arendt pursues a consistent concern in her work, namely, the connection between totalitarian evil and the modern tendency to escape responsibility. This claim builds on Jeff Love and Michael Meng's focus on the elimination of personal responsibility implied in "the banality of evil," but focuses on the complicity with this elimination by individuals rather than on its basis in modern bureaucracy as a system.[60]

Arendt's concern with responsibility in her late writings is influenced by her analysis of Eichmann's trial. While in *Origins* Arendt analyzes the destruction of responsibility from the viewpoint of the system, in *Eichmann in Jerusalem* and later writings she turns to the perspective of those who are complicit in this destruction. The question is no longer "how does totalitarianism eliminate responsibility?" but "why are people complicit in this elimination?" Although this question is not new in Arendt's work, the trial of Eichmann brought it to the center of her inquiries, in part because personal responsibility was crucial to the juridical process.[61] There is in this regard a clear resonance between the opening pages of *Eichmann in Jerusalem* and those of *Origins*, both of which warn against the tendency to narrate events as if the actors were representative of large historical tendencies, concealing their own motivations and choices. In the case of Eichmann, the problem was not only that the prosecutor tried to turn him into a representative of anti-Semitism in general, instead of focusing on his specific actions and motivations, but also, and more fundamentally, that Eichmann himself seemed to have acted with no motivations at all—as Arendt puts it in the epilogue, "except for an extraordinary diligence in looking out for his personal advancement, he had no motives at all."[62] It is precisely this seeming lack of motivations that made the adjudication of responsibility so difficult during the trial. Of course, Arendt's goal was not to exculpate Eichmann, but rather to face the novelty of his crimes as well as the challenges that they presented to our usual understanding of evil and responsibility.[63]

Eichmann's seeming lack of a sense of responsibility for his actions is linked to what Arendt describes as his "inability to think." She introduces this idea to characterize the perplexing fact that Eichmann described his initial years in charge of "the Jewish question" as if there had been a communion of interest between him and the Jews in the goal of relocation. This is an indication of an "almost total inability ever to look at anything from the other fellow's point of view."[64] This inability was supported, Arendt believes, by Eichmann's tendency to speak by means of a repetition of clichés and stock phrases, which worked as "the most reliable of all safeguards against the words and the presence of others," with the consequence that "no communication was possible with him."[65] For Eichmann, all that mattered when narrating a past event was the stock of words and phrases he had always linked to them, and which were often given to him as part of the "language rules" used by Nazi officials to conceal the true nature of what was happening (words like *extermination, liquidation,* or *killing* would be replaced by words like *final solution, evacuation,* and *especial treatment*).[66]

Despite this seeming inability to think about the meaning of his actions, Eichmann did not lack moral conscience altogether, but rather possessed an inverted kind of conscience. Arendt describes it in terms of an inversion of the feeling of pity, so that it ceases to work as an indication of criminality and becomes proof of a commitment to a historic task. Nazi officials, in Arendt's account, did not look for sadists and people who could enjoy killing innocent human beings, but rather sought people they could persuade to overcome their natural aversion to murder so as to fulfill their duty.[67] The point was that murdering an innocent person had to be seen not as a crime against that person but as a weight on the murderer, so that "instead of saying: What horrible things I did to people!, the murderers would be able to say: What horrible things I had to watch in the pursuance of my duties, how heavily the task weighed upon my shoulders!"[68] Thus the usual indications of criminality were reversed and became a signal of compliance with moral duty. This is one essential reason why, according to Arendt, it was so difficult to impute evil motivations to Eichmann. In complying with duty against his own private interest, he could insist that he had always been a "good citizen." A perplexing example of this logic is Eichmann's discomfort during the trial with the fact that he had made two exceptions to his duty: helping a half-Jewish cousin and a Jewish couple in Vienna to avoid the camps. The source of the discomfort is the fact that, for Eichmann, making no exceptions represented "the proof that he had always acted against his 'inclinations,' whether they were sentimental or inspired by interest, that he had always done his 'duty.'"[69] As long as one disregards one's personal interests and complies with duty, Eichmann reasoned, there is no ground on which one's actions can be judged to be criminal.

Following Arendt's analysis, the essential reason why it was so difficult to hold Eichmann responsible for his crimes is that he had indeed acted in accordance with the moral standards that were generally considered valid at the time. Eichmann certainly did not transgress any of the laws of the Third Reich in sending innocent people to their death, because sending innocent people to their death was precisely the law.[70] It is this coincidence between criminality and compliance with the law that constitutes, Arendt claims, the "moral point of the matter," which is reached "only when we realize that this happened within the frame of a legal order and that the cornerstone of this 'new law' consisted of the command 'Thou shalt kill,' not thy enemy but innocent people who were not even potentially dangerous."[71] In this regard, Eichmann's "inverted moral conscience" seemed to be strikingly close to a normal moral conscience, which equates compliance with duty with virtue. As a consequence, even the feeling of guilt ceased to be reliable as a source of moral guidance, for "guilt-feelings can . . . be aroused through a conflict between old habits and new commands . . . but they can just as well be aroused by the opposite: once killing or whatever the 'new morality' demands has become a habit and is accepted by everyone, the same man will feel guilty if he does not conform."[72] Even temptation, one of the clearest indications of evil, ceased working as a standard of criminality, for in the Third Reich one was "tempted" not to kill innocent people, and it required an effort to overcome this temptation and fulfill one's duty.[73] The problem of holding Eichmann and other Nazi criminals responsible is that they seemed to have acted according to all the standards that we usually associate with virtue.

In order to find a ground of responsibility that is different from the prevailing moral standards of one's political community, Arendt turns to a conception of moral conscience inspired by Socrates. In her view, moral conscience does not stem from a moral code, but rather from the dialogue between the self and itself: "I cannot do certain things, because having done them I shall no longer be able to live with myself."[74] In order to have a moral conscience, it is first of all necessary to experience this duality within ourselves, that is, the fact we are two-in-one. This duality takes place in the activity of thinking, in which "I speak with myself about whatever happens to concern me."[75] In speaking with myself, I become my own company, thus developing a concern with who I am that is at the root of moral considerations. According to Arendt, the validity of the fundamental formula of morality, according to which "it is better to suffer wrong than to do wrong," stems from the insight "that it is better to be at odds with the whole world than, being one, to be at odds with myself."[76] The ultimate standard of morality is therefore whether the self is in harmony or disharmony with itself. If we can tell the difference between right and wrong even against the opinion of everyone around us, it is because we are always in the company of ourselves and must consequently decide whether we want to be our own company: "it is better to suffer wrong than to do wrong, because you can remain the friend of the sufferer; who would want to be the friend of and have to live together with a murderer? Not even another murderer."[77] This inner dialogue, Arendt claims, does not require any standard given to it from without.[78] The only standard for distinguishing right from wrong is whether, in doing something, we can be in harmony with ourselves.

But a second condition is necessary, following Arendt, for the person to care about who he will be as an effect of his actions, namely, that he remembers them. This capacity to remember what we have done is what Arendt calls "moral personality," which also stems from thinking. To talk to oneself about the meaning of what one has done is indispensable for remembering it, for "no one can remember what he has not thought through in talking about it with himself."[79] This is why thinking is the precondition for being a person, namely, a stable self that remains one throughout its individual acts. Through the process of thought, "I explicitly constitute myself as a person, and I shall remain one to the extent that I am capable of such constitution ever again and anew."[80] Arendt compares this constitution of the self to "root-striking," which means one's thoughts and memories become the root of the self, which will be our company wherever we go.[81] The root sets a limit to what we are capable of doing, because we do not want to be in the company of someone who has done certain things. "Personality" thus refers to the quality of being a stable self that remains throughout its multiple states and deeds. For Arendt, there is nothing given about being a person, because it is the result of the activity of thinking and the remembrance that stems from it. If we suspend this activity, we cease to be persons and our actions become a series of events without an underlying identity.

We can see why lack of thinking entails a lack of responsibility. To be responsible for one's own deeds, there must be a self behind them that can be punished or forgiven for them. If I do not remember what I do, I cannot take responsibility for my actions, for the simple reason that I do not recognize them as "mine." Thus loss of thinking, in Arendt's words, entails "the loss of the self that constitutes the person."[82] This is precisely the reason why "rootless evil," as Arendt characterizes Eichmann's evil in a letter to Gershom Scholem, is unforgivable, for "in granting pardon, it is the person and not the crime that is forgiven; in rootless evil there is no person left whom one could ever forgive."[83] It is in this sense that Eichmann's crimes are not "radical," but rather "rootless" or "shallow." Those who do not strike roots are capable of doing anything, because they "skid only over the surface of events," and "permit themselves to be carried away without ever penetrating into whatever depth they may be capable of."[84] This superficiality enables people to engage in the most extreme forms of evil because they do not care about what they do. Those who have a root in their own person cannot do certain things because they will not be able to live with themselves, which is why "extreme evil is possible only where these self-grown roots, which automatically limit the possibilities, are entirely absent."[85] As a consequence, Arendt claims, "the greatest evildoers are those who don't remember because they have never given thought to the matter, and, without remembrance, nothing can hold them back."[86]

Arendt's remarks suggest that the reason why it is difficult to hold totalitarian criminals like Eichmann responsible for their actions is that they have eliminated their own personality, and thus feel no need to take responsibility for their actions beyond the standards of the world in which they were performed. Arendt's account of Eichmann seemed exculpatory precisely because this "new type of criminal," as she described him, does not act on the basis of a sense of responsibility as we usually understand it. Instead of insisting that Eichmann was responsible in the usual sense of the term, Arendt strived to reconsider responsibility in a way that would make the crime understandable. Following Benjamin Schupmann's and Sophie Cloutier's readings of Arendt's writings on evil, we may interpret Arendt as uncovering a more fundamental responsibility that determines whether we assume or deny responsibility for action to begin with.[87] As Pitkin notes, Arendt's terminology is ambiguous and sounds exculpatory at some points, which explains why some readers have criticized her for remaining within the philosophical association of evil with an intellectual deficiency—as if evil was determined by an incapacity to think.[88] However, some passages in Arendt's writings show that she is aware that "inability to think" involves some sort of willful choice. In *The Life of the Mind*, she claims that thinking "is not a prerogative of the few but an ever-present faculty in everybody," so "everybody may come to shun that intercourse with oneself."[89] In "Some Questions of Moral Philosophy," she claims that the reason why Eichmann and other Nazi criminals seem to lack responsibility is that "they renounced voluntarily all personal qualities, as if nobody were left to be either punished of forgiven."[90] Clearly, Arendt at least suspects that the absence of a sense of responsibility characteristic of totalitarian criminals stems from a decision to eliminate responsibility as such.

As we have seen, Arendt repeatedly characterizes totalitarian evil as stemming from the destruction of the sense of responsibility. This destruction can be interpreted as "radical evil," insofar as it involves a motivation beyond the usual motivations associated with evil-doing (egoism, lust for power, hatred), as Arendt suggests in *Origins*. It can also be interpreted as a "banal" kind of evil, insofar as it appears as an utter lack of motivations due to the person's thoughtlessness. Although there is an apparent tension between both perspectives, as Dana Villa claims, there is no "contradiction" between the two "at the level of philosophical reflection on the nature of evil," as he maintains.[91] Instead, as Peg Birmingham has recently argued, while radical evil characterizes the production of superfluousness (or, in my reading, the destruction of responsibility), "the banality of evil" characterizes the complicity of superfluous individuals (or individuals who lack a sense of responsibility) in this production.[92] The nature of totalitarian evil, whether "radical" or "banal," is linked to the attempt to eliminate the ground of responsibility for action. In *The Human Condition*, this ground is located in the appearance of the actor to others through action, while in Arendt's later writings, it is located in the faculty of thinking. One question that remains open is whether the two sources of responsibility share an element in common, that is, whether thinking also involves uncertainty and the establishment of relationships with others.

Responsibility between Thinking and Action

In this section, I show that although Arendt claims that thinking, unlike action, can take place in solitude, she suggests in several passages in her work that it often depends on the existence of others. By stressing the link between thinking and the establishment of relationships with others, I argue that it, like action, involves an experience of uncertainty that is essential for responsibility. This interpretation of Arendt's essays on thinking departs from Rosalyn Diprose's claim that for Arendt thinking is inherently individual and runs counter to the collective nature of action.[93] As we will see, Arendt believes that there is a link between the experience of communicating our ideas to others and the dialogue between the self and itself that is essential for remembering our actions, and thus for taking responsibility for them. In some passages, Arendt suggests that even in solitude thinking demands that one's own self becomes the representative of other viewpoints. If this is the case, then thinking involves the establishment of relationships with others and the ensuing exposure to uncertainty. The "thoughtlessness" characteristic of "the banality of evil" stems from a desire to eliminate this second source of uncertainty, namely, the one that takes place when we establish relationships with other viewpoints by sharing our thoughts. Let us keep in mind that Arendt describes Eichmann's inability to think as an "almost total inability ever to look at anything from the other fellow's point of view."

In order to avoid confusion, it is important to note that Arendt sees thinking and action as different and often in tension with one another. One important difference between thinking and action is that the former, unlike the latter, can withdraw from the presence of others, which is why it can work as a moral safeguard against their viewpoints when they turn complicit in crimes. In her lectures on responsibility, Arendt considers thinking, as well as the moral propositions that stem from it, as "politically a borderline phenomenon."[94] The reason is that a moral truth, such as "it is better to suffer wrong than to do wrong," "has nothing whatsoever to do with action." Moreover, Arendt claims that "politically speaking—that is, from the viewpoint of the community or of the world we live in—it is irresponsible; its standard is the self and not the world, neither its improvement nor change."[95] Political responsibility implies a concern with the world, and is therefore inherently collective because the world is never exclusively of our own making. Moral or personal responsibility, or what she designates as "guilt," implies concern with the self, and is therefore strictly individual.[96] Given that moral considerations do not tell us how to engage with the world, they remain entirely negative with regard to action, in the sense that they only tell us not to act under certain circumstances. It is only in situations where political and personal responsibility enter in conflict with one another that the latter becomes politically relevant.

Despite the apparently stark contrast between the two, Arendt's views on the relation between thinking and action are ambivalent. Although at some points she sees them as contrary to one another, linking action to politics and thinking to solitude, there are passages where she suggests that both action and thinking involve the establishment of relationships with others. In *Origins*, Arendt claims that the dialogue of the two-in-one of thinking "does not lose contact with the world of my fellow-men because they are represented in the self with whom I lead the dialogue of thought," and that "this two-in-one needs the others in order to become one again: one unchangeable individual whose identity can never be mistaken for that of any other."[97] Arendt develops this idea extensively in *The Life of the Mind*, where she addresses the relationship between thinking and acting through an analysis of Socrates. The importance of Socrates stems from the fact that, unlike later "professional philosophers" entirely devoted to the activity of thinking in solitude, he "unified two apparently contradictory passions, for thinking and acting," because he was "equally at home in both spheres and able to move from one sphere to the other with the greatest apparent ease."[98] The reason why Socrates could dwell both in solitude and in public is that, as opposed to "the inclination to find solutions for riddles and then demonstrate them to others," he "felt the urge to check with his fellow-men to learn whether his perplexities were shared by them."[99]

Socrates' thinking is essential for responsibility because, by putting the person in relation to others, it makes him examine his own viewpoints. The goal is not to reach a common viewpoint, but to share the perplexities that emerge when confronting my viewpoint with that of others: "if the wind of thinking . . . has shaken you from your sleep and made you fully awake and alive, then you will see that you have nothing in your grasp but perplexities, and the best we can do with them is share them with each other."[100] This kind of thinking does not produce any teaching that may orient our actions, but rather dissolves all established doctrines. It is therefore politically dangerous and potentially leads to nihilism.[101] However, it influences political action insofar as it prevents us from adopting a code of conduct as if it were the only valid one. Thinking may not tell us what is right, but "non-thinking, which seems so recommendable a state for political and moral affairs, also has its perils," because "by shielding people from the dangers of examination, it teaches them to hold fast to whatever the prescribed rules of conduct may be at a given time in a given society."[102] Thinking, then, allows us to examine our rules of conduct, and although this examination requires that we temporarily withdraw from the public, it also requires that we communicate our perplexities to others.

Arendt stresses the importance of others for thinking even more forcefully in her remarks on what she calls "representative thinking." In the *Lectures on Kant's Political Philosophy*, she claims that "critical thinking . . . exposes itself to 'the test of free and open examination,' and this means that the more people participate in it, the better."[103] Critical thinking is not merely a preparation for a more valid truth or doctrine than the predominant one, but rather the open-ended examination of one's own beliefs. As a consequence, it needs the involvement of others to whom one can communicate one's beliefs, so that they are open to examination. Even if thinking proceeds only in solitude, "unless you can somehow communicate and expose to the test of others . . . whatever you may have found out when you were alone, this faculty exerted in solitude will disappear."[104] Even in solitude the thinker needs to take into account others, given that "even if I shun all company or am completely isolated while forming an opinion, I am not simply together only with myself in the solitude of philosophical thought; I remain in this world of universal interdependence, where I can make myself the representative of everybody else."[105] Representative thinking takes place in solitude, where I am in the company of myself. But this self with whom I speak is a representative of everybody else, and thus of a potential public. Thus even in solitude, Arendt suggests, I am not completely withdrawn from the world, but only distanced from it in such a way that it becomes possible to examine my thoughts and beliefs.

These remarks on representative thinking suggest that there is one important aspect in common between the inner dialogue of conscience that is essential to thinking and the world of appearances that is essential to action. Arendt describes the inner dialogue of thinking as a process of "striking roots," in the sense that by thinking about who I am as a consequence of my actions, I remember them, and thus become a durable person who can take responsibility for them. But in order to think, one must be willing to be responsible to begin with. In the *Lectures*, Arendt claims that the examination of opinions characteristic of critical thinking "presupposes that everyone is willing and able to render an account of what he thinks and says."¹⁰⁶ In this specific sense, and notwithstanding Arendt's frequent opposition between the two, philosophy and politics share something important in common: just like Plato departed from earlier "wise men" in that he gave an account of his thoughts, "to render accounts is what Athenian citizens asked of their politicians, not only in money matters but in matters of politics. They could be held responsible."¹⁰⁷

We can see that although Arendt claims at some points that thinking and action are different and in conflict with one another, there are passages where she suggests that they both depend on willingness to assume responsibility by establishing relationships with others. I believe that these passages are important to avoid the conclusion that thinking and moral responsibility are inherently independent of relationships with others. Certainly, action and thinking are different, because the former depends on appearing to others in a way that the latter does not. Sometimes it may even be necessary to rely on thinking in solitude in order to prevent action from losing all moral orientation. But Arendt's remarks on Socrates make clear that thinking often depends on sharing our opinions with others. Without others, we would take our viewpoint, including our code of conduct, as self-evident, and never consider how our actions will be seen by them. If, as Arendt claims, thinking about our actions is a condition for remembering them and becoming a moral person, then a refusal to relate to others through thinking involves absence of personality and, consequently, of responsibility as well. Acting on the basis of a code of conduct does not require that we think about what we do, in the sense of considering how our actions may look from someone else's standpoint. This is why, following Arendt's remarks on the relationship between thinking and remembering, actions that simply comply with a code of conduct are not remembered, in the sense of belonging to a person that is willing to take responsibility for them. Taking responsibility for our actions demands considering how they will look from other perspectives, and thus exposure to multiple viewpoints.

Ultimately, one idea to which Arendt returns repeatedly throughout her work is that responsibility stems from our capacity to relate to others by means of either action or thinking, thus facing the uncertainty involved in responses by others. Arendt never developed a systematic theory of responsibility, and her uses of this term are not always consistent throughout her writings. However, as I have been arguing, there is one trend of thought linking responsibility to the capacity to establish relationships with others. The reason why totalitarian criminals, whether "superfluous" (unable to relate to others through action as beginning) or "thoughtless" (unable to relate to others through thinking) are unpunishable and unforgivable, is because they refuse to take responsibility for their actions. Shielded from relationships with others by means of ideologies and clichés, totalitarian criminals cease to care about the meaning of what they do beyond conformity with the law of the land. Caring for the ethical implications of our actions, as Arendt claims in her writings on moral philosophy, requires an enduring personality that is constituted in the establishment of relations with others. While we may err and do bad things when we act and think with others, refusing to establish relationships by means of action and thinking is at the core of the worst kind of evil, namely, the kind of evil that stems from utter indifference to our own actions.

Conclusion

Despite Arendt's shifts on the nature of totalitarian evil, there is a persistent concern in her work with the link between this kind of evil and the destruction of responsibility. The reason why totalitarian crimes are "unpunishable" and "unforgivable" is that they lack a stable personality behind them, as if the deeds were performed by no one. This observation led Arendt to explore the ground of responsibility. In *The Human Condition*, she locates this ground in the actor's capacity to begin, which is intertwined with disclosure to others. Because beginning entails an insertion into a web of human relationships, we are never in control either of the meaning or of the outcome of our actions. Yet by disclosing ourselves to others, we acquire an enduring identity that can take responsibility for its deeds, and which may be either forgiven or punished for them. Responsibility for action does not presuppose complete control over what we do, but rather the capacity to "risk our disclosure" and establish relations that exceed our control. After *Eichmann in Jerusalem*, Arendt's concern with responsibility shifted to the faculty of thinking which, by virtue of making us remember what we do, constitutes an enduring person who outlives her actions. While thinking and action are different activities that take place in different realms (solitude and the public), Arendt's analysis of "representative thinking" shows that the two are connected. Both action and representative thinking presuppose the presence of others, and it is by taking these others into account, either in our disclosure through action or in the examination of our beliefs in thinking, that we are capable of taking responsibility for our deeds and thoughts. In both cases, responsibility presupposes that we establish relationships with others, thus exposing ourselves to processes and viewpoints that we cannot control.

We have seen that Arendt is concerned from early on with the modern tendency to escape responsibility, which is at the root of the development of modern ideologies. Because it is only possible in the presence of others, action entails a twofold frustration: we do not know what its outcome and its meaning will be, and as a consequence, we do not know who we will be as a result of it. Therefore, action demands courage—not only in the usual sense of willingness to face dangers to our well-being, but also in the sense of willingness to expose our very identity to the view and to the reactions of others. There is no guarantee that our action will succeed, that is, that we will have been who we intended to be at the moment of action, which is why forgiveness and punishment are essential for limiting the risk we face when entering the public realm. This uncertainty creates two possibilities: either to accept a responsibility that is inherently limited, in the sense that it exposes us to meanings and outcomes that we can neither control nor foresee, or to withdraw from responsibility, either by leaving the public realm or, what is much more dangerous, by seeking to turn the public realm into a perfectly predictable process. Those who choose this latter path are not only the ones in charge of the project of making the world entirely predictable, but also the ones who happily subject themselves to it—"happily" because they enjoy the liberation from responsibility that the project entails.

In this regard, the focus on responsibility illuminates what I see as the essence of "the banality of evil": it is an active, willful destruction of one's own capacity for responsible action. It is therefore no coincidence that Arendt's analysis of Eichmann's trial seemed "exculpatory." The reason for this is not that Arendt believed that Eichmann had no responsibility for his actions, but rather that Eichmann himself truly believed so, and acted on the basis of this belief. This self-exculpatory mentality should not be understood as the mere absence of a faculty. The essential point, following my reading, is that to erase one's own responsibility, and thus to become "unpunishable" and "unforgivable," stems in itself from a decision either to act as if we were responsible for what we do or as if we were mere executioners of a larger process. Eichmann's unyielding commitment to his duty, even against his own self-interest, shows to what extent the elimination of responsibility can become an end in itself. In order to become thoughtless, one must actively shun the exposure to uncertainty involved in acting and thinking with others, and this "shunning" has no other goal than the liberation from uncertainty. It is by shunning responsibility that people become superfluous, and it is by virtue of being superfluous that they are released from the uncertainty and unpredictability involved in responsibility.

Chapter 2

Kant on the Deceptiveness of Evil

Totalitarian evil, following my reading of Arendt in the previous chapter, consists in the elimination of responsibility. Eichmann as well as other functionaries in charge of or complicit in mass murder did not act on the basis of cruelty, hatred, or selfishness, which are the motivations usually associated with the image of evil as deficiency, but rather of an utter indifference to their own actions. This indifference stems from a decision to refuse the uncertainty inherent in appearing to others through action, which is essential for the constitution of an enduring self that can take responsibility for what he or she has done. Despite the seeming stupidity and superficiality characteristic of complicity in totalitarianism, which are at the core of Arendt's polemical description of Eichmann during his trial, her analysis of evil points to a much deeper problem. In order for the totalitarian regime to rely on thoughtless, superficial individuals to carry out the leader's orders, it is necessary that these individuals choose to erase their personality, that is, their ability to take responsibility for their actions. This elimination of the sense of responsibility is at the core of totalitarian evil.

In this chapter, I connect Arendt's inquiries into the ground of responsibility and the desire to eliminate it with Immanuel Kant's thesis of radical evil in *Religion within the Boundaries of Mere Reason*. I turn to Kant not because I believe he has a better insight into evil and responsibility than Arendt. Evidently, having lived through totalitarianism and witnessed some of the developments of modern ideologies, Arendt had a broader perspective on the forms and sources of evil in modern politics. Instead, I turn to Kant because he pays closer attention to an aspect of evil that Arendt hints at, but does not analyze systematically, namely, the faculty of choice. If "the banality of evil," as we have seen, consists in a decision to eliminate one's own responsibility, it is because our capacity to choose what to do, which is a precondition of responsibility, must contain a desire to eliminate itself. It is this desire, I will argue, that is at the core of Kant's famous thesis of "radical evil." Evil is "radical," according to Kant, because it corrupts the core of freedom, which is, in his view, the willingness to assume responsibility for action.

The center of my reading of Kant is the connection between responsibility and choice or *Willkür*, which involves a fundamental uncertainty regarding one's own moral character. I show that the same faculty that makes us responsible for our actions, namely, choice, makes our moral character inscrutable. In order to be responsible for our actions, they must stem from a personal character that is freely chosen, and in order to be freely chosen, the character must remain inscrutable. If we had insight into the ultimate ground determining our character, it would cease to be free, and thus we would cease to be responsible for our actions. Therefore, assuming responsibility for our actions involves accepting a fundamental uncertainty regarding their moral worth. Radical evil consists in the attempt to overcome this uncertainty by subordinating our actions to moral rituals that serve as a guarantee of moral virtue. This view of evil as elimination of uncertainty, I will show, had an influence in Arendt's mentors Karl Jaspers and Martin Heidegger, which explains some of the connections between Kant's thesis of radical evil and Arendt's notion of "the banality of evil." Both notions coincide in the idea that evil takes place when the person attempts to eliminate a core of uncertainty that is constitutive of action.

In addition to clarifying the connection between Arendt's "the banality of evil" and Kant's "radical evil" through the problem of responsibility for action, my reading of Kant presents two contributions to our understanding of Kant's *Religion*. First, a focus on the problem of responsibility clarifies some of the apparent paradoxes of Kant's thesis of radical evil and its role in the development of his understanding of action. A number of political theorists have criticized Kant's practical philosophy on the grounds that it disavows the contingency of politics by subordinating action to a transcendental moral law.[1] Recently, Shalini Satkunanandan has challenged this view and argued that the moral law is not an epistemological formula that we can use to know what a good action is, but rather an ontological experience of our capacity to think and transform ourselves, thus awakening a sense of responsibility that is beyond compliance with rules.[2] Following Satkunanandan's perspective, I argue that a focus on the problem of evil and responsibility in Kant's *Religion* shows a concern with the ritualization of moral action, and an attempt to affirm the constitutive uncertainty involved in it. Second, the place of *Religion* in the context of Kant's practical philosophy has been the subject of debate in recent years. While J. B. Schneewind and Henry Allison read the text as complementing and completing Kant's conception of moral action as based on autonomy, Susan Shell, Peter Fenves, and Ian Hunter have emphasized the ways in which it departs from such conception and problematizes the Enlightenment's identification of freedom with self-knowledge and self-mastery.[3] My reading supports this second stance by showing that Kant's understanding of responsibility and evil in *Religion* represents a partial but significant departure from the one that predominates in the central texts of his practical philosophy.

Arendt, Eichmann, Kant

Interpreting Kant's thesis of radical evil in the context of discussions around the nature of totalitarianism is not a purely theoretical exercise. As Arendt recounts in *Eichmann in Jerusalem*, Eichmann himself brought Kant into the scene when he claimed before his trial that he had lived his whole life according to Kant's moral precepts and to his definition of duty. It would be pointless to discuss whether Eichmann's use of Kant was correct or plausible, for all ideas can be appropriated and manipulated to serve all kinds of actions in different contexts. However, this does not mean that we should dismiss Eichmann's reference to Kant altogether, especially given that, according to Arendt, this reference showed at least some accurate understanding of Kant's moral philosophy. Analyzing Eichmann's own use of Kant can illuminate some of the challenges and dangers that Kant's moral categories encounter when they enter the political realm. Judith Butler has claimed that Arendt's later writings can be understood to some extent as an attempt to mobilize Kant's philosophy in a way that departs from its usage by Eichmann.[4] Building on Butler's perspective, I reconstruct in this section the impact of Eichmann's reference to Kant in Arendt's later reflections on Kant's moral philosophy. I show that these reflections led her to inquire into the faculty of choice, which is precisely Kant's central concern in his essay on radical evil. In the following sections, I read the thesis of radical evil on the basis of the problem posed by the notion of "the banality of evil," namely, the source and possible elimination of our sense of responsibility.

Eichmann's reference to Kant appears in a central moment of Arendt's reconstruction of the trial. Arendt recounts that during the police interrogation prior to the trial, Eichmann claimed that he had lived his whole life according to Kant's moral precepts and to his definition of duty. When asked to clarify what he had meant, he answered with "an approximately correct definition of the categorical imperative," according to Arendt: "I meant by my remark about Kant that the principle of my will must always be such that it can become the principle of general laws."[5] Eichmann, who claimed that he had read the *Critique of Practical Reason*, added that he knew that "from the moment he was charged with carrying out the Final Solution he had ceased to live according to Kantian principles," but "he had consoled himself with the thought that he no longer 'was master of his own deeds,' that he was 'unable to change anything.'"[6] Arendt believes, however, that Eichmann did not dismiss Kant's moral philosophy altogether, but rather distorted it so that it would fit "the categorical imperative in the Third Reich": "act as if the principle of your actions were the same as that of the legislator or of the law of the land."[7] This constitutes what Eichmann himself called "the version of Kant 'for the household use of the little man.'" The one aspect of this "household use" that preserves the spirit of Kant, Arendt claims, is the demand that "a man do more than obey the law, that he go beyond the mere call of obedience and identify his own will with the principle behind the law."[8] For Eichmann, this principle was "the will of the Führer." According to Arendt, it is this complete identification with the principle behind the law of the land that explains Eichmann's thoroughness in performing his duty: "a law was a law, there could be no exceptions." This "no exception" mentality was so ingrained in Eichmann's understanding of duty that he felt ashamed about the two instances in which he had helped Jewish acquaintances to avoid the camps.[9] From Eichmann's viewpoint, this represented an exception to his compliance with duty driven by personal motives.

Eichmann's invocation of Kant served the idea that he had simply been a replaceable cog in the totalitarian regime, and thus that he bore no responsibility for his actions beyond compliance with duty. The reasoning would seem to confirm Arendt's long-standing distrust of the philosophy of the will, and especially of its modern introduction into the public realm by Rousseau and the French Revolution. In *On Revolution*, Arendt establishes a link between the development of terror and Rousseau's "general will," which she describes as "the articulation of a general interest, the interest of the people or the nation as a whole," adding that "because this interest or will is general, its very existence hinges on its being opposed to each interest or will in particular."[10] The contrast between the general and the particular will is at the core of the equation of virtue with "selflessness," which was popularized by the French Revolution, and according to which "the value of a man may be judged by the extent to which he acts against his own interest and against his own will."[11] The connection between this idea and Eichmann's self-justification is not difficult to see: no matter what a person does, the sacrifice of his or her personal interests and feelings is the ultimate standard of virtue. Arendt identifies a twofold problem in this idea. First, it conceals the fact that people may do evil without any egoistic motivation, and that they may even be driven to evildoing by their attachment to self-sacrifice, as seen in the different outbursts of terror in modernity. Second, insofar as the source of duty is independent of all personal interests and feelings, it would seem like the person bears no responsibility for his or her actions. From Eichmann's perspective, since he had thoroughly complied with the law, only the source of the law could be held accountable for what he had done. This disavowal of one's own choice and motivations as a source of action is the reason why it was so difficult during the trial to adjudicate responsibility to Eichmann—is not thorough compliance with the law the clearest sign of virtue?

Influenced by her encounter with Eichmann, Arendt became interested in the notion of the will in her later writings, and in Kant's thoughts on it in particular. Most of her remarks criticize Kant on the grounds that his conception of the will misunderstands the essence of freedom. The source of her concern is Kant's subordination of the will to practical reason, which in an early note in her *Journals of Thought* she attributes to his indebtedness to Rousseau: "Practical reason as the voice of everyone (in Rousseau) or the voice of humanity in the individual (in Kant) prescribes what is to be willed."[12] In her later writings, Arendt explains that the obedience of the will to practical reason undermines its freedom, for the latter "borrows its obligatory power from the compulsion exerted on the mind by self-evident truth or logical reasoning."[13] Thus if reason commands the will, Arendt claims in another essay, then it "would no longer be free but would stand under the dictate of reason."[14] Kant sought to avoid this conclusion by defining freedom as obedience to a law of which one is the legislator (that is, as autonomy), and locating the source of such law in practical reason. But Arendt finds this solution unsuccessful, for insofar as freedom is subordinated to a general law, then it is mistaken with obedience to a fixed command, which eliminates spontaneity in the sense of beginning something new. Moreover, Eichmann showed that the demand of obedience is more firm than the authority of reason: in its "household use," Kant's notion of the will tells us that we must obey the law, whatever the law is, and that the authority of its source is unquestionable and above personal feelings and opinions. Therefore, when Eichmann claimed that not him but the Führer was responsible for what he had done, he preserved one essential aspect of Kant's subordination of the will to practical reason: the authority of the law is prior to and independent of the person's feelings and opinions.

Arendt criticizes Kant's conception of evil, or at least its implications for our understanding of totalitarianism, in similar terms. In her view, the crimes of totalitarianism cannot be explained in terms of the traditional motivations linked to evildoing, such as self-interest, greed, or resentment.[15] These motivations are present to some degree in all human beings, which renders the deeds that stem from them comprehensible. Totalitarian crimes, by contrast, obey no recognizable motivation, which is why Arendt characterizes them in *The Origins of Totalitarianism* as an "absolute" evil. Kant, Arendt claims, must have suspected this form of evil when he coined the notion of "radical evil," but "he immediately rationalized it in the concept of a 'perverted ill will' that could be explained by comprehensible motives."[16] This critical stance toward Kant's conception of evil remains after Arendt's shift to a view of totalitarian crimes as "banal" or "rootless," in the sense of lacking motivations at all. In "Some Question of Moral Philosophy," she claims that "all transgressions are explained by Kant as exceptions that a man is tempted to make from a law which he otherwise recognizes as valid."[17] In Arendt's view, Kant remained within the traditional philosophical denial of the positivity of evil, which locates its source in limitations that prevent us from doing good. Totalitarian evil, either "absolute" or "rootless," showed that this is not the case: people may do evil because of motives that do not stem from a limitation that prevents them from complying with a law that they recognize as valid.

Although Arendt found the philosophy of the will mostly unable to cope with Eichmann's seeming lack of responsibility, she did not dismiss it altogether. At the beginning of her more extensive engagement with this philosophy in *The Life of the Mind*, she claims that aside from its paradoxes and self-contradictions, she shall "follow a parallel development in the history of the Will," in which it "creates the *person* that can be blamed or praised and anyhow held responsible not merely for its actions but its whole 'Being,' its *character*."[18] Arendt's interest in this development is influenced by her view that Eichmann lacked personality, namely, an enduring self that can be held accountable for its actions. Given that Eichmann did not think about who he would be as a result of his actions, he was unable to remember and to assume responsibility for them.[19] Although most of Arendt's reflections on moral personality focus on the faculty of thinking, she considered the importance of choice as the faculty that constitutes our moral character. Most of her remarks on this topic in her later writings are presented in connection to Duns Scotus. In *The Life of the Mind*, she claims that willing fashions the self "into an 'enduring I' that directs all particular acts of volition," and that "it creates the self's *character* and therefore was sometimes understood as the *principium individuationis*, the source of the person's specific identity."[20] In her essay "Some Questions of Moral Philosophy," she claims that "the will is the arbiter between reason and desire, and as such the will alone is free," adding that "while reason reveals what is common to all men, and desires what is common to all living organisms, only the will is entirely my own."[21] She notes in her unpublished manuscript "Basic Moral Propositions" that the will is free "as the faculty of choosing," and that "by willing I decide. And this is the faculty of freedom."[22] The idea that the will, understood as choice, is the faculty of freedom contradicts most of Arendt's remarks throughout her work, and brings her strikingly close to Kant's analysis of choice in his only text specifically concerned with it, namely, *Religion within the Boundaries of Mere Reason*. This is not surprising, however, given that Kant's inquiry in this text responds to the same concern that Arendt pursued, namely, how to hold people responsible for evil actions.

I will return to the theoretical connection between Arendt's and Kant's insights on evil and responsibility in the last section of this chapter, but it is worth noting a historical link that further justifies examining this connection. Scholars have frequently noted that the first suggestion that totalitarian evil, contrary to Arendt's original characterization of it as "absolute," must be confronted in its "total banality," appears in a letter by Jaspers from 1946.[23] However, no scholar to my knowledge has pointed out that in 1935, two years after Hitler's coming to power, Jaspers published an essay on Kant's "radical evil" and its importance for a critical understanding of modernity. Although Kant is not explicitly mentioned in Jaspers's letter, it is evident that its main point, which is that Nazi crimes are not "demonic" but "banal," is strongly influenced by Kant's thoughts on evil. Arendt acknowledged the pertinence of Jaspers's perspective in her response letter and, years later, the term that he had suggested would appear in the subtitle of her book on Eichmann.[24] Thus indirectly, and most likely inadvertently, Arendt's thoughts on totalitarian evil were influenced by Kant, via Jaspers. This intellectual trajectory connecting Kant, Jaspers, and Arendt, I will argue, is linked to a political concern running through the three thinkers, namely, the emergence of a new form of evil that consists in the elimination of responsibility, taking place with the increasing ritualization and bureaucratization of moral action.

Freedom and the Ground of Imputability

What is responsibility for Kant? On the one hand, the answer to this question seems simple: we are responsible for the choice to either comply with the moral law or pursue our self-interest. Yet the nature of this choice is much more complicated than it looks at first sight, and it poses difficult problems for our understanding of evil. There is, first, the problem that if the choice for either the moral law or self-interest is free, and therefore undetermined by anything external to us, it appears to be arbitrary, which means that there is no possible insight into the constitution of our moral character. Second, given that the choice is purely noumenal, that is, independent from natural causality, we have no phenomenal access to it, and therefore we cannot know what the person has chosen. These may sound like obscure theological questions, and it is no coincidence that Kant addresses them in a text on religion. But we should keep in mind that, as Allen Wood has shown, questions of morality and of religion are intertwined in Kant's thought.[25] Responsibility for action generates multiple paradoxes and perplexities that often call for theological ideas. In this section, I reconstruct Kant's remarks on responsibility in his moral philosophy. In the sections that follow, I show how *Religion*, and the thesis of radical evil in particular, responds to some latent problems in this understanding of responsibility.

Kant's earliest consideration of the ground of responsibility in his critical practical philosophy situates it in transcendental freedom. He introduces this concept in the third antinomy of reason, which is concerned with the question of whether all events have a prior cause in time, or an event without a prior cause is possible. The solution consists in showing that the two possibilities are not mutually exclusive. As appearances, all events have a prior cause in time. But appearances do not exhaust the field of all things, which includes their source, the "things in themselves." Therefore, it is at least possible that there are things in the world capable of starting a series of events that is not determined by a prior cause in time. This capacity is precisely transcendental freedom which, Kant claims in a remark, "constitutes only that of the absolute spontaneity of an action, as the real ground of its imputability [*Imputabilität*]."[26] Kant defines transcendental freedom as "the faculty of beginning a state **from itself**, the causality of which does not in turn stand under another cause determining it in time in accordance with the law of nature."[27] The existence of this capacity cannot be proved, because all experience is ruled by the law of natural causality. However, it cannot be disproved either, and so it is legitimate to presuppose its existence for practical purposes.

While transcendental freedom is the ground of imputability, its object, or that for which we are responsible, proceeds from practical freedom. In order to be responsible for our actions, we must not only be independent from external determinations, but also possess a standard by which to evaluate our actions. Kant defines practical freedom as "the independence of the power of choice [*Willkür*] from necessitation by impulses of sensibility."[28] While sensible impulses subject us to the law of natural causality, practical freedom "presupposes that although something has not happened, it nevertheless **ought** to have happened."[29] The source of the idea that something ought to happen, or what Kant calls "imperatives," is reason. This is the only faculty capable of "complete spontaneity," because it is the only faculty that is altogether independent of affection by sensibility, and so "it makes its own order according to ideas, to which it fits the empirical conditions and according to which it even declares actions to be necessary that yet **have not occurred** and perhaps will not occur."[30] Reason can produce imperatives for action based on ideas, independently of natural necessitation. These imperatives are the basis of moral judgments, for "however many natural grounds or sensible stimuli there may be that impel me to **will**, they cannot produce the **ought** but only a willing . . . , over against which the ought that reason pronounces sets a measure and a goal, indeed, a prohibition and authorization."³¹ Spontaneity is thus the ground of imputability in a twofold sense: it allows us to act independently of external determinations (transcendental freedom) and it allows reason to produce imperatives for action (practical freedom).

Kant's remarks explain the possibility of moral imperatives as a source of action, but they leave open the problem of imputability for evil actions. Kant claims that spontaneity renders choice independent of necessitation by sensible impulses, but he acknowledges that it is nevertheless affected by them. In the only passage specifically devoted to Willkür in the Critique of Pure Reason, Kant explains that

> a power of choice [Willkür] is **sensible** insofar as it is **pathologically affected** (through moving-causes of sensibility); it is called an **animal** power of choice (arbitrium brutum) if it can be **pathologically necessitated.** The human power of choice [Willkür] is indeed an arbitrium sensitivum, yet not brutum but liberum, because sensibility does not render its action necessary, but in the human being there is a faculty of determining oneself from oneself, independently of necessitation by sensible impulses.³²

Kant defines the human Willkür or arbitrium as both "sensitivum" and "liberum," which lays out the contrast between sensibility and freedom. The contrast preserves the distinction between choice and freedom that was present in both Wolff and Baumgarten. Following Leibniz, Wolff conceives of choice as the capacity to act on the basis of an internal ground, and freedom as the capacity to understand this ground by means of reason.³³ Baumgarten introduces an innovation that Kant takes up, namely, the contrast between a sensible and a nonsensible choice. While only nonsensible choice is free, both nonsensible and sensible choices are "mixed" in human choice.³⁴ For Kant, while sensibility subjects choice to the law of natural causality, freedom consists in a sort of self-determination ("*sich von selbst zu bestimmen*"; "to determine oneself from oneself") that is independent from it. Given that reason is the only faculty endowed with complete spontaneity, namely, with the capacity to act with complete independence of natural necessitation, freedom and reason would seem to be one and the same thing. If this is the case, however, it remains unclear what sort of agency is left for *Willkür*—why would a human being choose either reason or sensibility as the source of action? And if sensibility subordinates choice to natural necessitation, in what sense is the human being imputable for a choice that is pathologically affected? Given that complete spontaneity pertains only to reason, and that spontaneity is the ground of imputability, it would seem that one is only imputable for acting on the basis of reason. If this were the case, however, we would not be imputable for actions that are determined by sensible stimuli and transgress reason's imperatives—that is, we would not be imputable for evil actions.

The connection between responsibility and evil represents one of the most persistent problems in Kant's practical philosophy, and has been the subject of critique ever since its contemporaries.[35] Part of the reason for this persistence is that, in his central writings on moral philosophy, Kant does not systematically analyze *Willkür*.[36] In these writings, *arbitrium liberum* becomes the will, which Kant equates with both reason and freedom. This is the basis of Kant's notion of autonomy, according to which freedom consists in complying with a law of which one is the legislator. In the *Groundwork of the Metaphysics of Morals*, Kant claims that reason is "pure self-activity," and that it shows "a spontaneity so pure that it thereby goes far beyond anything that sensibility can ever afford to it."[37] Given that reason is the only faculty completely independent of natural causality, it is the only faculty capable of pure spontaneity, and thus of legislating what ought to be done independently of what is. If, as Kant had already suggested in the *First Critique*, freedom and spontaneity are one and the same thing, then reason is the only faculty that is completely free. Sensible impulses, by contrast, are given to us from without or "heteronomously," that is, independently of our freedom. Therefore, the question remains open: in what sense are we imputable for actions that stem from sensibility?

This question appears to have no answer in the *Groundwork*, where Kant draws a stark distinction between the will and the inclinations. He claims that "the human being claims for himself a will which lets nothing be put to his account that belongs merely to his desires and inclinations," and so, by means of this will, he thinks possible "actions that can be done only by disregarding all desires and sensible incitements," whose causality "lies in him as intelligence and in the laws of effects and actions in accordance with principles of the intelligible world."[38] Following this view, Kant suggests that responsibility is independent from a person's inclinations and impulses and stems instead from laws of the intelligible world, which is why

> he does not hold himself accountable for the former [*die erstere nicht verantwortet*; does not take responsibility for the former] or ascribe them to his proper self, that is, to his will, though he does ascribe to it the indulgence [*Nachsicht*] he would show them if he allowed them to influence his maxims to the detriment of the rational laws of his will.[39]

These words reflect a tension in Kant's conception of responsibility. On the one hand, the person is not responsible for his inclinations, since they do not belong to his "proper self," which is the free self or the will. On the other hand, the self is capable of "indulgence" to the inclinations, which can be ascribed to it. This latter point implies that freedom can yield to its opposite, namely, the inclinations. But it is unclear how this is possible, given that freedom stems from spontaneity, and reason is the only spontaneous faculty.

A similar tension takes place in the *Critique of Practical Reason*, where the possibility of choosing to act on the basis of the inclinations stems from the will's lack of "resistance" ("*Widerstand*") to them. Given that sensible incentives for action are external to the will and, consequently, to the proper self of the human being, the will's autonomy consists in resisting them:

> A choice [*Willkür*] that is pathologically affected (though not thereby determined, hence still free) brings with it a wish arising from *subjective* causes because of which it can often be opposed to the pure objective determining ground and thus needs a resistance [*Widerstand*] of practical reason which, as moral necessitation, may be called an internal but intellectual constraint.[40]

Insofar as choice is pathologically affected, which means that there are subjective causes (inclinations) opposing the pure objective determining ground of the will (the moral law), the will (which, as we have seen, is equivalent to practical reason) cannot but resist these pathological incentives. But insofar as practical reason is freedom itself, conceived as independence from natural causality, freedom seems to consist merely in resisting this causality. This implies that deeds transgressing the moral law proceed from a failure to resist, that is, from a failure by practical reason to "constrain" pathological incentives. Given that these incentives oppose freedom, and given that only such incentives lead to actions that transgress the moral law, evil deeds cannot be freely chosen. It is only insofar as the person fails to act freely by not resisting the influence of the inclinations that evil deeds are possible.

While Kant's remarks on the tension between the will, or practical reason, and the inclinations in his main writings on practical philosophy suggest a conception of evil as deficiency, he is not entirely consistent on this point. If actions that transgress imperatives of reason are the effect of the will's "indulgence" or lack of "resistance," then the source of evil would lie in reason's incapacity to execute its own commands. If this is the case, freedom stems from the strength of reason to resist the assault of the inclinations, as in a battle between two opposing forces. Kant suggests a different possibility in his *Lectures on Ethics*, developed briefly after the *Groundwork*, where he explicitly addresses the problem of "imputation." Here, he establishes a distinction between "weakness," which "consists in its want of sufficient moral goodness to make the action adequate to the moral law," and "frailty," which consists "also in the prevalence therein of even the strongest principles and motivations to ill-doing."[41] This is the source of what Kant defines as a "positive" or "moral" evil, which "arises from freedom, since otherwise it would not be *moral* evil, and however prone we may also be to this by nature, our evil actions still arise from freedom, on which account they are also debited to us as vices."[42] If vices can be imputed to us, they must stem from freedom rather than weakness. This would imply, however, that freedom lies beyond reason, and therefore beyond autonomy. Kant explores this possibility in *Religion*.

The Choice of Evil

Scholars in recent years have stressed the importance of *Religion* for a comprehensive understanding of Kant's practical philosophy. While the text is mostly known for its account of evil and its attempt to provide a rational justification of Christianity, it also plays a crucial role in clarifying problematic aspects of Kant's conception of freedom and moral action. Wood reads *Religion* as continuing Kant's earlier inquiries into the beliefs that are presupposed by moral agency.[43] Allison interprets it as the completion of what he calls the "incorporation thesis," according to which any incentive for action becomes effective only insofar as it is incorporated into a maxim, that is, a general rule or principle.[44] Schneewind claims that *Religion* completes Kant's conception of freedom as autonomy. Although he is careful to point out that Kant's confidence in self-governance is nuanced by the idea of freedom as choice, he sees self-governance and choice as complementary rather than as in tension with one another.[45] The reading of *Religion* that I will present departs from these interpretations in two ways. First, I clam that Kant's identification of freedom with choice departs from his earlier identification of freedom with reason. Therefore, *Religion* is not a completion, but rather a partial departure from Kant's earlier insights. Second, as a consequence of this departure, Kant identifies and stresses a constitutive uncertainty in our moral character. Briefly stated, the same faculty that makes us responsible for the constitution of our moral character, namely, choice, makes such character inaccessible to us, which means that the moral worth of our actions is inherently uncertain. This reading supports and builds on Shell's and Hunter's interpretations, according to which Kant's late work stresses some of the insurmountable mysteries involved in moral agency.[46]

One of Kant's central concerns in *Religion* is to identify the ground of responsibility for evil deeds, which, as we have seen in the previous section, represents a persistent problem in his moral philosophy. Relying on the link between freedom, spontaneity, and imputability that he had laid out in the *First Critique*, Kant claims that in order for evil deeds to be imputable, they must stem from freedom, as opposed to be determined by natural causality. The problem is that our natural impulses or inclinations, which subject us to the law of natural causality, are not free. If only reason is free, then it is unclear on what grounds a person would freely perform deeds that stem from the inclinations, and thus be imputable for them. Kant's solution consists in shifting freedom and spontaneity from reason to choice, which determines whether a person acts on the basis of reason or on the basis of the inclinations. The crucial concept mediating between choice and either reason or the inclinations is "maxim": "the freedom of the power of choice [*Freiheit der Willkür*] has the characteristic, entirely peculiar to it, that it cannot be determined to action through any incentive *except so far as the human being has incorporated it into his maxim*."[47] In the *Groundwork*, Kant defines a maxim as a "subjective principle of volition" or "a subjective principle of acting," and distinguishes it from an objective principle that establishes how the subject ought to act.[48] While reason and the inclinations provide the two fundamental incentives for action, choice produces a maxim that determines which one of the two will determine action. This means that even when we act with the aim of satisfying our inclinations, we do so on the basis of a free choice, which is why "the ground of evil [*Grund des Bösen*] cannot lie in any object *determining* the power of choice [*Willkür*] through inclination, not in any natural impulses, but only in a rule that the power of choice itself produces for the exercise of its freedom, i.e., in a maxim."[49] The ground of evil is not the inclinations, but rather choice, which freely determines whether a person's action will be performed on the basis of reason or the inclination.

By placing spontaneity in choice, as opposed to reason, Kant deprives freedom of a ground that determines what to do. If only reason is spontaneous, then acting freely and adopting a maxim stemming from reason are one and the same thing. If, by contrast, choice is spontaneous, then freedom has no determining ground, for both good and evil maxims are freely chosen. Because of this absence of a ground, Kant claims that the choice of maxim is "inscrutable":

> That the first subjective ground of the adoption of moral maxims is inscrutable [*unerforschlich*] can be seen provisionally from this: Since the adoption is free, its ground . . . must not be sought in any incentive of nature, but always again in a maxim; and, since any such maxim must have its ground as well, yet apart from a maxim no *determining ground* of the free power of choice [*freien Willkür*] ought to, or can, be adduced, we are endlessly referred back in the series of subjective determining grounds, without ever being able to come to the first ground.[50]

In order to explain the free choice of a maxim, we would need to rely on a prior maxim that determines choice, and so on to infinity. Therefore, the first maxim, or the "first subjective ground," is, and even ought to be (for otherwise the adoption of a maxim would not be free), "inscrutable." If we were able to identify such ground, the choice of a maxim would cease to be free, which means that we would not be imputable for it. Gordon E. Michalson has claimed that, given this infinite regress, Kant's thesis of the inscrutability of moral maxims falls into an "argumentative flaw" and a "frustrating conceptual logjam." However, as Jean-Luc Nancy and Ian Hunter point out, Kant's goal is not to explain imputability so that it becomes fully knowable and understandable, but rather to show that imputability presupposes a limit in our capacity to know and to explain the ground of action.[51] If we could find a ground behind the adoption of an evil maxim (or a good maxim, for that matter), such maxim would cease to be freely chosen and thus imputable—strictly speaking, it would cease to be evil at all. Therefore, Kant claims that the choice of a maxim must be represented as always already having taken place, or as "innate," even if the person remains imputable for it.

But even if the first ground for the adoption of a maxim is inscrutable, the very possibility of choosing an evil maxim shows that choice is susceptible to evil. Kant locates this susceptibility in what he calls a "propensity [*Hang*] to evil," which he defines as "the subjective ground of the possibility of an inclination (habitual desire, *concupiscentia*), insofar as this possibility is contingent for humanity in general."[52] Humanity is capable of acting on the basis of the inclinations, but only contingently, that is, depending on a free choice. A propensity is the possibility of this choice. The idea of a propensity to evil seems to be redundant: evil must be freely chosen in order to be evil at all, and in order for a free choice of evil to be possible, the power of choice must have a propensity to it. However, Kant introduces an example that clarifies how the propensity to evil may lead people to freely adopt maxims that serve the inclinations:

> All savages [*rohe Menschen*] have a propensity for intoxicants; for although many of them have no acquaintance at all with intoxicants, and hence absolutely no desire for the things that produce it, let them try these things but once, and there is aroused in them an almost inextinguishable desire for them.[53]

The example is illuminating because it suggests that the propensity to evil involves a deception regarding the true ground of action. The savages do not know that they have chosen the inclinations as the supreme incentive of their maxim for action, simply because they have not yet encountered the object that arouses them. However, from the moment they are capable of acting on the basis of the inclinations, they are already evil, even if their character has not yet become manifest. This means that the propensity to evil involves a corruption of the maxim for action, which appears to be good even though it conceals evil motives.

It is important to stress that, for Kant, maxims always contain multiple incentives for action. What determines the moral worth of a maxim is not whether it contains the moral law or the inclination as the only incentive, but how they are ordered in the determination of action: "the difference, whether the human being is good or evil, must not lie in the difference between the incentives that he incorporates into his maxim . . . but in their *subordination* . . . : *which of the two he makes the condition of the other*."[54] The propensity to evil does not consist in choosing to act on the basis of the inclinations against the moral law, but rather in subordinating compliance with the law to the inclinations: "the human being (even the best) is evil only because he reverses the moral order of his incentives in incorporating them into his maxims."[55] The propensity to evil involves a reversal of the incentives for action, in such a way that actions appear to be good even though the maxim that orients them is evil, that is, it has the inclinations as its supreme incentive.

Kant's claim that evil is "radical" ("*radikal*") refers to this propensity of the power of choice to corrupt all maxims, even those that appear to be morally good. He claims that "this evil is *radical*, since it corrupts the ground of all maxims."[56] This concern with the corruption of even apparently good maxims is not entirely new in Kant's thought. In the *Groundwork*, he warns against the "coolness of a scoundrel" ["*kalte Blut eines Bösewichts*"; "the cold blood of the villain"], which "makes him not only far more dangerous but also immediately more abominable in our eyes than we would have taken him to be without it."[57] While a savage may simply lack the use of reason to prevent him from a moral misuse of his inclinations, the cold blood of the villain produces what Kant calls a "propensity to rationalize" ("*Hang zu vernünfteln*"), that is, to question the purity and strictness of the moral law, and "to make them better suited to our wishes and inclinations, that is, to corrupt them."[58] The villain with cold blood does not simply transgress the law, but uses his reason to corrupt it in a way that serves his own interests. Kant reinforces this idea in *Religion* by showing that an evil disposition does not only stem from a propensity to rationalize our transgressions to the law, but also to conceal our disposition behind empirical compliance with it, in such a way that "the empirical character is then good but the intelligible character still evil."[59] Kant claims that "the attitude of mind that construes the absence of vice as already being conformity of the *disposition* to the law of duty (i.e., as *virtue*) is nonetheless itself to be named a radical perversity in the human heart."⁶⁰ This kind of thinking consists in "dishonesty" regarding our incentives, and in

> a certain *perfidy* on the part of the human heart . . . in deceiving itself [*selbst zu betrügen*] as regards its own good or evil disposition and, provided that its actions do not result in evil (which they could well do because of their maxims), in not troubling itself on account of its disposition but rather considering itself justified before the law.⁶¹

Given that the maxim of our actions is inscrutable, radical evil conceals itself behind dishonesty, which consists in taking empirical compliance with duty as proof of moral virtue. Consequently, radical evil "puts out of tune [*verstimmt*] the moral ability to judge [*moralische Urteilskraft*] what to think of a human being, and renders any imputability [*Zurechnung*] entirely uncertain, whether internal or external."⁶² Because of the natural propensity to deceive oneself and others, all moral judgments are inherently uncertain. This way, the same capacity that makes the person responsible for her actions, that is, the choice of the maxim for action, makes any judgment holding her responsible uncertain.

Before proceeding to Kant's analysis of the mechanisms that conceal uncertainty and facilitate moral deception, let us note one implication of Kant's shift in his understanding of evil regarding his views on the public role of reason and philosophy in fighting against it. If evil stems from reason's weakness, as Kant suggests in the *Groundwork* and the *Second Critique*, then the victory of moral virtue over evil depends on strengthening reason so that it does not yield to the inclinations. This leads to the idea that philosophers play a crucial public role, above that of theologians. The view would represent a continuation of what Hunter identifies as a "philosophical theology" emerging with Leibniz, in which philosophy takes up the role traditionally assigned to theologians, namely, the salvation of the soul.⁶³ If, by contrast, evil stems from a choice that is prior to reason, then the role of philosophy is much more limited, as long as philosophy is identified with rational thinking. No matter how strong a person's reason, she is perfectly capable of choosing evil by virtue of her freedom of choice. Moreover, reason in the hands of an evil person is far more dangerous than its absence. Kant's thesis of radical evil thus represents a warning against some of the dangers of the Enlightenment's confidence in rational thinking. Rational villains are much more pervasive than irrational ones, which means that the task of the philosopher is not only to teach how to think rationally but also, and perhaps more fundamentally, to expose the conditions under which reason is misused. If this is the case, the thesis of radical evil is part of what Dieter Henrich identifies as Kant's turn from an ethics based on an abstract formula (given by reason) to another one based on the "assent" [*Zustimmung*] to the formula by the self, as part of which Kant attempts "to oppose the sophistry of reason, which stands in the service of want, and so to back the insight of the good against its dialectical tricks."[64] Philosophy is as much an agent in the development of reason as in the exposure of its tricks at the service of evil.

Deception

The social context surrounding the writing of *Religion* provides important clues for understanding Kant's concern with the link between religious practices and the moral deception characteristic of radical evil. Two political developments—one immediate and the second one unfolding throughout decades—are especially relevant in this regard. The first development, pointed out by a series of recent studies, is the growing public censorship in matters of theology and philosophy. Fredrick the Great, the "Enlightened monarch" celebrated by Kant in "What Is Enlightenment?" for his support for freedom of speech, died in 1786. His son, Fredrick Wilhelm II, had more conservative views regarding religious toleration, as evidenced by the appointment as minister of Education and Religious Affairs in 1788 of Johann Christoph Wöllner, a reactionary whose ideas were at odds with the Enlightenment. That same year, Wöllner promulgated a new edict restraining religious innovation by demanding that all teachers of theology adhere to the guidelines of their professed creed, and by reactivating censorship in matters of religion.[65] The aim and scope of Wöllner's edict are the subject of historical debate, but Kant was clearly aware that it would affect his ability to convey his thoughts honestly to the public—as the eventual censorship of *Religion*, most of which could only be published after the death of Fredrick Wilhelm II, would confirm. Susan Shell and Steven Lestition have analyzed in detail how the new political situation restrained Kant's confidence in the Enlightenment.[66] This had two implications for Kant's views on evil. First, evil is no longer seen as stemming from impulses that reason fails to overcome. If an enlightened era can be followed by an unenlightened one, the root of evil must be resistant to the progress of civilization, and may even be intertwined with it. Second, the reinstatement of censorship and the demand of public declaration of faith lead to the problem of public insincerity. It seems likely that, under a nonenlightened monarch, the enlightened will have to lie about their true beliefs or, even worse, adapt them to the new circumstances.

These issues are connected to Kant's broader concern with the deceptiveness of religious rituals in moral matters. Kant biographers Ernst Cassirer and Manfred Kuehn suggest that the strong discipline and control that characterized Kant's early Pietist education at the *Collegium Fridericianum* left a long-standing negative impression in him.[67] The *Fridericianum* was founded in Königsberg with the support of the two main figures of the Pietist movement, Philipp Jackob Spener and August Hermann Francke.[68] Spener, the founder of the movement, called for a transformation of the Lutheran church that shifted the emphasis from doctrinal orthodoxy to the experience of conversion and its manifestation through the performance of good deeds for the neighbor. His goal was to make religion more attuned to the needs and experiences of the laymen, by contrast to the observance of rituals and the learning of dogmas.[69] Spener's disciple Francke, a clever political strategist, played a crucial role in expanding the influence of Pietism by exploiting its affinities with the monarch's views and projects, especially in matters of education. At the time of the emergence of Pietism, the Prussian State was undergoing a process of rapid modernization under Fredrick Wilhelm I, who shared the worldly oriented mentality of the new religious movement.[70] Crucial to this process was the development of the army and the bureaucracy, with their characteristic sense of discipline and obedience. The Pietist emphasis on worldly deeds over ritual, and on spiritual transformation over intellectual clarification, was functional to the development of this mentality.[71] Exploiting these affinities, Francke maneuvered to increase the number of Pietist teachers in schools, as well as the number of Pietist orphanages, which became the central institution of the movement. By Kant's time, the Pietist educational philosophy was widespread in Prussia.

Although Spener's views emerged as an attempt to reinvigorate personal religious experience against ossified symbols and rituals, Pietism under Francke led to a growing sense of discipline and control over people's actions. While both Spener and Francke emphasized the need to go through a "devotional rebirth" and overcome one's sinful self, Francke stressed the experience of repentance and uncertainty leading to it.[72] Anxiety regarding one's own moral condition translated into a growing need of purifying one's own practices, so as to prove oneself and others that one had regenerated himself.[73] Given that every proof of regeneration was uncertain, the demand for discipline and self-scrutiny was virtually inexhaustible. The only means to confirm a person's devotion was to thoroughly comply with the rules handed down by the educational and religious authorities.[74] As a consequence, some Pietist circles turned to an extreme regulation of all the spheres of life and an ethics of blind obedience. Somewhat contrary to the original spirit of the movement, compliance with externally given rules became more important than inner regeneration—not because the latter ceased to be essential, but because external rules were its only available signs.[75] With time, many people would see these signs of internal devotion as a potential source of manipulation and deception—as indicated by Prince Wilhelm's (later Kaiser Wilhelm I) definition of a Pietist, in the context of a conversation with Otto von Bismarck in 1853, as "a man who feigns in religion in order to make a career."[76] Kant was certainly familiar with this tendency to conflate religious practices and obedience with careerism, both through his early education at the *Fridericianum* and, very likely, through his observation of religious practices in the Königsberg of his time. If this experience made him distrustful of strict discipline and obedience in matters of religion from early on, as evidenced by his negative remarks on his childhood education, Wöllner's edict could not but intensify the fear of opportunistic insincerity in public speech and action.

This brief historical overview underscores to what extent Kant's remarks on evil and imputability in *Religion* respond to the phenomenon of deception regarding the moral worth of action. The concern with deception becomes explicit in the fourth part of the text, titled "Concerning Service and Counterfeit Service under the Dominion of the Good Principle." Kant introduces here the distinction between moral religion, which consists in the fulfillment of one's moral duty represented as divine commands, and statutory religion, which is concerned with commands given by God in history.[77] True religion, according to Kant, is moral religion, but this does not mean that statutory religion should be disregarded altogether, given "the natural need of all human beings to demand for even the highest concepts and grounds of reason something that *the senses can hold on to.*"[78] This demand for sensuous mediation is both indispensable and dangerous. Kant defines it as a "vehicle" [*Leitmittel*] between the universality of the true church and the "particular validity" of a historically grounded church.[79] It is indispensable because sensuous beings cannot have access to the rational ground of religion without the guidance of historically given commands and doctrines—just like children, Kant explains, need to obey seemingly arbitrary commands before they can understand the reasons behind them.[80] It is also dangerous because the sensuous mediation tends to become autonomous regarding its mediating function. Ideas and practices that are meant to give a sensuous representation to moral duty are taken to be duty itself, thus transforming service into "mere *fetishism*" ("*bloßes* Fetischmachen"; "mere fetish-making").[81] Kant calls this attitude "delusion of religion" ("*Religionswahn*").

Delusion of religion consists in practices by which the evil disposition conceals itself. This sort of deception is self-inflicted, for it is "not merely an unpremeditated deception [*unvorsätzliche Täuschung*] but a maxim by which we attribute intrinsic value to the means rather than the end."[82] This maxim to deceive oneself is part of the "hidden inclination to deceit" that, as we have seen, is intertwined with an evil disposition. The deception has a curious structure, for it is a deception whose object (the moral character) is inherently inscrutable. Instead of accepting the uncertainty of moral judgments that, as we have seen, is a consequence of radical evil, human beings have a tendency to pretend to reveal their moral disposition through ritualized moral practices.[83] Different kinds of rituals can serve this purpose. Kant claims, however, that "sacrifices" ["*Aufopferungen*"] are particularly effective in this regard, for "just because they have absolutely no use in the world, and yet cost effort, they seem to be aimed solely at attesting devotion to God."[84] The deception, Kant believes, can go as far as to serve no personal interest. By sacrificing ourselves for no visible purpose whatsoever, we seem to comply with the law. The maxim to deceit thus becomes as powerful as the evil maxim to serve our inclinations, and may even take primacy over it. At some point, the more we act against our own self-interest, the more we seem to be complying with the law. Sacrifice becomes an end in itself.

Given this propensity to deception, Kant believes that the right moral attitude involves mistrust toward visible signs of virtue. A moral character is unattainable, yet we have a duty to strive for it. The propensity to deceive oneself consists in believing that one is virtuous, as opposed to striving for virtue. According to Kant, "the distance between the goodness which we ought to effect in ourselves and the evil from which we start is . . . infinite," which is why "it is not exhaustible in any time."[85] Given that we can never achieve virtue, but only move toward it, "the deed, as a continuous advance *in infinitum* from a defective good to something better, always remains defective, so that we are bound to consider the good as it appears in us, i.e., according to the *deed*, as *at each instant* inadequate to a holy law."[86] There is no such thing as a moral deed, but only deeds that move toward moral virtue. Therefore, the goal of religious practices is not to bring our actions in agreement with the law, which Kant repeatedly claims would involve a deception. Rather, the goal is to lead people to persevere in the striving for virtue.

Lack of moral certainty, Kant believes, is beneficial to a moral disposition because it promotes striving toward it. If the main source of evil is moral self-deception, it is natural that self-doubt be a source of virtue. Kant explicitly reproaches those who feel that they have a pure moral disposition, for "one is never more easily deceived than in what promotes a good opinion of oneself."[87] In order to persevere in the striving for virtue, one should feel confidence in his or her capacity to improve, as opposed to certainty regarding his or her moral character:

> Certainty with respect to the latter is neither possible to the human being, nor, so far we can see, morally beneficial. For (be it well noted) we cannot base this confidence upon an immediate consciousness of the immutability of our disposition, since we cannot see through to the latter but must at best infer it from the consequence that it has on the conduct of our life.[88]

Given the impossibility of knowing our moral disposition, expecting moral certainty has no benefit for morality. Instead, confidence in our capacity to become moral must be based on a constant striving which, although at each instant inadequate to morality as such, allows us to represent it as a progression toward the better.

From Radical Evil to the Banality of Evil

Self-deception is an essential attribute of what Arendt called "the banality of evil." As we have seen, Eichmann claimed during the trial that, since he had done nothing but thoroughly comply with the law of the land, he could not be held personally responsible for his actions. Given the traditional contrast between egoistic self-interest and duty, Eichmann's willingness to sacrifice himself for the latter served in his eyes as proof of moral virtue. If there was anyone responsible for the moral implications of his deeds, it was the source of the law. For Arendt, this reasoning was not simply a lie, but rather a reflection of a long-standing conception of virtue on which Eichmann relied as a means to conceal his responsibility. Arendt believed that the philosophy of the will, of which Kant was a representative, was for the most part complicit in this elimination of responsibility. In her later writings, however, she searched for an alternative conception of the will, according to which it does not simply give a law, but rather chooses and constitutes a character. Arendt's goal was to find the source of that which Eichmann seemed to lack, namely, a sense of responsibility for his actions. The challenge was twofold: first, to understand on what grounds Eichmann could be held responsible for his actions; second, to understand the mechanism by which a person refuses responsibility and destroys the very sense of being responsible, beyond blind compliance with duty.

Kant's analysis of evil and imputability in *Religion* presents a response to both challenges. The ground of responsibility lies in choice, which ought to remain inscrutable in order to be a free choice at all. This is indeed what we could call the "paradox of responsibility" in Kant: in order to have a moral character that is responsible for our actions, the character must be freely chosen, and in order to be freely chosen, it must remain inscrutable. Every new action works as a sign of our moral character, but it can never reveal it. Radical evil, according to Kant, consists in deceiving ourselves regarding our disposition, precisely by attempting to turn it into an object of experience—a fetish. Eichmann's unbreakable commitment to his duty beyond all self-interest, which made it so difficult to judge his actions as evil, can therefore be read as a mechanism by which he destroyed his own responsibility. It is precisely because radical evil conceals itself behind empirical signs of virtue that it becomes deceitful and, consequently, utterly pervasive. Kant shows that this concealment is itself freely chosen. The reason why people appear to be thoughtless individuals unable to respond for their actions beyond blind compliance with duty is that they have decided to conceal the uncertainty involved in choosing a maxim for action behind ritualized displays of virtue.

The theoretical links between Kant's thesis of "radical evil" and Arendt's reflections on "the banality of evil" are not a coincidence, given the historical and intellectual trend connecting the two. Historian Richard Gawthrop claims that the extreme discipline and control developing in Pietist institutions represents an antecedent to the totalizing views of modern ideologies, in which people voluntarily subordinate themselves to the rules sanctioned by a group believed to hold the truth.[89] This discipline was seen as a way to bridge the gap between worldly deeds and the inscrutable moral worth of the inner self. This development, together with the emergence of censorship and of public regulations on profession of faith with Fredrick Wilhelm II, which encouraged the subordination of inner convection to public displays of moral virtue, made Kant aware of a dangerous tendency to fetishize external signs of virtue. His emphasis on the inscrutability of our disposition and his analysis of religious delusion can therefore be read as warnings against the development of a proto-totalitarian mentality, in which individuals hold fast to whatever rituals of morality they are given at a certain point. The identification with these rituals conceals responsibility because the person acts as if the only morally right choice were to comply with such rituals, independently of how they emerge or what purpose they serve.

The historical trajectory connecting Kant's *Religion* with the social developments of the twentieth century did not go unnoticed within German philosophy. Arendt's analysis of totalitarianism was directly influenced by her reading of Kant, but also mediated by interpretations of Kant by her two mentors, Heidegger and Jaspers. Both philosophers were concerned with uncovering a more original notion of responsibility, which is not subordinated to pregiven norms, but is rather the precondition for any norm. "Guilt," according to Heidegger and Jaspers, is not an effect of not complying with a norm, but rather a constitutive condition of our existence.[90] Of course, we do feel guilty for transgressing particular norms, but this would not be possible if we were not willing to assume responsibility for our own actions to begin with. To derive the experience of guilt from a specific norm is already a way to misunderstand it, for it is reduced to compliance with commands for whose content we are unable to respond. Following this idea, Jaspers reads Kant's analysis of radical evil as showing that attempts to find an objective distinction between good and evil conceal responsibility for interrogating such distinction. This objectification, Jaspers claims, is the first moral deception, and it is operational in most philosophical systems, where every time evil is almost looked over in that, by being turned into an object of observation (and even into a grandiose appearance), it becomes harmless. Why now this obstinacy to find possible objectifications of evil in all directions? Because each time one would miss, through the becoming palpable of evil, the chance to find the possibility of improvement in myself.[91]

According to Jaspers, the aim of Kant's practical philosophy consists in resisting this objectification by showing the limits of what we can know and control, thus opening up the possibility of an open-ended transformation. To objectify evil is already a way to externalize it, and thus to blur our responsibility to improve ourselves. For Jaspers, responsibility does not stem from an objective rule that distinguishes between good and evil, but rather from the drawing of the distinction itself.

It should be clear that the concealment of one's responsibility behind objectified signs of moral virtue has nothing to do with the concealment of a "true intention." This is the way Allison interprets the link between radical evil and the banality of evil. According to Allison, Eichmann is an example of the deception at play in Kant's understanding of evil, in which "immoral maxims appear to pass the universalizability test only because they ignore or obscure morally salient features of a situation."[92] The problem with this reading is that it ignores Kant's thesis of the inscrutability of our maxims and its effects (the "putting out of tune") on our ability to make moral judgments. According to Kant, there is no access to our "actual intention," which lies beyond anything given to us through our senses. There are therefore no empirical features that can serve as a test for grasping our moral maxims. As Alenka Zupančič has pointed out in response to Allison, the first deception consists precisely in taking empirical signs as a proof of moral virtue, as if our disposition could be turned into an object of experience.[93] We must understand the self-deception operative in radical evil as the attempt to turn empirical deeds into means of moral certainty, which relieve us from the need to judge each one of our deeds anew. In the words of Olivier Reboul's classical study, for Kant "evil is sanctimony, the fact of believing oneself justified by one's deeds, one's 'good works,' or of taking one's exterior non-culpability for innocence."[94] The thesis of radical evil does not represent a call to overcome deception and acknowledge our true intention, which can only lead to an even more radical delusion, but rather a call to accept the inscrutability of our intentions and thus the uncertainty of our moral disposition as constitutive of our responsibility for action.

Conclusion

Eichmann claimed that, in complying with the law of the land as thoroughly as possible, he had followed a version of Kant's practical philosophy adapted to the circumstances he was living in. According to Arendt, the one aspect of this "household Kant" that preserved his original spirit was the demand that one always sacrifices his own self-interest and makes no exception to compliance with duty. Because of the predominant view of evil as stemming from some sort of egoistic motivation, there seemed to be no ground from which to hold Eichmann responsible for his deeds. However, we have seen that Kant, in his later writings, does not think of evil as stemming primarily from self-interest. Although Arendt took Kant's notion of radical evil as a contrast to "the banality of evil" that she attributed to Eichmann, the notions are closely connected. Kant's notion or radical evil emerged as a response to a phenomenon that resembled an essential aspect of totalitarianism, namely, the concealment of one's own responsibility behind moral rituals and attachment to self-sacrifice. For Kant, the ground of responsibility does not stem from externally given rules, but rather from our capacity to choose the maxim of our actions. Given that this maxim is inscrutable, it can never be regulated by any sort of ritualized practice. The attempt to overcome the inscrutability of our moral disposition by holding fast to empirical signs of virtue, such as self-sacrifice, constitutes an active deception regarding our own responsibility. We can never know the disposition that underlies each one of our deeds, yet it is precisely because of this hiddenness that every new deed involves a demand for self-transformation—not in the sense of a more thorough compliance with the law, but rather of transforming the character that determines such compliance.

Kant's thesis of radical evil illuminates another aspect of the central problem involved in "the banality of evil," namely, the identification of the ground of responsibility for action. We saw in the previous chapter that, according to Arendt, the uncertainty to which action exposes us creates the temptation to replace appearing to others with ideology. For Arendt, this uncertainty stems from the fact that action presupposes the presence of others who will necessarily interpret it and react to it, thus conditioning its meaning and its outcome. Kant shows another, yet related, source of uncertainty. By virtue of the gap between the action as appearance, or as it is perceived by others and by oneself, and the inscrutable maxim that is the necessary condition of moral responsibility, we are necessarily unable to know our moral character. The same condition that makes us responsible for our actions limits knowledge of our moral worth. The ritualization of action that, as we have seen, is an antecedent to the development of modern ideologies, provides a delusional solution to this limitation in the form of visible rules for action. Instead of facing the moral uncertainty that is inherent to responsibility, people may choose to submit their actions to all sorts of objective standards that determine what is "good" and what is "evil." These standards, Kant points out, usually share some visible element of morality, such as the overcoming of our self-interest by means of sacrifice. When someone like Eichmann uses his self-sacrifice as evidence of nonculpability, he is not simply lying about his true motivations. He is rather using visible signs of morality as a means to escape the moral uncertainty that is constitutive of responsibility.

PART 2

Judgment

Chapter 3

Kant on the Sublime and the Judgment of Action

While the first part of the book was concerned with the problem that evil poses to our understanding of action, this second part is concerned with the relationship between evil and judgment. I showed in the first part that both Arendt and Kant identify a kind of evil that corrupts responsibility, which depends on a fundamental uncertainty regarding the meaning of action. In this second part, I will show that evil also corrupts judgment by replacing its constitutive uncertainty with a rule whose validity is posited as certain. The turn to judgment further pursues Arendt's concern with the "inability to judge" characteristic of "the banality of evil." Building on Arendt's inquiries, I will examine how Kant and Lyotard (whose views are deeply influenced by Kant) develop a conception of judgment that responds to their reflections on evil. One common idea in Kant's and Lyotard's conceptions of judgment is that at least certain kinds of judgment that demand universal approval involve a fundamental uncertainty regarding their validity. Judgments rely on rules, but in some cases we do not know if the rule we are relying on is universally valid. This uncertainty regarding the validity of rules for judgment does not mean that there is no ground for the expectation that others will agree with it. Instead, the very need to judge in the absence of a rule produces an expectation that our judgment will call for the agreement of everyone. In some cases, the experience of uncertainty is itself the ground for the expectation of universal agreement.

In this chapter, I read Kant's analysis of the judgment of the sublime as a response to the problem of judging actions on the basis of moral ideas. The judgment of the sublime, I argue, represents an alternative to the kind of moral self-deception characteristic of radical evil, which I examined in chapter 2. We saw that, according to Kant, radical evil puts "out of tune" the moral ability to judge, given the propensity to self-deception inherent to our capacity to freely choose the moral maxim that orients our actions. Now, I will show that the problem of making judgments on actions based on moral ideas runs through Kant's moral philosophy. On the basis of this analysis, I will argue that Kant's "Analytic of the Sublime" represents a response to this problem, because it illuminates a possible link between moral ideas and actions based on the feeling of the sublime. This way, the feeling of the sublime works as an alternative to the delusion that makes us feel certain about the moral worth of our actions. In considering this contrast, it is worth keeping in mind that the *Critique of the Power of Judgment* appeared two years before the publication of Kant's essay on radical evil, and therefore it is likely that the problem of evil was already a prominent concern for Kant as he was developing the theory of aesthetic judgment. However, given that Kant only hinted at this link indirectly, it will be necessary to trace it by means of careful textual analysis. I will show that, in relevant passages of *Religion*, as well as of the *Third Critique*, Kant presents the feeling of the sublime as an alternative ground for judgment to the "delusion of the sense" characteristic of radical evil.

My reading of Kant's analysis of the sublime in connection to the problem of the judgment of action has two goals. First, the connection will contribute to clarify the source of the demand of approval by everyone in the judgment of action, which has been at the center of recent debates around judgment in Kant and Arendt. Lack of attention to Kant's analysis of the sublime has led most scholars to neglect an important point of connection between Kant and Arendt on this issue.[1] Most of Arendt's remarks on the problem of the validity of judgment locate it in the capacity to take into account multiple perspectives, an idea that has drawn criticism on grounds that it makes validity dependent on the empirical agreement of one's community. However, Arendt also considered the possibility that the validity of judgment stems from a universal idea, which she calls "the idea of mankind," and which connects the principle of judgment with the principle of action, allowing us to judge from the widest possible perspective. This idea, I will argue, is close to what Kant calls "the idea of humanity" in his analysis of the judgment of the sublime, which is the ground of the claim to universal approval. The second goal of my reading of the "Analytic of the Sublime" in connection to the judgment of action is to show its importance in the development of Kant's practical philosophy. Against a number of studies that read the "Analytic of the Sublime" as situated exclusively within Kant's investigation of the nature of aesthetic judgment, I follow the view of Jean-François Lyotard, Paul Crowther, John H. Zammito, and Robert R. Clewis, according to which the sublime represents an important development in Kant's practical philosophy.[2] One central element in this regard consists in clarifying how it is possible to make a judgment based on moral ideas upon actions as they appear in experience.

Arendt's Turn to Kant's *Third Critique*

As a consequence of her description of Adolf Eichmann's "inability to judge" in *Eichmann in Jerusalem*, Arendt became increasingly concerned with the faculty of judgment and, in particular, with Kant's analysis of the judgment of taste in the *Third Critique*. In his seminal study of Arendt's *Lectures on Kant's Political Philosophy*, Ronald Beiner identifies two reasons for Arendt's later concern with judgment: first, Eichmann's own lack of judgment showed the importance of the faculty of judgment for our public life; second, it was by no means evident how one was to judge Eichmann from a third-person standpoint—for example, the standpoint of the judges in Jerusalem.[3] Both issues are connected with a broader problem that concerned Arendt throughout her work, namely, the absence of stable, reliable standards for judgment in the modern world.[4] Eichmann showed to what extent the idea that, because of the absence of such standards, we can dispense with the need to judge altogether, works as a mechanism of self-exculpation, while the difficulty of casting judgment on him showed to what extent this mechanism is a public problem rather than a merely individual subterfuge. As Arendt claims in an essay, "behind the unwillingness to judge lurks the suspicion that no one is a free agent, and hence the doubt that anyone is responsible or could be expected to answer for what he has done."[5] The refusal to judge our actions as well as the actions of others contributes to a generalized self-exculpation, in which no one feels personally responsible for what he or she does. The question that follows is: how do we judge action in the absence of universally shared standards?

This question emerges in part from Arendt's observations on Eichmann's "inability to judge." In Arendt's account, this inability becomes evident when Eichmann adapted to his new task of extermination as the person in charge of the Final Solution, of which he was informed during the Wannsee Conference in 1942. During those days, Eichmann witnessed how "the élite of the good old Civil Service" was more than willing to take part in the enterprise of mass murder. He took this as a sign that there was nothing morally reprehensible about his new role, given that if people of higher social status had no guilty conscience, "*who was he to judge?*"[6] Seeing that the views of the "respectable society" around him approved the murderous duty he had to perform, Eichmann felt relieved of the need to judge his own actions.

Eichmann's inability to judge showed the importance of casting judgments independently of the standards of one's community. In the Postscript to *Eichmann in Jerusalem*, Arendt claims that Eichmann's trial demanded "that human beings be capable of telling right from wrong even when all they have to guide them is their own judgment which, moreover, happens to be completely at odds with what they must regard as the unanimous opinion of all those around them."[7] At the same time, however, Arendt does not believe that universal moral standards are a reliable ground for distinguishing right and wrong, which explains her insistence on separating judgments from what she calls "moral propositions."[8] In her view, holding fast to moral norms is no guarantee against adapting to a new situation in which those norms no longer hold. As she claims in "Personal Responsibility under Dictatorship," we know after totalitarianism "that moral norms and standards can be changed overnight, and that all that then will be left is the mere habit of holding fast to something."[9]

Arendt's distrust in our attachment to moral norms is influenced by her description of Eichmann as someone who had always been seeking an "Idea" for which he could sacrifice everything, and thus give meaning to his life. This attitude was also evident in Eichmann's claim that until his role in the Final Solution he had lived his whole life according to Kant's definition of duty, only to switch to a new version (a "household" version) of the categorical imperative when it seemed impossible to comply with the original one. In response to this attitude, Arendt claims that it is not those who cherish a system of moral values, but rather the "doubters and skeptics" who are "used to examine things and to make up their own minds," who preserve the capacity for autonomous judgment beyond the contingent standards of a given context. If judgment on right and wrong is still possible in a situation in which all customary standards are suddenly subverted, it is not because the faculty of judgment possesses immutable standards independent of context, but rather because it "functions spontaneously, that is to say, is not bound by standards and rules under which particular cases are simply subsumed, but on the contrary, produces its own principles by virtue of the judging activity itself."[10]

It is precisely the idea that the power of judgment can produce its own principles, independently of either communitarian or transcendental rules, that led Arendt to Kant's *Third Critique*. Arendt's reading focuses on the judgment of taste, and especially on the notion of common sense, although her interpretation departs significantly from Kant's own framework. By contrast to cognitive and moral standards, which are objective because they are given to the power of judgment independently of the situation and of the presence of others, common sense is inherently "intersubjective."[11] Arendt describes it as "that sense which fits us into a community with others, makes us members of it and enables us to communicate things given by our five private senses."[12] Unlike moral and cognitive judgments, which apply a general rule to a particular case, the judgment of taste makes communicable a private perspective of an object. This communicability stems from the combined operation of imagination and common sense. Imagination, Arendt claims, "transforms an object into something I do not have to be directly confronted with," so that "one now has, by means of representation, established the proper distance, the remoteness or uninvolvedness or disinterestedness, that is requisite . . . for evaluating something at its proper worth."[13] By taking distance from an object through representation, we are able to transcend our immediate perception of it, thus acquiring what Arendt calls (following Kant) "impartiality." Then, common sense puts our own perspective in relation with the perspective of others, so that we "overcome our special subjective conditions for the sake of others."[14] This is done by considering what the object looks like from the viewpoint of others, so that the person who judges "claims the assent from others because in judging he has already taken them into account and hence hopes that his judgments will carry a certain general, though perhaps not universal, validity."[15] The communicability of our judgment does not stem from correctly applying a rule independently of perspectives, but rather from considering other perspectives at the moment we judge. The more perspectives we take into account, the more valid our judgment will be.

One problem in Arendt's conception of judgment, which has attracted a number of criticisms, is that it seems to restrict the validity of judgment to the empirical agreement of those in one's own community. Although Arendt repeatedly rejects this idea, she does not clearly explain how exactly our judgments can be valid beyond this empirical agreement. As we have seen, Arendt believes that we must often judge "against the unanimous opinion" of all around us. Taking into account others when judging "does not mean that I conform in my judgment to theirs," because "I still speak with my own voice and I do not count noses in order to arrive at what I think is right."[16] And although "one judges always as a member of a community, guided by one's community sense, one's *sensus community*," in the last analysis "one is a member of a world community by the sheer fact of being a human; this is one's 'cosmopolitan existence.'"[17] Common sense allows us to transcend our particular perspective so as to take into account to perspective of others, but it neither leaves behind our perspective nor does it stop at the perspective of our community. Even if we can consider how an object appears from other standpoints, we must also be able to consider standpoints beyond all those familiar to us, to the point of challenging the views of those around us. The question that Arendt leaves open is how common sense, the sense that "fits us into a community with others," can make us members of a "world community" to which we belong by the sheer fact of being human.

This problem has led a number of commentators to criticize Arendt's stark separation of the judgment of taste from the moral judgment. The criticism is shared by Ronald Beiner, Seyla Benhabib, and Robert Dostal, who argue that by leaving aside Kant's concern with moral foundations, Arendt could not find a viable alternative between a strictly communitarian and a transcendental, universalist conception of judgment. According to Beiner, Arendt's attempt to separate Kant's analysis of the judgment of taste from his practical philosophy, something that a systematic reconstruction of the *Third Critique* would not allow, confuses rather than clarify the problem of the validity of judgment.[18] This is so for two interconnected reasons: first, Kant conceives both the practical judgment and the judgment of taste under the ideal of autonomy, which means that the individual's judgment is independent from the community to which she belongs; second, the categories used by Kant to analyze the judgment of taste are transcendental rather than social, which means that its standards of validity are (again) independent from any empirical community. Beiner finds in John Rawls an example of how Kant's analysis of the aesthetic judgment could be read as a model for political judgment without disregarding its connection to his practical philosophy. Rawls's idea of an original position from which to evaluate the justice of actions and institutions, Beiner claims, "involves an experiment of moral reflection engaged in by one representative rational agent."[19] While this operation relies on representative thinking, in the sense of transcending one's particular viewpoint and imagining what the world looks like from the viewpoint of others, it is performed by an autonomous rational agent, whose moral standards are independent of the standards of the concrete community to which he or she belongs.

Benhabib's criticism of Arendt is connected to Beiner's, although she is more distrustful of the capacity of Kant's moral philosophy to solve the seemingly "communitarian" implications of Arendt's analysis. Like Beiner, Benhabib is critical of Arendt's attempt to disregard moral foundations in the judgment of action. Also like Beiner, she relies on Rawls's interpretation of Kant to argue that "there is a moral foundation to politics insofar as any political system embodies principles of justice."[20] Arendt's analysis of the judgment of taste in connection to representative thinking should therefore be read not as an alternative to moral foundations, but rather as a procedure by which to apply such foundations to concrete situations, thus preserving the "universalist-egalitarian kernel of Kantian morality."[21] On this point, Benhabib finds a deficit in Kant's practical philosophy, which holds that, because morality depends on the intentions driving the act, "we can never know if an action was morally virtuous in this sense at all, since the morally good defies embodiment in the phenomenal world."[22] Arendt's interpretation of the aesthetic judgment, Benhabib claims, compensates for this deficit by providing a procedure with which to overcome the gap between intentions and phenomenal action. The operation of common sense, which Benhabib translates into two concrete formulas for judgment, works as a standard by which to describe the phenomenal action in such a way that its moral value is taken into consideration. This way, we can combine the universalist foundation of Kantian morality with a contextual thinking that makes it applicable to specific situations.

A similar attempt to turn the aesthetic judgment into a means by which to apply moral foundations to experience is presented by Dostal. In his view, however, this procedure is implicitly developed by Kant himself. Like Benhabib, Dostal agrees with Arendt that the role of the imagination in the judgment of taste can be applied to the judgment of action, while rejecting the idea that this kind of judgment can be independent of practical reason. The challenge, then, is to connect the imagination with Kant's analysis of the practical judgment in the *Critique of Practical Reason*, which is concerned with pure moral principles rather than with their application to phenomenal actions. According to Dostal, this is achieved by supplementing the analysis of the practical judgment with the *Metaphysics of Morals*, in such a way that the latter becomes an exercise of the imagination by which to apply practical judgments to experience. Through this operation, "one comes to see what Kant himself did not clearly see—that Kant is asking one to imagine reflectively a human world where such an action might occur."[23] For Dostal, the *Metaphysics of Morals* plays the same role that Rawls's original position plays for Beiner and Benhabib, namely, allowing us to imagine a situation that works as a guide for the application of moral principles to experience, in such a way that we can judge the moral value of empirical actions. This way, Dostal claims, the function of the imagination in moral matters is analogous to the function that Kant assigned to it in the *Critique of Pure Reason*. While here the imagination applies the concepts of the understanding to empirical objects, the *Metaphysics of Morals* is an example of how it can apply ideas of reason to empirical actions.[24]

The three criticisms of Arendt just described stress the lack of universal standards for judgment in her thought, but they leave aside Arendt's own remarks on the question of the universality of judgment. These remarks suggest a different connection with Kant. Arendt's awareness of the problem of the universality of judgment is evident in her claim that the validity of the judgment of taste does not depend on the empirical agreement of others, but rather on the degree of generality attained by our *sensus communis*—a degree that need not remain within the boundaries of any given community.[25] Although Arendt says little about the "world community" to which we belong by the fact of "being human," she refers at one point in her *Lectures* to "the necessary condition for the greatest possible enlargement of the enlarged mentality."[26] This condition is "the idea of an original compact, dictated by mankind itself," which in the context of the *Third Critique* refers to a state of perfect communication in which all our pleasures can be communicated to others.[27] Arendt's own use of this idea, however, departs significantly from Kant, and is closer to what he calls "the idea of humanity." Arendt claims that it is by virtue of "the idea of mankind, present in every single man, that men are human, and they can be called civilized or humane to the extent that this idea becomes the principle not only of their judgments but of their actions."[28] Through this idea, "actor and spectator become united," because "the maxim of the actor and the maxim . . . according to which the spectator judges the spectacle of the world, become one."[29] The idea of mankind allows us to attain the greatest possible enlargement of our enlarged mentality, which is the condition for the validity of our judgments, and to bridge the gap between action and judgment.

These brief remarks on the role of the idea of mankind in action and judgment are closely connected to some of Kant's central concerns in the analysis of the judgment of the sublime. As we will see farther down, it is in this kind of judgment that principles of action and principles of judgment relate to one another, producing a judgment on action that can legitimately claim universal approval. The sublime provides an alternative response to the relationship between aesthetic judgment and moral ideas to the ones proposed by Beiner, Benhabib, and Dostal.[30] While their interpretations subordinate aesthetic judgment to moral judgment, Kant shows that it is possible to relate the two kinds of judgment without subordinating one to the other. In this regard, Kant is as distrustful as Arendt of the direct application of moral standards to the judgment of action. Unlike Arendt, however, Kant believes that this kind of judgment demands a relation to moral ideas, because they are the source of universal principles for action. The question is whether it is possible to relate moral ideas to experience without turning the imagination into an instrument with which to apply the former to the latter, thus subordinating the aesthetic judgment to the moral judgment. In addressing this question by means of the judgment of the sublime, I depart from Arendt's strict separation between aesthetic and moral judgments, while avoiding the tendency to reground the former on the latter present in Beiner's, Benhabib's, and Dostal's approaches. Kant, I will show, had both theoretical and practical reasons for avoiding this apparently "Kantian" solution, which is why he developed an alternative in his analysis of the sublime. But in order to understand the importance of the sublime for Kant's understanding of the relationship between moral ideas and actions, it is first necessary to consider the problematic nature of this relationship in his practical philosophy.

Judgment between the Empirical and the Intelligible

In the context of Kant's practical philosophy, the problem of the judgment of action appears in the discussion of freedom as a cosmological idea in the *Critique of Pure Reason*. In the third antinomy of reason, Kant shows that the idea of freedom is not incompatible with the law of natural causality: as objects of experience, everything that happens is determined by a previous cause in time, while as "things in themselves," that is, as the things that are the source of appearances, freedom is possible. We cannot observe a free event in experience, yet for practical purposes, or for the purpose of adjudicating moral responsibility and judging action on the basis of it, we presuppose its existence. This means that the causality of objects endowed with freedom can be considered "from two sides ["*auf zwei Seiten*"]: "as **intelligible** in its **action** as a thing in itself, and as **sensible** in the **effects** of that action as an appearance in the world of sense."[31] The actions of free beings must therefore be considered in a twofold manner, as caused at once by freedom (and so as "actions" properly speaking) and by a natural cause (and so as "effects"). Kant claims that every cause has "a law of its causality," which he calls a "character."[32] A free being has both an "empirical character, through which its actions, as appearances, would stand through and through in connection with other appearances in accordance with constant natural laws," and an "intelligible character, through which it is indeed the cause of those actions as appearances, but which does not stand under any conditions of sensibility and is not itself appearances."[33] The empirical character is constituted by the series of appearances that determine one another according to the law of natural causality, while the intelligible character determines appearances without being itself an appearance. The "law" of the intelligible character, Kant claims, is given by imperatives, which determine what a person "ought to" do in accordance with reason, independently of sensible determinations. Yet precisely because it is independent of sensible determinations, the intelligible character does not appear—it is a "thing in itself."[34]

The gap between the empirical and the intelligible character is the source of an important difficulty in Kant's understanding of the judgment of action. Kant claims that the intelligible character, which he also calls the "transcendental subject," is "empirically unknown to us." The reason is that "although the effects of this thinking and acting of the pure understanding are encountered among appearances, these must nonetheless be able to be explained perfectly from their causes in appearance . . . by following its merely empirical character," while "the intelligible character, which is the transcendental cause of the former, is passed over as entirely unknown, except insofar as it is indicated through the empirical character as only its sensible sign [*Zeichen*]."[35]

The idea that empirical causes can work as a "sign" of our noumenal character is intriguing, given that the term has no systematic meaning in Kant's work. A possible source for Kant's use of it is Baumgarten's *Metaphysics*, where a sign is defined as "the means for knowing the existence of another thing."[36] For Baumgarten, however, this "other thing" is located in either the past, the present or the future, which cannot be the case with an intelligible character which, as a thing in itself, is atemporal. This explains why we do not know the "mode of thought" of the intelligible character, even if Kant preserves the idea that somehow "it is indicated through appearances" (*"Die letztere kennen wir aber nicht, sondern bezeichnen sie durch Erscheinungen"*; "We do not know the latter, but we designate it through appearances").[37] If this were not the case, the power of judgment would have nothing to hold on to in order to judge the morality of action. Yet Kant admits that the "judgment of imputation," which is the judgment concerned with adjudicating merit or blame to an act, cannot ultimately bridge the gap between empirical and intelligible character:

> The real morality of actions (their merit and guilt), even that of our own conduct, therefore remains entirely hidden from us. Our imputations [*Zurechnungen*] can be referred only to the empirical character. How much of it is to be ascribed to mere nature and innocent defects of temperament or to its happy constitution (*merito fortunae*) this no one can discover, and hence no one can judge it with complete justice.[38]

Although empirical actions are the only signs we have of our intelligible character, the latter remains nevertheless "entirely hidden" from us, and so no moral judgment can be completely just. It is always possible that a seemingly moral action is an effect of luck, rather than of the moral constitution of our intelligible character.

Kant's skepticism regarding the judgment of imputation runs through his main writings on practical philosophy. In the *Groundwork of the Metaphysics of Morals*, Kant claims that the morality of action is determined by its maxim, that is, by the principle on the basis of which it is performed. This means that the same empirical action may be moral or not depending on its underlying maxim. If the maxim motivating a seemingly moral act is compliance with the imperative of reason, or the moral law, it is performed "from duty" and is consequently moral, whereas if the maxim is some sort of self-interest, it is merely "in conformity with duty," and is not moral. Evidently, maxims cannot be observed, which is why it is seemingly impossible to differentiate an action that is performed "from duty" from one that is performed merely "in conformity with duty." Kant suggests that an acute power of judgment is aware of this distinction, and consequently distrustful of the real morality of action:

> One need not be an enemy of virtue but only a cool observer, who does not take the liveliest wish for the good straightaway as its reality, to become doubtful at certain moments (especially with increasing years, when experience has made one's judgment [*Urtheilskraft*; power of judgment] partly more shrewd and partly more acute in observation) whether any true virtue is to be found in the world.[39]

As experience makes our power of judgment "more acute," and insofar as we are capable of separating our observation of actions from our wish for the good, we become doubtful regarding whether virtue even exists in the world. This doubtfulness, Kant believes, plays a positive role for morality insofar as it allows the power of judgment to distinguish its true ground, which is reason, from a spurious ground, which is the subordination of reason to self-interest. Thus, while an acute power of judgment shows that seemingly good actions are not truly moral if they are not grounded on a maxim of reason, "reason by itself and independently of all appearances commands what ought to happen."[40] As a consequence, Kant claims, "actions of which the world has perhaps so far given no example, and whose very practicability might be very much doubted by one who bases everything on experience, are still inflexibly commanded by reason."[41] Insofar as morality is grounded on reason, it never appears in experience, and therefore any judgment based on experience cannot but play a negative function, namely, to make us doubtful regarding its correspondence with morality. Even if all that judgments on experience show is that no moral action has ever existed, and most likely will never exist, reason still commands that it ought to exist.

The problem for judgment presented by the split between experience and moral maxims reappears in the *Critique of Practical Reason*, in the section titled "On the Typic of Pure Practical Judgment." This section represents Kant's first systematic analysis of the relationship between moral ideas and phenomenal actions. Kant explains that we can judge actions as natural events by considering them as effects of a cause. In this case, the imagination possesses a procedure, or what Kant calls a "schema," for applying the category of causality to the sensible intuition of the action. As Kant explains in the *Critique of Pure Reason*, the imagination plays an essential role in the constitution of objects of experience, because it mediates between concepts, which are given by the understanding, and intuitions, which are given by sensibility. The schema is the procedure by which the imagination applies a concept to intuitions, so that, for example, the concept of cause is applied to a concrete event that is then judged to be the empirical cause of a certain effect. In the case of moral ideas, however, the imagination lacks a procedure, for "no intuition can be put under the law of freedom . . . and hence no schema on behalf of its application *in concreto*."[42] The law of freedom (the moral law) cannot be applied to experience, because there is no intuition that corresponds to it. The question, then, is how a practical judgment is possible at all, namely, how it is possible to apply the ideas of good and evil to empirical actions.

In the absence of a schema guiding the imagination, Kant locates the possibility of applying ideas to concrete actions in what he calls a "type." While a schema mediates between concepts of the understanding and intuitions, the type mediates between ideas of reason and what ought to happen in intuition. The practical judgment is not concerned with what is, but rather with what ought to be, for "to appraise [*die Beurtheilung*; the judging] whether or not something is an object of *pure* practical reason is only to distinguish the possibility or impossibility of *willing* the action by which . . . a certain object would be made real."[43] In order to know whether it is possible to will a concrete action on the basis of the moral law, we need a procedure by which we can apply this law to experience. Kant claims that this application is not performed by the imagination (through a schema) but rather by the understanding: "what the understanding can put under an idea of reason is not a *schema* of sensibility but a law, such a law, however, as can be presented *in concreto* in objects of the senses and hence a law of nature, though only as to its form."[44] The form of the moral law as can be presented in objects of experience is what Kant calls the "type of the moral law," and it is given by the law of nature. While the moral law determines what ought to be, independently of experience, the law of nature determines what is given in experience. In order to make the moral law applicable to experience, the understanding provides reason with the form of the law of nature in order to determine whether a certain action is in accordance with the moral law. This produces the formula of the practical judgment: "Ask yourself whether, if the action you propose were to take place by a law of the nature of which you were yourself a part, you could indeed regard it as possible through your will."[45] In order to judge whether an action is or is not morally good, that is, whether it is a case of an action under the moral law, the power of judgment borrows the form of the law from the understanding, and then asks whether we could will that this law existed.

The analysis of the practical judgment shows that the power of judgment plays a role in the determination of action, but it does not address the possibility of judging actions as they appear in experience, or what Kant calls "judgments of imputation" in the *First Critique*. Although the formula of the practical judgment is not entirely clear in this regard, Kant states that its object is not the action as such, but rather its underlying maxim, that is, the principle on the basis of which it is performed: "If the maxim of the action is not so constituted that it can stand the test as to the form of a law of nature in general, then it is morally impossible."[46] The distinction, often neglected by commentators, is important because the maxim of an action is not observable.[47] According to Kant, every action has an underlying maxim, which is the general principle by which we determine what to do. A moral action is one whose underlying maxim is compliance with duty, while an evil action is one whose underlying maxim is the satisfaction of one's own interests. But because maxims are not observable, we cannot unequivocally judge whether an action is good or evil. The practical judgment tells us what the form of a good maxim is, but it does not provide any means to determine the moral worth of an empirical action. Therefore, it is a mistake to read the type of the moral law, following Felicitas Munzel, as a mediation between intelligible and empirical character, thus neglecting the difference between the type and the schema, and between the imagination (which relates to intuitions) and the understanding (which relates to rules).[48] As Henry Allison points out, the practical judgment determines types of action, not particular actions as they appear in experience.[49]

The seeming impossibility of judging the morality of action becomes an important concern in *Religion*, in connection to the problem of evil. Here, Kant explicitly states that the maxim of an action is beyond observation, which is why "the judgment that an agent is an evil human being cannot reliably be based on experience [*nicht mit Sicherheit auf Erfahrung gründen*; one cannot securely ground it upon experience]."⁵⁰ This is not merely a theoretical, but also a moral problem. According to Kant, the difficulties that the power of judgment encounters when assessing the morality of action can be manipulated so as to deceive oneself and others. An empirically good action ("in conformity with duty") can be used to conceal a maxim that is not moral—as when, for example, a person does not lie out of a concern with his own reputation, as opposed to compliance with moral duty. Kant links this deception to a form of "perfidy" ("*Tücke*") which consists in "the human heart . . . deceiving itself as regards its own good or evil disposition [*guten oder bösen Gesinnungen*] and, provided that its actions do not result in evil (which they could well do because of their maxims), in not troubling itself on account of its disposition but rather considering itself justified before the law."⁵¹ An empirically good action can be motivated by an evil maxim, in which case it is morally evil.

Given that the maxim of action is inscrutable, we can distort our judgment to conceal an evil disposition under the guise of empirically good actions. This is one of the effects of what Kant calls "radical evil," which is the propensity to subordinate compliance with moral duty to self-interest as the supreme incentive in the maxims of our actions. Because this inversion of the incentives leads most of the times to empirically good actions (it is usually in our own self-interest to do what is morally good), radical evil "puts out of tune [*verstimmt*] the moral ability to judge [*moralische Urtheilskraft*; moral power of judgment] what to think of a human being, and renders any imputability [*die Zurechnung*; the imputation] entirely uncertain, whether internal or external."⁵² The theoretical problem of judging the morality of action thus becomes a moral problem in its own right, for it is in our own self-interest to deceive the power of judgment so as to confuse actions "from duty" with actions that are merely "in conformity with duty." And given that our moral disposition is beyond observation, there would seem to be no way to overcome the evil propensity to deceive, and thus the conclusion that judgments of imputation are impossible.

Kant addresses this problem by mentioning two ways to counter the evil propensity to deceive and to put the power of judgment "out of tune," as part of his reflections on moral education. The first one, which further develops his earlier insight in the *Groundwork*, is the use of examples in a negative way, namely, as a means to train the power of judgment to detect the impurity in the incentives of seemingly good actions, thus "allowing our apprentices in morality to judge the impurity of certain maxims on the basis of the incentives actually behind their actions [*aus den wirklichen Triebfedern ihrer Handlungen*; from the real incentives of their actions]."⁵³ The judgment that apparently moral actions stem from impure incentives gradually becomes an "attitude of mind," according to which "*duty* merely for itself begins to acquire in the apprentice's heart a noticeable importance." In this negative use of judgment, the person becomes aware that duty is important "merely for itself" by separating it from impure incentives. According to Kant, "even the most limited human being is capable of all the greater a respect for a dutiful action the more he removes from it, in thought, other incentives which might have influence upon its maxim through self-love."⁵⁴ By judging the impurity behind virtuous actions, we acquire respect for the idea of acting from duty. And given that an action from duty is merely an idea, we can only use examples negatively, namely, as a means to distinguish this idea from nonmoral incentives.

The second way to counter the evil propensity to deceive the power of judgment is positive and more enigmatic. Kant claims that "there is one thing in our soul which, if we duly fix our eye on it, we cannot cease viewing with the highest wonder, and for which admiration [*Bewunderung*] is legitimate and uplifting [*seelenerhebend*; elevating of the soul] as well. And that is the original moral predisposition in us, as such."⁵⁵ The idea of "fixing our eye" on "the original moral predisposition in us" is intriguing, since such predisposition is beyond observation. Kant adds that

> the very incomprehensibility of this predisposition, proclaiming as it does a divine origin, must have an effect on the mind, even to the point of exaltation [*Begeisterung*], and must strengthen it for the sacrifices which respect for duty may perhaps impose upon it. Often to arouse this feeling of the sublimity of our moral vocation is especially praiseworthy as a means of awakening moral dispositions, since it directly counters the innate propensity to pervert [*Hange zur Verkehrung*] the incentives in the maxims of our power of choice.⁵⁶

Arousing a feeling of the sublimity of our moral vocation is a means to counter the propensity to pervert the incentives for action, which is the essence of what Kant calls "radical evil." The question, then, is what arouses this feeling of sublimity, considering Kant's repeated assertion that nothing in experience corresponds to moral ideas. This is a central issue in Kant's "Analytic of the Sublime" in the *Third Critique*.

A Sublime Judgment

The relationship between the sublime and Kant's practical philosophy has been the subject of debate in recent years. One problematic aspect is that while Kant presents the judgment of the sublime as a kind of aesthetic judgment, its interrelation with moral categories seems to put its purely aesthetic nature into question. In a classical study, Paul Crowther argues that Kant provides insufficient grounds for distinguishing the aesthetic feeling of the sublime from the moral feeling of respect for the moral law, and develops an alternative formulation of the sublime that accounts for its aesthetic (as opposed to moral) nature.[57] While more recent studies by Patricia M. Matthews, Henry E. Allison, and Rodolphe Gasché have explicitly or implicitly challenged Crowther's criticism of Kant, they share the concern with emphasizing the aesthetic, as opposed to moral character of the judgment of the sublime.[58] However, in their attempts to make Kant's text amenable to a clear distinction between aesthetic and moral judgments, these studies give little or no room to Kant's discussion of human actions and affects as cases of sublimity, with the consequence that the relationship between sublimity and morality is not subject to a systematic scrutiny. A recent study by Clewis addresses this issue by focusing on the relationship between the sublime, morality, and enthusiasm, stressing the importance of the sublime for the experience of moral ideas.[59] My reading of Kant's analysis of the sublime shares Clewis's approach, but with disagreements I will address farther down. I follow more closely Milton Nahm's suggestion (in an essay from 1956) that the sublime represents a response to the problematic status of the judgment on action in Kant's practical philosophy, in part because it concerns the relationship between the two faculties that must be involved in a judgment of this kind: the imagination and reason.[60] By exploring the relationship between these two faculties in the judgment of action, which will be the focus of my reading, we can better understand the practical implications of Kant's analysis of the sublime.

The role of the imagination in the power of judgment represents one of the main innovations in Kant's analysis of the aesthetic judgment in the *Third Critique*. We have seen that the imagination plays no role whatsoever in the practical judgment. Moral ideas belong to reason, and nothing corresponds to them in experience, which means that there is no possible representation of a good action, or an action that corresponds to the idea of the moral law. In cognitive judgments, the imagination plays a subordinate role: the understanding provides the concepts with which to constitute objects of experience, and the imagination gives form to intuitions in accordance with these concepts. In the aesthetic judgment, by contrast, the imagination becomes relatively autonomous in relation to the other faculties. The reason is that, like in a cognitive judgment, the aesthetic judgment is concerned with objects given in experience, but unlike the former, there is no concept under which to subsume them. As a consequence,

> the power of judgment, which has no concept ready for the given intuition, holds the imagination (merely in the apprehension of the object) together with the understanding (in the presentation of a concept in general) and perceives a relation of the two faculties of cognition which constitutes the subjective, merely sensitive condition of the objective use of the power of judgment in general (namely the agreement of those two faculties with each other).[61]

The description corresponds to the judgment of taste, rather than the sublime. The important point now is that the role of the imagination is not to apprehend an object on the basis of a determined concept, but rather on the basis on of a "concept in general." As a consequence, imagination and understanding reach an agreement without either one of the two subordinating the other: the imagination attempts to give form to intuitions as if there were a concept, and the understanding provides "a concept in general," or a concept without a determinate content. This agreement is the "subjective condition" of the objective use of the power of judgment, that is, of the determinative and cognitive judgment. In cognitive judgments, there is agreement between the two faculties because the imagination follows the rules or concepts of the understanding. In the aesthetic judgment, by contrast, there is no concept ready to guide the imagination, but only "a concept in general." In the second Introduction to the *Third Critique*, Kant describes the agreement between the imagination and the understanding as a "free play," in which "no determinate concept restricts them to a particular rule of cognition."[62] Given that there is no determinate concept ruling the imagination, yet the imagination strives to give intuitions a certain form, it must establish a play with the understanding without the latter providing a rule on how to proceed.

The agreement between the faculties explains why the judgment of taste produces a pleasure that demands the agreement of everyone. A second important innovation in Kant's analysis of the aesthetic judgment concerns the role of the faculty of pleasure and displeasure, which until that point in his work had been considered to be entirely private, in the sense of depending on purely subjective conditions. In the *Third Critique*, Kant distinguishes between "the agreeable" and "the beautiful": while the former pleases our inclinations and appetites, the latter pleases by virtue of the "state of mind" that it produces. Given that this state of mind is an effect of the accord between our cognitive faculties, which all human beings possess, the pleasure occasioned by the beautiful demands universal agreement: "it is the universal capacity for the communication of the state of mind in the given representation which, as the subjective condition of the judgment of taste, must serve as its ground and have the pleasure in the object as a consequence."[63] When we judge an object as beautiful, we are not merely implying that it pleases us individually, but rather that it pleases us by virtue of producing a state of mind that we can expect to be shared by others who contemplate the same object. This state of mind is the same as the one reached in cognitive judgments, with the difference that in the aesthetic judgment there is no determinate concept regulating the agreement. Therefore, there is no a priori rule determining whether an aesthetic judgment is communicable or not, and thus no "proof" regarding its validity.[64] However, it is possible to compel the agreement of others on the basis of the state of mind produced in us by the object.

The judgment of the sublime resembles the judgment of taste in that the imagination relates to indeterminate concepts, but in this case they are concepts of reason. This introduces an important difference in the role of the imagination, as well as in the structure of its relationship with the other faculty involved. Concepts of the understanding are concepts of experience, that is, concepts whose sole purpose is to give form to intuitions. By contrast, concepts of reason, or what Kant more commonly calls "ideas," have no experiential content. Rational ideas like the world as a whole (the totality of objects in the infinity of space and time) or freedom (a cause that is not in its turn the effect of a previous cause in time), do not have a corresponding object in intuition. Therefore, while "the beautiful in nature concerns the form of the object, which consists in limitation . . . the sublime, by contrast, is to be found in a formless object insofar as limitlessness is represented in it, or at its instance, and yet it is also thought as a totality."[65] Because concepts of the understanding give form to intuitions, the free play between the imagination and the understanding involves a limited, yet undetermined form. Ideas of reason, by contrast, have no form, and so the imagination can only relate to reason by encountering objects that are formless, and consequently allow for limitlessness to be represented in them. Evidently, there is no such thing as a formless object in intuition. However, as we will see, there are objects that challenge the imagination's capacity to give form to intuitions. It is these objects that awaken the feeling of the sublime.

Kant analyzes two kinds of sublime: mathematical and dynamical. While it is in the analysis of the latter that the relationship between judgment and action comes to the fore, the explanation of the mathematically sublime lays out the foundations for understanding the judgment of the sublime in general. The mathematically sublime is that which is "absolutely great," that is, great beyond comparison. Kant suggests that this is the meaning of the word *great* in a judgment like "the man is great," for "if I simply say that something is great, it seems that I do not have in mind any comparison at all . . . , since it is not thereby determined at all how great the object is."[66] Greatness, however, is not a concept for determining an object, but rather a "comparative concept." The judgment of magnitude requires a unit of measurement for determining how great something is, and this unit requires in turn something else to be compared with—a kilometer is great in comparison with a meter, but small in comparison with a mile. The question, then, is what in the contemplation of the object produces the idea of greatness independently of comparison. On this point, Kant claims,

> Nothing that can be an object of the senses is . . . to be called sublime. But just because there is in our imagination a striving to advance to the infinite, while in our reason there lies a claim to absolute totality, as to a real idea, the very inadequacy of our faculty for estimating the magnitude of the things of the sensible world awakens [*ist . . . die Erweckung*] the feeling of a supersensible faculty in us; and the use that the power of judgment naturally makes in behalf of the latter

(feeling), though not the object of the senses, is absolutely great, while in contrast to it any other use is small.[67]

The feeling of the sublime is awakened by the inadequacy between the imagination and reason. The imagination strives to present the infinite on behalf of reason's claim to absolute totality. But this is impossible, for there is no possible presentation of infinity. Yet in its very striving for the infinite, the imagination awakens the feeling of a supersensible faculty in us, which is reason. Thus in judging an object as sublime, the use of the power of judgment is absolutely great, because it serves a faculty of the mind that has no limitations.

The inadequacy between imagination and reason is occasioned by objects that challenge the imagination's capacity to estimate their magnitude. Kant explains that this estimation depends on two operations: apprehension and comprehension. In apprehension, the imagination presents an individual sensuous perception to the mind. In comprehension, it retains the series of presentations in order to form an object. The sublime is awakened by a disruption in comprehension,

> for when apprehension [*Auffassung*] has gone so far that the partial representations of the intuition of the senses that were apprehended first already begin to fade in the imagination as the latter proceeds on to the apprehension of further ones, then it loses on one side as much as it gains on the other, and there is in the comprehension [*Zusammenfassung*] a greatest point beyond which it cannot go.[68]

In the presence of certain objects, the imagination finds itself unable to comprehend all partial apprehensions. Kant's examples are the pyramids and Saint Peter's Basilica, which suggest objects whose magnitude challenges our capacity to comprehend all its parts into one whole representation. As the imagination runs through these objects, it encounters difficulties retaining apprehensions as it must proceed to new ones. Ultimately, given that the imagination is finite, it encounters a point beyond which it cannot go, and comprehension fails.

The failure of the imagination in representing the object produces the thought of infinity, thus arousing the feeling of respect. Reason is a supersensible faculty, which means that it lies beyond the limitation of the senses. Consequently, in its demand to present all the elements in a series, it "does not exempt from this requirement even the infinite (space and past time), but rather makes it unavoidable for us to think of it (in the judgment of common reason) as **given entirely** (in its totality)."[69] In its relation with the imagination, reason demands what is impossible for the latter, namely, to comprehend the infinity of space and time. It is the failure of comprehension produced by this demand that makes it unavoidable for us to think of this totality, even if it cannot be presented. Thus, what is a failure from the viewpoint of presentation becomes a victory from the viewpoint of thinking: we cannot present the totality of space and time, but the very attempt to do so shows that we are capable of thinking it. It is this capacity that awakens the feeling of "respect" ("*Achtung*"), which Kant defines as "the feeling of the inadequacy of our capacity for the attainment of an idea **that is a law for us**."[70] In its effort to present an idea of reason, the imagination meets its inadequacy, but "at the same time its vocation for adequately realizing that idea as a law," which shows that "the feeling of the sublime in nature is respect for our own vocation, which we show to an object in nature through a certain subreption [*Supreption*] (substitution of a respect for the object instead of for the idea of humanity [*Idee der Menschheit*] in our subject)."[71] Although the failure of the imagination is felt as displeasure, it also "arouses [*rege macht*] the feeling of our supersensible vocation in us, in accordance with which it is purposive and thus a pleasure to find every standard of sensibility inadequate for the ideas of the understanding [*Ideen der Vernunft*; ideas of reason]."[72] Therefore, even in their contrast, imagination and reason find a sort of harmony in disharmony, for the latter is felt as having a purpose, namely, to arouse the feeling of the supersensible vocation of our mind.

Before proceeding to the implications of this analysis for the judgment of action, let us note one important contrast between the feeling of the sublime and the feeling of the beautiful. The feeling of the beautiful, as we have seen, stems from the harmony achieved in the interaction between the imagination and the understanding. The feeling of the sublime is more complex. On the one hand, the judgment of the sublime involves harmony between the imagination and reason, even though this harmony is mediated by disharmony. But the feeling of the sublime is not simply the feeling of this harmony—according to Kant, it is the "feeling of the supersensible vocation in us," that is, respect. Without this feeling for the supersensible, there would be no harmony between the faculties, because the failure of the imagination would not lead us to hear the voice of reason. Consequently, Kant claims, "the pleasure in the sublime in nature . . . presupposes another feeling, namely that of its supersensible vocation, which, no matter how obscure it might be, has a moral foundation."[73] Commentators who emphasize the continuities between the beautiful and the sublime tend to leave aside these and other descriptions of the feeling of the sublime as dependent on the (moral) feeling of respect, and overlook that the former, unlike the feeling of pleasure in the beautiful, does not result from the harmony between the faculties.[74] As Paul Guyer points out, the harmony between the faculties in the sublime is a "psychological state" that characterizes the aesthetic judgment in general, which does not imply that the phenomenological structure of the feeling of the sublime or the source of the claim to universal approval of the judgment (which I will address in the next section) are the same in both kinds of judgment.[75] Regarding these two elements, Kant is clear that the feeling of the sublime, unlike the feeling of the beautiful, depends on our capacity to feel the supersensible vocation of our mind, which is why it has a moral foundation.[76] This interrelation between the feeling of the sublime and the feeling for ideas of reason comes to the fore in the analysis of the dynamically sublime.

A Supersensible Power

Kant comes closer to the analysis of the judgment of action in his analysis of the dynamically sublime and in the general remarks that follow it. While the mathematically sublime is related to the faculty of cognition, the dynamically sublime is related to the faculty of desire, which is the faculty that determines action.[77] It is therefore no coincidence that in the analysis of the dynamically sublime human actions and affects are introduced as examples of sublimity. This does not mean, however, that actions belong to a specific kind of sublime, as Crowther and Clewis have proposed in different ways. Rather, the analysis of the sublime in general shows that a judgment of action on the basis of ideas of reason is possible. This is evident if we consider that already in the analysis of the mathematically sublime Kant mentions "the man is great" as an example of a judgment of the sublime, and refers to "the magnitude of a certain virtue" as one possible object of this kind of judgment.[78] The view that the judgment of action constitutes a special kind of sublime not only departs from Kant's text, but also, and more importantly, neglects the relationship between the aesthetic and the moral components of the judgment of the sublime, which will be the focus of my reading in what follows.

While the mathematically sublime emerges out of the attempt to represent magnitude, the dynamically sublime emerges out of the attempt to represent power. Kant introduces this idea as follows:

> **Power [*Macht*]** is a capacity that is superior to great obstacles. The same thing is called **dominion [*Gewalt*]** if it is also superior to the resistance of something that itself possesses power. Nature considered in aesthetic judgment as a power that has no dominion over us is **dynamically sublime**.[79]

In the dynamically sublime, nature is considered as a power, yet not as powerful enough to have dominion over us. As a consequence, the object arouses admiration for our own power over nature. This is an effect of contemplating an object that produces fear by virtue of overcoming our capacity to resist it. Powerful objects in nature, such as "bold, overhanging, as it were threatening cliffs, thunder clouds towering up into the heavens, bringing with them flashes of lightning and crashes of thunder, volcanoes with their all-destroying violence . . . , make our capacity to resist into an insignificant trifle in comparison with their power."[80] Even if these objects are fearful, Kant claims, "the sight of them only becomes all the more attractive the more fearful it is," given that "they elevate [*erhöhen*] the strength of our soul above its usual level, and allow us to discover within ourselves a capacity for resistance of quite another kind, which gives us the courage to measure ourselves against the apparent all-powerfulness [*Allgewalt*] of nature."[81] In contemplating a violent volcano, we experience a power that makes our capacity to resist insignificant. Yet even if we are afraid of it, we can "**think of** the case in which we might wish to resist it."[82] And even if resisting the power of a volcano would be futile, the very thought of this resistance elevates our soul to experience a different kind of resistance, one that does not depend on physical power. The thought that we may want to resist nature, with its apparent all-powerfulness, shows that there is a power in us of a different kind, unconstrained by the boundaries of physical power.

The contrast between nature and resistance to it resembles Kant's contrast between our empirical and our intelligible characters. We have seen that while our empirical character is subject to the law of nature, our intelligible character is independent from it. Therefore, just like the mathematically sublime revealed a superiority of reason over nature by virtue of the latter's incapacity to match its ideas,

> likewise the irresistibility of its power certainly makes us, considered as natural beings, recognize our physical powerlessness, but at the same time it reveals a capacity for judging ourselves as independent of it and a superiority over nature on which is grounded a self-preservation of quite another kind than that which can be threatened and endangered by nature outside us, whereby the humanity in our person remains undemeaned even though the human being must submit to that dominion.[83]

While our self-preservation can always be threatened by nature "outside of us," there is a self-preservation of another kind that remains undemeaned by it. This is what Kant calls "the humanity in our person," which stems from our capacity to act on the basis of moral principles, in such a way that our principles for action are universally communicable.[84] By raising the imagination to a case in which we might resist nature in all its power, we regard our own natural incentives for action, that is, "those things about which we are concerned (goods, health and life)," as trivial in comparison with "our highest principles," which stem from the moral law.[85] This way, the irresistibility of nature "outside of us" raises the imagination to a power over nature inside of us, because no natural incentive is powerful enough to make us disregard the moral law as an object of admiration. As with the mathematically sublime, every standard for assessing the value of natural incentives for action is trivial in comparison with the moral law, which calls us to resist such incentives.

The connection between the representation of nature and the idea of a resistance to it discloses a new possibility for the power of judgment, which is crucial for relating it to actions. We have seen that all objects of experience, including actions, are ruled by the law of natural causality. This means that as objects of experience all actions are determined by the inclinations, and so actions performed out of moral ideas simply do not exist in experience. However, if there are objects which, by virtue of their resistance to our capacity to represent them as a purely natural power, arouse the feeling of a vocation of the mind that is beyond natural necessitation, then a new possibility opens up for the representation of action. As objects of experience, all actions are ruled by the law of natural causality. But there are actions that challenge our ability to represent them as a power of nature, and thus arouse the idea of a supersensible power. Kant mentions the warrior as "an object of the greatest admiration [*grösten Bewunderung*]," whom aesthetic judgment determines as deserving respect.[86] By appearing to sacrifice all inclinations and putting all self-interest at risk, the warrior surpasses our capacity to represent his actions as determined by nature, that is, by his inclinations, thus arousing the idea of a supersensible power. Therefore, Kant claims that the mentality of the people conducting war is "all the more sublime, the more dangers it has been exposed to and before which it has been able to assert its courage."[87]

Kant's reference to human actions seems to depart from his own definition of the dynamically sublime as a power that stretches the imagination to its limit, which has led commentators to consider it as a new type of sublime. According to Crowther, the example of the warrior constitutes "a subcategory of dynamic sublimity whose origin is to be found in our affective response to rationally significant *human deeds*."[88] This affective response does not consist in stretching the imagination to the limit of what it can present, as Kant defines the dynamically sublime, but rather in leading the imagination "to envisage possibilities of moral action."[89] In a similar vein, Clewis claims that the references to actions constitute a "moral sublime" that is different from both the mathematically and the dynamically sublime, and which consists in "a response to the moral law (or a representation or embodiment thereof) and more directly reveals the human capacity for morality."[90] Both interpretations neglect the fact that there is no such thing as an action that embodies or represents compliance with duty, and there is no reason to assume that Kant is being inconsistent on this point. An action that overcomes great obstacles of sensibility is not an example of moral action, but rather an object that, by virtue of surpassing the capacity of the imagination to represent it as a natural power, arouses the idea of a supersensible power in us. In this regard, the sublimity of war is no different from that of the power of a great volcano, for "sublimity is not contained in anything in nature, but only in our mind, insofar as we can become conscious of being superior to nature within us and thus also to nature outside us (insofar as it influences us)."[91]

This consideration is important for understanding the precise sense in which a judgment of action is possible. A morally good action, as we have seen, is an action performed on the basis of compliance with the moral law, which is an idea of reason that lacks any possible presentation in experience. In the *Second Critique*, Kant explain that we are aware of the moral law through the feeling of respect, which "is produced by a purely intellectual ground," and is therefore independent of sensuous perceptions or sensations.[92] The feeling of the sublime is aesthetic, which means that it is connected to sensuous perceptions, but it also depends on ideas of reason, for otherwise the imagination would not feel the demand to overstep its boundaries. This is why Kant claims that the feeling of the sublime has its foundation "in the predisposition to the feeling for (practical) ideas, i.e., to that which is moral," which "is the ground for the necessity of the assent [*Beistimmung*; approval] of the judgment of other people concerning the sublime to our own."[93] In order to judge an object as sublime, we need to feel respect for the moral law, for otherwise we would not experience the failure of the imagination in the representation of an object as serving a purpose for the mind that is universally communicable. Consequently, while, on the one hand, the feeling of the sublime is awakened by an object that challenges our capacity to represent it, on the other hand, it requires the feeling of respect. This means that the representation of the morally good has both an aesthetic and an intellectual "side," as Kant explains in the following passage:

> The object of a pure and unconditioned intellectual satisfaction is the moral law in all its power, which it exercises in us over each and every incentive of the mind **antecedent to it**; and, since this power actually makes itself aesthetically knowable only through sacrifices . . . , the satisfaction on the aesthetic side (in relation to sensibility) is negative, i.e., contrary to this interest, but considered from the intellectual side it is positive, and combined with an interest. From this it follows that the intellectual, intrinsically purposive (moral) good, judged aesthetically [*ästhetisch beurtheilt*], must not be represented so much as beautiful but rather as sublime, so that it arouses [*erwecke*; awakens] . . . the feeling of respect (which scorns charm).[94]

Although the moral law is the object of a purely intellectual satisfaction through the feeling of respect, its power is only aesthetically knowable through sacrifices, that is, through the overcoming of sensible incentives for action. The aesthetic representation, however, is only negative, and works by means of awakening the feeling of respect for the moral law, which is purely intellectual. Therefore, the representation of the morally good is never purely aesthetic, for without the feeling of respect, sacrifices would not arouse the idea of the moral law. The two sides of the sublime feeling, aesthetic and intellectual, are necessary for the representation of the morally good. The judgment of action, like action itself (according to Kant's description of it in the *First Critique*, as we have seen), has two "sides": one purely intellectual and one accessible to the senses.

It is this twofold nature of the judgment of the sublime that allows us to judge on the basis of ideas, without disregarding their incommensurability with anything given in experience. The imagination cannot subordinate intuitions to ideas and bridge the gap between our noumenal and our empirical characters, because there is no correspondence between the realm of freedom and the realm of experience. But objects in experience can arouse ideas of reason by driving the imagination to the limit of what it can represent. It is the "arousal" or "awakening" of respect for ideas by virtue of this stretching of the imagination that constitutes the sublime feeling. The judgment of the sublime thus relates ideas and actions while preserving their heterogeneity: no action can represent compliance with duty, but an action can arouse the feeling of a power that is beyond natural necessity, and thus respect for the idea of duty. Superiority over nature is the negative side of the sublime feeling, but by itself it is not enough to ground a judgment claiming universal approval. The source of this claim is the positive side, which is the feeling of respect for the moral law. There is no middle term between these two sides because, as we have seen, the sublime feeling emerges out of the inadequacy between two faculties, and it is this inadequacy that puts them in relation to one another. As Lyotard puts it, "the differend cannot be resolved. But it can be felt as such, as differend. This is the sublime feeling."[95] The experience of a discordance between the object and our capacity to represent it awakens in us the feeling for ideas, which is the basis for making a judgment on action claiming universal approval.

Between Enthusiasm and Sublimity

Let us now go back to the original question of this chapter. I considered the possibility, hinted at by Arendt, of judging from the viewpoint of the "idea of mankind," which connects the perspective of the actor and that of the spectator. To act or to judge on the basis of the idea of mankind means to act and to judge in a way that everyone will in principle approve. Following Kant, we see that this idea has no phenomenal manifestation, in the sense that no object corresponds to it. Arendt suggests that we can approach this idea by enlarging the imagination and considering other viewpoints. But to approximate an infinite number of possible viewpoints seems self-defeating, for the power of our imagination is inherently limited. Kant's alternative consists in grounding our judgment on the feeling aroused by the idea of mankind, that is, the idea of a viewpoint that is beyond the limitation of phenomenal representation. Certain actions, Kant believes, can arouse a feeling for ideas that exceed any possible representation, without the need to know the moral disposition behind the act. On the basis of this feeling, it is possible to make a judgment on action that demands universal approval. When we judge that a person is "great," we expect that others will agree—not on the basis of our knowledge of the person's moral character, but rather of the feeling of respect for the idea of greatness aroused by the action.

The sublime as a ground for the judgment of action represents an alternative to the deception involved in taking seemingly good actions as proof of moral virtue. The alternative becomes clear if we consider Kant's distinction between the sublime and enthusiasm (*Enthusiasmus*) in the *Third Critique*. As we have seen, the judgment of the sublime has an "aesthetic side," which is the feeling of superiority over obstacles of sensibility, and an "intellectual side," which is respect for the moral law. Enthusiasm is a state of mind that is produced by the feeling of the sublime, but without a connection to the feeling of respect, in such a way that superiority over obstacles of sensibility becomes an end in itself. Kant describes enthusiasm as "the idea of the good with affect," adding that "this state of mind seems to be sublime." The explanation of why this state of mind only "seems" to be sublime follows:

> Now, however, every affect is blind, either in the choice of its end, or, even if this is given by reason, in its implementation; for it is that movement of the mind that makes it incapable of engaging in free consideration of principles, in order to determine itself in accordance with them. Thus it cannot in any way merit a satisfaction of reason. Nevertheless, enthusiasm is aesthetically sublime [*ästhetisch gleichwohl ist der*

Enthusiasmus erhaben; aesthetically nevertheless enthusiasm is sublime], because it is a stretching of the powers through ideas, which give the mind a momentum that acts far more powerfully and persistently than the impetus given by sensory representations.[96]

The movement of the mind that makes one capable of engaging in "free consideration of principles" requires the feeling of respect for the moral law. Without this free consideration of principles, the aesthetic feeling of sublimity (the feeling of superiority over nature) remains "blind," in the sense that superiority over sensible obstacles is not linked to the pure idea of the moral law. Kant's example is "indignation, as anger," which suggests an affect that shares with the idea of the good the disregard for sensuous self-interest, but which does not necessarily involve a free consideration of principles for action and their implementation in accordance with reason. A sense of indignation can predispose us to overcome our inclinations, but this predisposition does not necessarily involve respect for the idea of the law, which is why enthusiasm "cannot merit any satisfaction of reason." Considered aesthetically, enthusiasm is sublime because it produces a momentum in the mind that exceeds the power produced by any sensory representations. But because it is not related to the purely intellectual regard for the law, and thus to a free consideration of principles, it lacks the nonaesthetic, ideal component that is essential for the judgment of the sublime. This enthusiasm, Kant claims, can be compared to a "delusion of sense" ("*Wahnsinn*"; literally, "madness"), that is, to the idea that sensuous representations are equivalent to that which they represent—so that superiority over the inclinations is not taken to be a representation of morality, but rather to be morality as such.

Kant's concern with enthusiasm shows the essential twofold nature (both aesthetic and intellectual) of the judgment of the sublime. In *Religion*, Kant identifies "delusion of sense" as part of the deceptive religious practices that he calls "delusion of religion" ("*Religionswahnn*"), which consists in "the habit of taking a mere representation (of the imagination) for the presence of the thing itself, and to value it as such."[97] In religion, the "mere representation" is given by the practice that expresses our moral disposition, while the "thing itself" is the disposition as such. Significantly, Kant mentions rituals of self-sacrifice as one of the delusional practices we often confuse with morality, because we take its aesthetic component (the overcoming of our inclinations) as the thing itself. The judgment of the morality of action only in terms of its aesthetic component, without a free consideration of principles, becomes a source of delusion, that is, an attachment to the appearance of virtue without a regard for the moral ideas that underlie it. As we have seen, this delusion is not merely a theoretical mistake, but rather a manipulation of the power of judgment stemming from what Kant calls "radical evil." The attempt to make the morality of action directly accessible to sensibility cannot but deceive the power of judgment, erasing the gap between sensible representations and moral ideas. As Kant puts it in his remarks on affects,

> Even tumultuous movements of the mind, whether they be associated with ideas of religion, under the name of edification, or, as belonging merely to culture, with ideas that contain a social interest, no matter how much they stretch the imagination, can in no way claim the honor of being a **sublime** presentation, if they do not leave behind a disposition of mind that, even if only indirectly, has influence on the consciousness of its strength and resolution in regard to that which brings with it intellectual purposiveness (the supersensible).[98]

No matter how noble the idea we are presenting (some of Kant's examples are courage, indignation, and humility), it is only sublime if it makes us conscious of our supersensible capacities. Otherwise, it remains at the level of enthusiasm, and potentially leads to delusion.

The contrast between enthusiasm and the sublime corresponds with the distinction between the attachment to ritualized forms of virtue and the capacity to judge actions independently of them. Arendt, as we have seen, believes that the attempt to ground our judgments on a given system of values leads to the mere habit of holding fast to something, that is, to whatever standards are given to us at any given moment. Her view is influenced by Eichmann's "idealism," which consisted in a desire to find an "Idea" for which he could sacrifice everything. This strange idealism, which finds satisfaction in the mere representation of virtue and disregards its true moral ground, is precisely what Kant calls enthusiasm. Sacrifice itself, according to Kant, merits no satisfaction of reason, for it lacks a relation to the purely intellectual source of moral ideas. The sublime feeling, by contrast, relates sacrifices to respect for the moral law, thus preserving its true ground. There is therefore a subtle but crucial difference between the state of mind in enthusiasm and in the feeling of the sublime: the former finds pleasure in sacrifice as an end in itself, while the latter finds pleasure in sacrifice only insofar as it arouses respect for the idea of duty. Because this idea is incommensurable with anything in experience, the state of mind in the feeling of the sublime involves an inadequacy between our faculties, that is, between the aesthetic representation of virtue by means of the imagination and the intellectual respect for ideas by means of reason. The judgment of the sublime does not overcome the inadequacy, but rather stems from it: it is the tension between the two sides of the sublime feeling (aesthetic and intellectual) that produces a state of mind that is communicable to everyone.

Conclusion

Arendt's turn to Kant's aesthetics, influenced by Eichmann's "inability to judge," represents an attempt to find an alternative between a communitarian and a transcendental standard for the judgment of action. The focus of this turn is the notion of common sense, which constitutes an "intersubjective" standard for judgment, in the sense that it stems from the capacity to take into account multiple standpoints. This conception leaves open an important problem, namely, the possibility that our judgment be valid beyond all viewpoints familiar to us. In order for our judgment on action to claim universal approval, it must have a ground in universal ideas, as Arendt suggests in her references to the "idea of mankind" and our "cosmopolitan existence." Kant's analysis of the sublime shows how it is possible to judge on the basis of ideas, thus avoiding a purely communitarian standard for judgment, but also an objective standard that would work as a fixed rule. Like Arendt, Kant is distrustful of our attachment to representations of moral virtue, because they tend to conceal the true ground of morality, which is the purely intellectual respect for the moral law. The judgment of the sublime represents an alternative to this attachment, because it does not consider the object as a representation of an idea, but rather as the occasion that arouses respect for the idea of humanity in those who contemplate it. It is on the basis of the feeling of respect for this idea, which must be present in any being capable of moral action, that we expect everyone will agree with our judgment.

Kant's analysis of the judgment of the sublime shows that it is possible to make judgments on the basis of moral ideas that aspire to the assent of everyone, without the need for rules and procedures that secure its validity. Political theorists often believe that uncertainty and universality are mutually exclusive—that either we know the fundamental principle of validity that grounds the assent of everyone, or otherwise the assent is contingent and limited. But the aspiration to the universality of judgment and the experience of uncertainty share a common root, namely, the striving for ideas that transcend particular viewpoints. To act and to judge on the basis of these ideas involves at once aspiration to universality and awareness that the ground of universality is unpresentable. This means that the experience of uncertainty is not a limitation to judgment but rather the condition that allows it to move beyond established standards and generate relations with a potentially infinite number of other judgments. While the experience of uncertainty generates the desire to turn to rules that secure the validity of judgment, it also enables an openness to indeterminate relations. According to Kant, it is this openness that preserves our receptivity to moral ideas, in contrast to their concealment under ritualized practices that deceive the power of judgment and lead to radical evil.

Chapter 4

Lyotard on Good and Evil in Postmodernity

In the context of value pluralism, it may seem that judgments based on moral ideas, which are by their very nature universal, are impossible. As we have seen in the previous chapter, Kant shows that we can judge on the basis of moral ideas while acknowledging that they are undeterminable. We make these judgments because an action arouses a feeling for moral ideas, even if we cannot turn these ideas into a representable object. This conception of judgment points to a possible articulation of universality and plurality: we feel our striving for a universal viewpoint beyond particular perspectives of the world, but we cannot reach it, which means that we cannot know whether our judgment is valid. In moral matters, universality is a striving rather than an object of knowledge. But what happens when there is disagreement on how to judge? What happens when different perspectives rely on different and even conflicting standards for judgment? Can we still rely on moral ideas to orient our political commitments in an increasingly pluralistic world?

One of the main theorists of the radical pluralism characteristic of postmodern societies, Jean-François Lyotard, believes that the ideas of good and evil are not independent of, but rather intertwined with such pluralism. In his central political book, *The Differend*, he claims that "politicians cannot have the good at stake, but they ought to have the lesser evil. Or, if you prefer, the lesser evil ought to be the political good." Although Lyotard does not write on the problem of evil extensively, the importance of this remark in his thought becomes apparent in a eulogy after his death, pronounced by his friend Jacques Derrida, who claimed that the question of what is even worse than radical evil "keeps a strange, uncanny spell for him."[1] As Lyotard defines it, evil is the "incessant interdiction of possible phrases, a defiance of the occurrence, the contempt for Being."[2] The terms *phrase*, *occurrence*, and *Being* refer to that which arrives unpredictably, without following a preexisting rule. All phrases and occurrences fall into a web of discourses, each one of which seeks to regulate the web under its rules, thus doing wrong to other discourses. The political good, according to Lyotard, consists in minimizing this wrong, in such a way that the conflict between discourses around the regulation of phrases does not lead to obliteration, as if all phrases had to belong to a single discourse. Attempting to regulate this lack of regulation under an absolute set of rules, as the philosophical discourse (as Lyotard understands it) has often attempted to do, would be self-defeating, for such rules would necessarily wrong other rules. However, if politics is still to have an orientation, and not fall into skepticism, it is necessary to have an idea of what the "lesser evil" would be. It would be necessary, in other words, to know how to minimize the wrong that takes place with each occurrence, with the ensuing conflict regarding how to regulate it—that is, the conflict around how to speak about the occurrence.

Like Arendt and Kant, Lyotard believes that the foundation of ethical commitments stems from our relation to a fundamental uncertainty—for him, the uncertainty of judgment. What he adds to Arendt's and Kant's perspectives is the focus on conflict. The source of uncertainty in judgment is not only the unavoidable relationship between different perspectives with different standards for judgment, but also the conflict that emerges from it. Plurality is essentially conflictive because even though there are multiple standards for judgment, only one set of standards can determine each individual judgment at each moment. Different standards for judgment are in constant tension with one another, making it uncertain which one will prevail at each instance. Evil, in Lyotard's view, stems from the desire to eliminate uncertainty by subordinating all judgments to a single set of standards.

My goal in this chapter is to show, following Lyotard, that good and evil are still operative political concepts in a context of postmodernity. Several scholars have mistakenly interpreted Lyotard's conception of postmodernity as advocating for a political skepticism or nihilism, according to which political judgment should abandon all aspirations to communicability and universality, and limit itself to local struggles and narratives.³ While it is true that Lyotard rejects totalizing narratives and universal standards for judgment, this does not entail the complete abandonment of the universalist aspiration of political judgment and action. Political action can still be judged as "just" or "good," on the condition that we do not ground justice and goodness on a pregiven set of norms that we can simply apply to a multiplicity of situations. Rather, a just or a good political action will be one that invents new means of communication in a situation that seems deprived of them, thus establishing a link between heterogeneous parties. The universal appeal of such action does not stem from a rule that grounds this linkage, but rather from the very need to communicate, even when there are no means by which to do so. The model for this kind of universality is Kant's judgment of the sublime. In Lyotard's view, the judgment of the sublime exposes the general procedure underlying Kant's critical philosophy, which is in itself a model for politics. By focusing closely on Lyotard's interpretation of Kant, I will show that universality and postmodernity are not mutually exclusive—rather, postmodernity, properly understood, exposes what universality truly is.

The Problem of Legitimacy and the Turn to Kant

In *The Postmodern Condition*, Lyotard succinctly defines "postmodern" as "incredulity toward metanarratives."⁴ Given that narratives play a crucial role in the legitimation of knowledge, this incredulity leads to a crisis of legitimacy. Modernity, according to Lyotard, is characterized by the attempt to legitimize scientific knowledge by means of a metadiscourse that explains its rules. The discourse in charge of this legitimation is philosophy, which ever since Plato has provided a narrative, such as the Allegory of the Cave, that accounts for the validity of scientific statements: "Scientific knowledge cannot know and make known that it is the true knowledge without resorting to the other, narrative, kind of knowledge, which from its point of view is no knowledge at all."⁵ The implications of this interrelation between narrative and knowledge, however, go far beyond the realm of science. Once knowledge has created a metadiscourse that legitimates it, this metadiscourse can be used to legitimate ethical and political norms. Philosophical narratives emerge originally from the need to legitimate scientific knowledge but, after the Enlightenment, "narrative knowledge makes a resurgence in the West as a way of solving the problem of legitimating the new authorities."⁶ When these narratives lose credibility, legitimacy is in crisis, for there is no single source that regulates the distinction between the true and the false, the just and the unjust, the beautiful and the ugly, the productive and the unproductive, and so on. As a consequence, there is a dispersion of "language games," each producing its own standards of legitimacy without a metalanguage that mediates between them.

This linguistic dispersion creates a new problem for the legitimacy of judgments. A language game can determine whether a specific statement is legitimate or not according to its own criteria, but there is no higher standard determining which criteria should apply in each case. In the absence of a metadiscourse that organizes the relationship between judgments, social pragmatics "is a monster formed by the interweaving of various networks of heteromorphous classes of utterances (denotative, prescriptive, performative, technical, evaluative, etc.)."⁷ As a consequence, we cannot expect that there will be consensus regarding the rules that determine the legitimacy of each utterance, or what Lyotard calls "metaprescriptives": "there is no reason to think that it would be possible to determine metaprescriptives common to all of these language games or that a revisable consensus . . . could embrace the totality of metaprescriptions regulating the totality of statements circulating in the social collectivity."⁸ Consensus, Lyotard claims, is a dated idea, for it presupposes that the heterogeneous language games that constitute social pragmatics could agree on common rules for regulating all utterances. In the absence of a credible metadiscourse, such agreement is simply not possible. This does not mean, however, that universal principles for judgment and action must be abandoned: "justice as a value is neither outmoded nor suspect. We must thus arrive at an idea and practice of justice that is not linked to that of consensus."⁹ The question that follows is how we can determine what justice is if consensus is impossible.

Lyotard's response to this question is that we need a transformed notion of justice that consists in the acknowledgment that it is impossible for any single language game to determine what justice is. Lyotard develops this idea in the dialogue *Just Gaming* (*Au juste*), where he claims that the "Idea of Justice" consists "in preserving the purity of each game, that is, for example, in insuring that the discourse of truth be considered as a 'specific' language game, that narration be played by its 'specific' rules."¹⁰ This is a contrast to what Lyotard calls "terror," which consists in one language game seeking to impose its rules on all others. While a just judgment acknowledges the heterogeneity between the rules of different language games, the terrorist judgment seeks to obliterate this heterogeneity. This is why, according to Lyotard, justice can only be an Idea in the Kantian sense: it is not the referent of a judgment, but a principle that orients how we judge. To judge on the basis of the Idea of Justice is to keep the "game of justice" open, in such a way that another judgment may disagree on what justice is. Terrorism, by contrast, consists in judging in such a way that one assumes that one knows what justice is, thus delegitimizing any judgment that disagrees: "any attempt to state the law, for example, to place oneself in the position of enunciator of the universal prescription is obviously infatuation itself and absolute injustice, in point of fact."[11] This is why the just judgment partakes in the "game of justice": it does not presuppose a definitive concept of justice, but listens to what other judgments have to say about this, in such a way that "one speaks only inasmuch as one listens, that is, one speaks as a listener, and not as an author."[12] Justice is a "game" in the sense that its meaning is defined by the mutual responses between the "players." Injustice, by contrast, precludes these responses, thus withdrawing from the game.

This conception of justice is essential for Lyotard's understanding of political judgment. Politics, according to Lyotard, presupposes an idea of justice, for it is this idea that supports prescriptions regarding what society should be like: "There is no politics if there is not at the very center of society . . . a questioning of existing institutions, a project to improve them, to make them more just."[13] Justice, as we have seen, is a game rather than a set of principles. This means that political judgments do not rely on an absolute conception of justice, as if they possessed the standards for determining what justice is, but rather respond to other judgments in an open-ended "game of justice." The game is played between different language games with specific rules, which is why the only "rule" of the game of justice, if it is not to become terror, is to respect the heterogeneity of rules. At the moment of uttering a judgment, one cannot presuppose any rule: "I judge. But if I am asked by what criteria do I judge, I will have no answer to give." Otherwise, Lyotard claims, "it would mean that there is actually a possible consensus on these criteria between the readers and me; we would not be then in a situation of modernity, but in classicism" (the contrast between modernity and classicism here corresponds to the contrast between postmodernity and modernity in later writings).[14]

Lyotard's interpretation of the Idea of Justice as a ground for judgment has been criticized as implicitly falling back into a philosophical universalism. David Ingram claims that Lyotard's denial of absolute standards for judgment brings about a new "communitarian ideal," according to which "the *plurality of voices* (or language games) would be preserved without the violence of hegemony."[15] In other words, Lyotard's idea of a judgment lacking absolute foundations would lead back to a new foundation under the form of a regulative idea—namely, that of a world in which all voices are respected. A similar argument is presented by Samuel Weber in his Afterword to *Just Gaming*, where he claims that "by prescribing that no game, especially not that of prescription, should dominate the others, one is doing exactly what it is simultaneously claimed is being avoided: one is dominating the other games in order to protect them from domination."[16] Jean-Luc Nancy further pursues this line of critique in his response to *Just Gaming*, claiming that "Lyotard says that justice must intervene in order to purify the games that are impure, such as narrations infiltrated by prescriptions: but where are the 'purities' in question determined from?"[17] According to Nancy, this question leaves Lyotard with two equally problematic options: either the purity of each discourse must be determined empirically, without a connection to the idea of justice, or the idea of justice has to be determined by a particular discourse, in which case it would cease to be universal. Thus, Lyotard's idea of justice would do either too little or too much: either it prescribes that particular judgments should follow empirical laws, which can hardly lead to justice, or it constitutes a new universal standard for judgment, which may be in its turn contaminated by the particular. Counterintuitively, according to these three critiques, Lyotard's postmodern conception of judgment is not as postmodern as it claims to be, but carries the essential elements of the philosophical universalism that it seeks to overcome.

Lyotard's later work, where ideas (in the Kantian sense) play a more prominent and systematic role, contains a response to this criticism, as we shall see in what follows. Lyotard's attempt to translate his diagnosis of a postmodern condition into a theory of political judgment proceeds through a reading of Kant, and especially of the *Third Critique*. The aesthetic judgment serves as a model for political judgment, because it does not presuppose any pregiven rule mediating between heterogeneous discourses. This does not mean, however, that it lacks any sort of orientation. Instead, political judgment stems from the feeling that one ought to judge even in the absence of standards by which to do so, thus inventing new standards by the very act of judging. It is this feeling, of which the feeling of the sublime serves as a model, that connects the power of judgment to universal ideas, such as justice or (as we will see) "humanity." In order to understand this relationship between heterogeneity, political judgment, and ideas, let us turn to Lyotard's reading of Kant.

Critical, Political, and Reflective Judgment

"There is an affinity between the critical (the 'tribunal' of critique, the 'judge' who examines the validity of the claims of various phrase families . . .) and the politico-historical: each has to make judgments without having a rule for making judgments, as opposed to the politico-juridical."[18] These opening words of *Enthusiasm*, Lyotard's collection of studies on Kant, summarize the link between political judgment and critical judgment. Critique, according to Lyotard, presupposes no doctrine, that is, no set of rules regulating a discourse, because its aim is to inquire into the legitimacy of all rules. Evidently, a rule for inquiring into the legitimacy of rules would lead to an infinite regress. While there are specific doctrines for specific realms of experience, such as knowledge and ethics, the critique of such doctrines, that is, the inquiry into their validity, cannot itself be a doctrine. Given Lyotard's conception of society as a web of language games without a metadiscourse, it is not difficult to understand in what sense there is an affinity between the political and the critical. The institution of society is determined by a plurality of language games interacting with one another, without any discourse regulating this interaction. Despite this lack of regulation, it is necessary to judge, which is why there are judgments that lack a prior regulation, that is, critical judgments. As we have seen, the political judgment must proceed without rules, acknowledging the heterogeneity of language games as irreducible to a common ground. Therefore, Lyotard suggests, "perhaps the critical . . . is the political in the universe of philosophical phrases, and perhaps the political is the critical . . . in the universe of sociohistorical phrases."[19] Just like critique emerges out of the need to adjudicate the validity of heterogeneous faculties on their respective realms, politics emerges out of the relationship between heterogeneous language games (science, art, economics, popular narrative, etc.).

According to Lyotard, Kant's fundamental analysis of how critical judgments proceed in the absence of rules takes place in the *Third Critique*, whose object is what Kant calls the "reflective judgment." The reason is that "the critical is determined in general as reflexive," in the sense that "it does not arise from a faculty, but from a quasi- or 'as if' faculty (the faculty of judgment, sentiment) inasmuch as its rule for determining which universes are pertinent to it entails some indeterminacy (the free play of the faculties among themselves)."[20] The reflective judgment does not proceed from a specific realm of objects (natural, moral, or aesthetic), but from the interaction between universes of phrases. As a consequence, the "faculty" of judgment is not really a faculty, because it does not regulate any specific realm; it emerges rather from the play between faculties. This is why critique is essentially reflective: it does not proceed from a faculty, but rather from the need to find new rules that relate the faculties to one another. In the absence of a rule for judgment, one must judge on the basis of the indeterminate relationship, or the "free play," between different sets of rules.

It is in order to understand the structure of the critical judgment, which proceeds by inspecting the legitimacy of judgments, that Lyotard turns to Kant's *Third Critique*. The procedure for legitimating cognitive judgments was the central concern of the *Critique of Pure Reason*, while the procedure for legitimating moral judgments was the central concern of the *Groundwork of the Metaphysics of Morals* and the *Critique of Practical Reason*. The *Critique of the Power of Judgment*, Lyotard claims, has "the mission of unifying the field of philosophy" by "making manifest . . . the reflexive manner of thinking that is at work in the critical text as a whole."[21] The reflective judgment is not just another kind of judgment, but the judgment that makes manifest the manner in which critical thinking proceeds in general. Lyotard is careful to stress Kant's distinction between "manner" and "method": while the latter "follows definite principles," the former "possesses no standard other that than the *feeling* of unity in the presentation."[22] A method provides thinking with definite principles by means of which to unify its presentations and produce a judgment on objects, while a manner provides only a feeling of this unity, without a rule for producing a judgment. This is what makes thinking critical: it lacks any fixed resting point that would put a halt to its quest for a judgment's legitimation.[23]

In the absence of rules that legitimate a judgment, critical thinking is oriented by the "aesthetic feeling" which, in the *Third Critique*, is the feeling of pleasure and displeasure. The reason is that only this feeling accompanies all the states of consciousness, and thus it is "able to pass through the different spheres of thought that the critique distinguishes."[24]

Whenever we think of something, whether an object of experience or an idea, we have a feeling of our own thinking. Lyotard calls this feeling "tautegorical," by which he means that it is a sign of thought to itself. Cognitive judgments are based, on the one hand, on the object to which they refer and, on the other, on principles that legitimate them (the categories and their deduction, as shown in the *First Critique*). Aesthetic judgments also refer to an object, but their legitimation is a subjective feeling. When I say "the flower is beautiful," I have nothing to rely on in order to legitimate the judgment, other than the feeling of pleasure. Properly speaking, the judgment says nothing about the object, but rather refers to the state of mind in the presence of the object. This state of mind does not need any rule or principle to be known: if I feel pleasure, I am aware of it immediately. This is why the "two aspects of judgment, referentiality and legitimacy, are but one in the aesthetic."[25] In the aesthetic judgment, the referent and that which legitimates my judgment on the referent are the same. The aesthetic judgment is therefore reflective: its object is the judging subject itself. The aesthetic feeling makes this judgment possible by informing the judging subject of its own state, which does not need the mediation of rules.

The central question of the aesthetic judgment concerns the communicability of this state. How can an inherently private sensation of pleasure be "universal" and "necessary," so that it demands the agreement of others? According to Kant, communicability stems from the accord between our faculties. Both theoretical and moral judgments are valid, and can therefore demand universal agreement, insofar as our faculties relate to one another following universally valid principles. In the theoretical judgment, the principles are given by the understanding, which legislates over the imagination, while in the practical judgment they are given by reason, which legislates over the understanding. In the reflective judgment, such principles are missing. However, if the judgment still demands to be communicated and be universally valid, it means that it stems from the same disposition of thinking present in the other two kinds of judgment.[26] Consequently, the demand to make aesthetic pleasure communicable reveals that there is a "unity of the faculties," which precedes "the unison required of other individuals by the individual who judges."[27] In making an aesthetic judgment, thinking feels the same disposition as when it makes a cognitive or practical judgment. Unlike these judgments, however, it lacks a definite principle that determines the accord between the faculties. Therefore, no "disputation" is possible regarding the legitimacy of an aesthetic judgment, because there are no objective grounds on which to decide whether it is valid or not. However, it is possible to "argue" about taste, which implies the hope to reach universal agreement without objective proofs.[28]

In the absence of a principle that regulates the interaction among the faculties, their agreement has to emerge spontaneously. But how can the faculties establish an accord without a rule that regulates it? There are two ways: the beautiful and the sublime. The agreement between our faculties in the beautiful, and the corresponding demand of communication, relies on what Lyotard calls "the supersensible." This idea appears as a solution to the antinomy of taste, according to which there is either a concept determining what is beautiful and what is not, and therefore taste is objective, or there is no concept of the beautiful at all, and therefore it is entirely subjective. The judgment of taste, however, demands to be communicated, which means that it is not merely subjective, but it does not proceed according to concepts, and is therefore not objective either. Kant's solution relies on what he calls an "indeterminate concept," that is, a concept that does not correspond to any intuition, which amounts to what he calls an idea.[29] This idea is precisely "the supersensible." According to Lyotard's interpretation, the idea appears in the antinomy of each of the faculties, as an effect of their striving for the unconditioned condition of their use: "The unconditioned of knowledge cannot be known. The absolute law of the faculty of desire cannot be desired. The supersensible principle that founds the demand for the universal communication of taste is not the object of an aesthetic pleasure."[30] The unconditioned in each of the faculties is a "limit-Idea," that is, an idea after which each faculty can and must strive without ever reaching it. In this striving, however, the faculties encounter an affinity with each other, which "is revealed by way of the similarity of their respective inconsistencies."[31] There is an affinity between heterogeneous faculties, not because there is a higher principle or faculty regulating their interaction, but because they are equally unable to totalize their respective fields.

The beautiful provides a model for the commonality within heterogeneity that characterizes what Kant calls *sensus communis*. In order to establish an accord between the faculties, it is first necessary to deny their striving for totalization. This cannot be done by means of a higher, totalizing principle that would determine the limit of each faculty, but only by means of each faculty immanently encountering its own limit. The discordance experienced by each faculty is a sign of its affinity with the other faculties, and so "one must think excessively, until one reaches a discordance, in order to hear the voice of concordance."[32] This discordance signals the need that each faculty moderate itself, so that "each lends itself to the play of the other." It is this free play that produces the aesthetic delight by which "thought succeeds in putting itself in the place of the other."[33] The communication of taste thus stems from thought experiencing its own heterogeneity. Without this experience, the free, indeterminate accord between the faculties, on which the aesthetic feeling depends, would be impossible. By reaching its own limit, thought becomes critical, in the sense of questioning the legitimacy of its claims (cognitive, moral, or aesthetic) and lending itself to an indeterminate argumentation. But does each faculty acknowledge its own limitation independently of the encounter with other faculties? Or does this acknowledgment stem from the disaccord produced by the interaction itself? It is this latter possibility that Lyotard's reading of the sublime explores.

The Sublime and the Differend

The sublime represents a commonality within heterogeneity that is different from that of the beautiful. The faculties do not communicate here by means of their free play with one another, but rather by means of the subjection of one to the other. This subjection is not mediated by rules, as in the theoretical and practical judgments. In a way, the sublime proceeds according to an absolute violence, to the point that Lyotard describes it as a sort of rape.[34] Reason, which is the faculty of ideas, subdues the imagination, which is the faculty of presentation. The heterogeneity is here extreme, for ideas are inherently nonpresentable, and thus reason's command is impossible to fulfill. The imagination attempts to present absolute ideas, such as the absolutely great and the absolutely forceful, but it fails, for every presentable magnitude or force can be surpassed by a greater one—the ideas of reason are infinite, while the imagination is finite. The failure is felt as displeasure, but it gives rise to the feeling of pleasure as we become aware of our mind's vocation for the supersensible:

> The feeling of the sublime is thus a feeling of displeasure from the inadequacy of the imagination in the aesthetic estimation of magnitude for the estimation by means of reason, and a

> pleasure that is thereby aroused at the same time from the correspondence of this very judgment of the inadequacy of the greatest sensible faculty in comparison with ideas of reason, insofar as striving for them is nevertheless a law for us.[35]

The heterogeneity between reason and the imagination lends itself to no agreement, not even one mediated by a disagreement. Rather, it is in the disagreement itself that the sublime feeling emerges, which is why aesthetic pleasure here is necessarily mixed with displeasure.

The discordance experienced in the sublime feeling is at the root of critical thinking. This kind of thinking, as we have seen, does not follow any fixed set of rules—if it did, it would be unable to inquire into the legitimacy of these rules. This is what happens in cognitive judgments, where we determine an object under a concept and, provided that we have followed the right procedure, we demand that everyone else agrees. In the judgment of the sublime, by contrast, no cognition is involved, but merely a feeling of pure thinking, that is, of thinking prior to any of its determinations, such as sensible forms, schemas, or concepts: "'before' all of this, thinking is the power to think . . . , irrelative, 'raw,' that comes from nothing other than itself."[36] Critical thinking, which is thinking prior to any determined form, is awakened by the dissonance that takes place when it encounters incommensurable forms. As a consequence, resistance is an essential component of the sublime feeling: if the imagination did not resist, by virtue of its finitude, the demands of reason, the heterogeneity between the two faculties would not be felt. This dissonance "is essential for thought to feel reflexively its heterogeneity when it brings itself to its own limits."[37] The dissonance produced by the judgment of the sublime is felt as a disposition of thought for which no standard for judgment is legitimate a priori, that is, as critical thought. This is why critical thought has no specific location: it is not one more discourse among others, but rather the feeling that takes place at the limit between discourses. The critical judgment is oriented by this feeling, which cannot be translated into a rule because it stems from the conflict between rules.

The heterogeneity of the faculties in the sublime serves as a model for any situation in which two heterogeneous discourses interact with one another, thus producing what Lyotard calls a "differend." The differend is the elementary political situation, which takes place when "something which must be able to be put into words cannot yet be."[38] The reason why something cannot be put into words is that it lacks an "idiom," that is, a discourse that is able to communicate it. One of Lyotard's examples is a Martinican who is considered a French citizen under French law. By being considered a French citizen, the Martinican suffers a wrong, for he does not consider himself a French citizen.[39] Yet any complaint that he can bring to the French authorities will be taken as a litigation under French law. The wrong thus lacks an idiom to express itself, for it is always translated into a discourse that is foreign to it. The question that follows is: if the wrong lacks an idiom in which to express itself, can it be communicated at all? How do we even know that it is there? It is on this point that the political import of the sublime feeling becomes evident.

The wrong suffered by one of the parties in a differend produces both a silence and a "call upon phrases which are in principle possible."[40] The differend is a state in which something cannot be put into phrases, yet this "something" is felt as a call to invent new phrases by means of which it can be expressed. Lyotard describes this feeling through an analogy that resembles the sublime:

> Suppose that an earthquake destroys not only lives, buildings, and objects but also the instruments used to measure earthquakes directly and indirectly. The impossibility of quantitatively measuring it does not prohibit, but rather inspires in the minds of the survivors the idea of a very great seismic force. The scholar claims to know nothing about it, but the common person has a complex feeling, the one aroused by the negative presentation of the indeterminate.[41]

The feeling that something is to be phrased is a negative presentation, which emerges from the impossibility of presenting an experience under any available idiom. The example of the earthquake refers to the impossibility of properly phrasing the wrong produced by the Nazi extermination camps: given that the means to prove the magnitude of the crime were destroyed, the feeling of the crime is incommensurable with any demonstration of it. Yet this failure of demonstration is felt as the presence of something that demands to be phrased. The impossibility of phrasing is felt as displeasure, while pleasure accompanies the invention of new phrases.[42]

The sublime feeling could be called the "feeling of heterogeneity." Heterogeneity can only be felt subjectively because there is no objective judgment that could designate it. A certain discourse can be "objectified" by another discourse so as to explain the rules that govern it. But there is no rule governing the interaction between heterogeneous discourses, just like there is no rule that determines how reason should relate to the imagination, which is why the relationship takes the form of an absolute violence. Similarly, there is no rule determining how French law should relate to someone who does not acknowledge it as his or her law, and so violence ensues. The incommensurability between the two discourses cannot be shown, for this would requires a metadiscourse that knows the rules for translating one language into the other. In the absence of a metalanguage, the gap separating one discourse from another can only be experienced as a feeling. Unlike a judgment, the feeling has no determined object. It is rather a sign that there is heterogeneity and, as an effect of it, a wrong that demands to be phrased. The political challenge consists in turning the feeling into a new idiom that can bring the two heterogeneous discourses into communication with one another, as opposed to subordinating one to the other.

The invention of new idioms does not overcome the heterogeneity between different discourses, but establishes connections between them. Lyotard describes this procedure through the symbol of an archipelago: "Each genre of discourse would be like an island; the faculty of judgment would be, at least in part, like an admiral or like a provisioner of ships who would launch expeditions from one island to the next, intended to present to one island what was found . . . in the other."[43] The faculty of judgment moves from one genre of discourse to another, with the aim of presenting to one genre what it has found in another. In order to do so, it invents "passages." Lyotard identifies a model of passage in what Kant calls the "type" in the *Second Critique*, which establishes a link between ethical and cognitive judgments so as to establish the categorical imperative. The type, according to Lyotard, makes an object of reason (the moral law) presentable to the understanding, whose objects are ruled by the law of natural causality. The goal of this passage is to make the moral law effective in the world, which is achieved through the formula of the categorical imperative: "Act as if the maxim of your action were to become by your will a *universal law of nature*." Here, the object of one faculty is presented to a different faculty "as if" it belonged to it. Through the "as if," the faculty of judgment acknowledges the heterogeneity between ethical and cognitive judgments, and "neither hollows out nor fills in the abyss" that separates them, but rather "passes or comes to pass over it, and takes it therefore into consideration."[44] The passage thus allows two different discourses or "islands" to communicate with one another without disavowing their heterogeneity—that is, without relying on an underlying commonality that subsumes their difference.

Lyotard's focus on the sublime shows that the ground of communicability is not a universally shared standard or rule, but rather the experience of dissensus. It certainly seems paradoxical that the invention of new means of communication stems from an incommunicable feeling, or of the feeling that there is no communication. Yet this is precisely why communication depends on invention rather than on the discovery of any procedure. For Lyotard, the encounter with an other with whom we cannot communicate and the feeling that there is a wrong summons us to "institute idioms which do not yet exist."[45] This institution has nothing to do with the discovery of a common ground mediating two standpoints. If this were the case, the experience of dissensus would be a means to discover an underlying consensus, which would serve as an "Archimedean viewpoint" from which to assess the validity of the conflicting judgments. If, by contrast, dissensus is irreducible to a higher consensus, then it is up to each party to produce new means of communication "from nowhere"—or, following Kant's term in his analysis of the sublime, from the "abyss" that a party encounters when it reaches the limit of what it can present.[46] It is on the basis of feeling this abyss that heterogenous discourses may invent passages that allow them to communicate with one another, as opposed to attempting to subordinate the other to a given procedure.

The sublime feeling is the ground of a political judgment that presupposes dissensus rather than agreement. Politics, according to Lyotard, is not a specific genre of discourse with its own specific rules, but rather it "bears witness to the nothingness which opens up with each occurring phrase and on the occasion of which the differend between genres of discourse is born."[47] When a new phrase occurs, a differend opens up between genres of discourse seeking to regulate it—as in the above-mentioned example, an identity claim by a Martinican will be described differently by the traditions of the nationals and by French law, and there is no rule to make the description of one discourse presentable to the other. Politics bears witness to this differend between genres of discourse and attempts to invent a passage by which the claim that is made in terms of local traditions can be presentable to French law. There is no rule guiding the invention of this passage, other than the principle that "heterogeneity ought to be respected in an affirmative manner."[48] Thus the political actor, like the critical philosopher, remains always between genres of discourse, refusing to accept any principle of legitimation without considering the wrongs that they produce. Politics cannot get out of the archipelago, but only navigate it indefinitely, wondering at the heterogeneity between islands and enjoying each invention of passages.

The notion that one ought to respect the differend certainly makes it sound like Lyotard has replaced one transcendental idea for another, as his critiques point out: instead of a law for subsuming differends under a rule, we have a law stating that we ought to respect differends. But let us note that there is no rule stating how we ought to respect them. The feeling of the differend (the sublime feeling) summons us to respect the differend and to create a new idiom by which the parties may communicate with one another, but it does provide us with a rule for doing so. As Geoffrey Bennington puts it, "the obligation to judge justly does not project an achieved state of justice as the end of history, but encourages the critical watcher . . . to discover ever more *torts* [wrongs] and *différends*, in the very effort made to find idioms to phrase those *torts* and *différends* already discovered."[49] The critical or political judgment is not ruled by a regulative idea (as Ingram suggests), but stems rather from the felt need to communicate what remains incommunicable, in an open-ended process with no preestablished end. If one judges on the basis of the idea of justice, it is only in the sense that one respects the heterogeneity of rules for judgment, and invents new rules by which to make communication possible between the heterogeneous parties. These new rules are not neutral: they create new wrongs that invite new political judgments. Consequently, as Bennington points out, the idea of justice has no end: it does not guide judgment to an ultimate state in which everything is communicable, but keeps us alert to the emergence and displacement of differends, and thus to the open-ended displacement of the boundary between the communicable and uncommunicable.

As it is clear, Lyotard is not simply rejecting the possibility of agreement so as to affirm disagreement, but rather rethinking the relationship between agreement and disagreement altogether. Linda Zerilli misses this when she criticizes "Lyotard's celebration of the Kantian sublime . . . : the affirmation of a *differend* or *Widerstreit*, that is, a conflict that permits no resolution whatsoever," claiming that this reading "tends to foreclose any possibility of a politically mediated agreement about community whatsoever."[50] Lyotard's point, however, is not that agreement is not possible, but rather that the principles by which we reach agreement are not external to disagreement. In other words, the principles that ground agreement are not waiting to be discovered, but are invented on the basis of the tension experienced in each particular disagreement. This is the central lesson of the sublime, in Lyotard's interpretation: the parties have no common language by which to communicate, yet the very fact that they relate to one another without a common language is felt as a sign that communication is nevertheless possible. It is this feeling aroused by the disagreement that orients the invention of new idioms by which the parties may agree. Yet because every new idiom creates new differends, the dividing line between agreement and disagreement is never clear-cut: disagreements generate the possibility of new agreements, while agreements generate new disagreements. Therefore, politics consists neither in seeking to overcome disagreement by finding unquestionable principles of agreement, nor in celebrating disagreement for its own sake. Rather, it consists in navigating disagreements with the aim of inventing partial agreements.

We are now in a position to understand the distinction between good and evil in a context of postmodernity. Clearly, any rule for determining what good and evil are would lead to terrorism, for such rule would wrong other rules. Indeed, judging those who judge differently as "evil" is perhaps the most extreme form of terrorism, for it equates different perspectives with moral faults. This does not mean, however, that the distinction between good and evil has ceased to exist. Political judgments institute new tribunals by which the parties of a differend can communicate with one another—and yet by inventing new rules that regulate differends, these judgments will in its turn produce new differends: "it is impossible that the judgments of the new tribunal would not create new wrongs, since they would regulate (or think they were regulating) differends as though they were litigations."[51] Thus, given that there is no way out of differends, "politicians cannot have the good at stake, but they ought to have the lesser evil. Or, if you prefer, the lesser evil ought to be the political good."[52] In postmodernity, the distinction between good and evil is not absolute, but it is still operative. The political good consists in minimizing evil, namely, the wrong suffered by discourses that lack the means to communicate. Yet this minimization cannot follow a preestablished procedure, for such procedure would necessarily wrong other procedures. The good, as a consequence, consists in remaining attentive to the open-ended displacement of the distinction between good and evil, in such a way that political actors minimize wrongs while acknowledging the creation of new wrongs.

Universality as a Sublime Sign

If politics takes place amid an archipelago, are universalist political judgments possible? In other words: if politics consists in the invention of passages that communicate heterogeneous discourses, can we make claims that appeal to everyone, beyond those involved in a particular differend? Lyotard's answer is yes, on condition that we properly understand what this "everyone" means. On this point, Lyotard is critical of a universalist politics that presupposes the existence of a universal subject, such as "humanity," which could be the referent of a judgment. Commenting on the Declaration of the Rights of Man, he claims that the Declaration fell into an unsolvable confusion between its addressor, that is, the French people, and its addressee, namely, humanity. Through this confusion, "the members of the Constituent Assembly would have been prey to a 'transcendental appearance' and even perhaps to a *dementia*. . . . They hallucinated humanity within the nation."[53] Here, Kant's distinction between concepts and ideas plays a crucial political role. For both Lyotard and Kant, "humanity" is an idea, that is, a concept without a corresponding object in experience. The "transcendental illusion" consists precisely in confusing the idea with a concept, in such a way that something in experience can correspond to it. By claiming to speak in the name of humanity, the Constituent Assembly confused the idea of humanity with the French Nation, thus opening the door to imperialism and terror. This illusion is common to all revolutionary politics, which "confuses what can be presented as an object for a cognitive phrase with what can be presented as an object for a speculative and/or ethical phrase."[54]

The critique of revolutionary politics does not imply, however, that universal claims should be abandoned. It is a usual mistake to interpret Lyotard as advocating for a particularist politics that disregards universal ideas. Claude Piché, for example, claims that for Lyotard the philosopher must develop an "aesthetic sensitivity" as he observes political events, departing from universalist aspirations: "the feelings of pleasure and pain which are intertwined in the sublime do not have to be shared by everyone. . . . Fragmentation and particularism become the lot of philosophy."[55] But this particularism is impossible after the emergence of modern, cosmopolitan discourses structured on the idea of a common humanity. To abandon the idea of this community would entail returning to a premodern state in which different communities do not share anything in common, and are therefore authorized to destroy one another. If there is an obligation, whatever it may be, to people from different communities, it is because all people belong to a cosmopolitan community called "humanity." The problem with this idea is that it has no referent—no one can show what "humanity" is, and no one can speak in its name. However, as Kant shows, the fact that ideas have no referent in experience does not mean that they have no possible connection to it. The political challenge consists in acting and judging on the basis of this idea, while avoiding the transcendental illusion that one can know it.

Lyotard finds an example of the relationship between political events and the idea of humanity in Kant's famous interpretation of the French Revolution in *The Conflict of the Faculties*, and more specifically, in the notion of the "sign of history." Kant introduces this notion as part of his attempt to respond to the question of whether the human race is morally progressing. This question, Kant claims, cannot be answered by means of observation, because we cannot foresee free actions, which are the actions that stem from a moral disposition. In order to know whether human beings will act morally in the future (and thus that they are morally progressing), we need to know their moral disposition, which is impossible. However, Kant claims,

> There must be some experience in the human race which, as an event, points to the disposition and capacity of the human race to be the cause of its own advance toward the better, and (since this should be the act of a being endowed with freedom), toward the human race as being the author of this advance.[56]

This occurrence, Kant adds, could not be considered in itself as the cause of history, "but only as an intimation, a historical sign . . . demonstrating the tendency of the human race viewed in its entirety."[57] The historical sign is then an occurrence in history that demonstrates that the human race has a good moral disposition, and is therefore on the path of moral progress. But how is this demonstration possible? Kant's solution to this problem consists in shifting the demonstration from the act itself to the "mode of thinking" of the spectators. Indeed, the occurrence that shows that the human race is progressing is not a deed, but rather "the mode of thinking of the spectators which reveals itself *publicly* in this game of great revolutions, and manifests such a universal yet disinterested sympathy for the players on one side against those of the other, even at the risk that this partiality could become very disadvantageous for them if discovered."[58] In the presence of certain deeds, the spectators experience a disinterested sympathy for one of the parties, and this sympathy is universal, in the sense that they expect that all spectators will participate in it. Given that the revolution does not serve the interests of the spectators, the only cause for this way of thinking is their moral disposition. Thus, the universal and disinterested sympathy for one of the parties in a revolution is the "historical sign" that demonstrates that the human race is progressing.

Lyotard interprets Kant's brief remarks on the French Revolution through an analysis of the sublime. In the *Critique of the Power of Judgment*, Kant claims that "aesthetically, enthusiasm is sublime, because it is a stretching of the powers through Ideas, which gives the mind a momentum that acts far more powerfully and persistently than the impetus given by sensory representations."[59] Observing a certain event, the imagination of the spectators is stretched to the point of arousing a feeling of that which lies beyond representation, namely, Ideas. But unlike the transcendental illusion, which mistakenly makes Ideas representable, enthusiasm only feels that which lies beyond representation, and remains at the threshold between the representable and the nonrepresentable. The sign, therefore, does not produce a unity between representation and Ideas, but rather remains in a zone of indeterminacy between the two: "the 'passage' does not take place; it is a 'passage' in the course of coming to pass, and its course, its motion, is a kind of agitation in place, within the impasse of incommensurability, over the abyss."[60] One cannot legitimately claim that a certain historical event is caused by a good moral disposition, because there is an abyss between Ideas and historical events. However, the agitation produced by certain events makes the spectators feel the abyss. Given that this feeling is only possible if the imagination is aroused to go beyond its limit by Ideas of reason, the feeling is in itself a sign of the presence of Ideas, even if we cannot "present" them.

The sublime, in this interpretation, constitutes a model for a specifically political kind of universality. According to Lyotard, there is an affinity between politics and aesthetics. Just like the importance of Kant's philosophy of the beautiful and the sublime "resides in the de-realizing of the object of aesthetic feelings, and at the same time, in the absence of a faculty of aesthetic cognition," the same goes "for the historico-political object, which has no reality in and of itself, and for a faculty of political cognition, which must remain nonexistent."[61] Both in politics and in aesthetics, we make universal claims regarding a certain object, without a rule that determines whether the claims are valid. Strictly speaking, we do not make judgments about the object, but rather about how we feel when contemplating an object—which is why the object of the aesthetic (or political) feeling "has no reality." This changes the sense in which the claim is "universal." The sublime feeling, Lyotard claims, "is not universal the way a well-formed and validated cognitive phrase can be; a judgment of cognition has its determining rules set 'before it,' while the sublime phrase judges in the absence of rules."[62] Therefore, while the cognitive judgment applies a rule that is given to it beforehand, the judgment of the sublime has a "rule in waiting, a rule with the 'promise' of universality."[63] The judgment of the sublime is universal only in the sense that those who judge expect that their judgment will be shared by others, without possessing a rule that grounds this expectation.

This promised universality constitutes a community that cannot be presented, or what Kant calls a *sensus communis*. In order to present an object in a way that can legitimately claim the agreement of others, one must possess beforehand the universal rule that grounds the presentation. *Sensus communis*, by contrast, is a communicability without a rule, whose ground is the aesthetic feeling. In the case of the beautiful, the feeling stems from the relationship between the understanding and the imagination. In the sublime, by contrast, the feeling stems from the relationship between the imagination and reason, which is the source of moral ideas. This is why only the sublime can be a sign of historical progress which, as we have seen, is moral progress. The capacity of the spectators to feel enthusiasm for certain events is a sign that they are "susceptible to Ideas," and this susceptibility is already moral. Thus, even if the sublime "is indicative only of a free causality," because it only indicates that those who feel it are susceptible to the Idea of morality, "it nonetheless has 'proof' value for the phrase that affirms progress, since the spectating humanity must already have made cultural progress in order to be able to make this sign, by its 'way of thinking' the revolution."[64] The very capacity to have the sublime feeling proves that we are susceptible to moral ideas. And given that this susceptibility is the aim of cultural progress, the sublime feeling also proves that humanity is progressing. Humanity is thus the name of an ethical community on the path to moral progress, whose only "proof" is the sublime feeling aroused by certain historical occurrences.

The analysis of *sensus communis* in connection to the French Revolution provides the link between the differend and universality. Lyotard explains this link through an analysis of Marxism and, more specifically, in response to the question: "Marxism has not come to an end, but how does it continue?" According to Lyotard, Marx, like most modern revolutionary thinkers, fell prey to the transcendental illusion of confusing the Idea of humanity with a concrete subject. Class struggle is a differend, for the proletarians suffer as an effect of capital, and their suffering does not find an idiom in which it can be expressed. As a consequence, "Marx tries to find the idiom which the suffering due to capital clamors for. . . . He thinks he hears the demand of the proletariat, which is the object of an Idea, an ideal of reason, namely an emancipated working humanity."[65] Now, as we know at this point, this idea has no referent, which means that it cannot be represented. Yet Marx fell into the transcendental illusion of confusing the enthusiasm felt by those who contemplate the proletarian struggles with a request by the proletarians to take part in a common being: "The referent of the Idea of communism is transcribed as a subject (addressor) who prescribes communism. The common being wants itself."[66] In other words, by virtue of the enthusiasm that proletarian struggles arouse in the spectators, the proletariat is mistakenly understood as a representative of the Idea of humanity. From this illusion, a second illusion follows, namely, that of giving this subject a political organization, which is the task of the party.

Is it possible to preserve the universal appeal of the proletarian's suffering, without turning the proletarian into the representative of a universal Idea? The sublime provides the answer. The feeling of enthusiasm that the spectators feel when contemplating the struggle of a wronged party does not stem from their common participation in a common being—as if, by virtue of the wrong suffered by the proletarian, everyone were being wronged. Rather, enthusiasm is a sign of the differend, which summons thought to be phrased. Lyotard expresses this, in a very condensed way, in the following complex passage on the wrong suffered by the proletarians:

> The wrong is expressed through the silence of feeling, through suffering. The wrong results from the fact that all phrase universes and all their linkages are or can be subordinated to the sole finality of capital . . . and judged accordingly. Because this finality seizes upon or can seize upon all phrases, it makes a claim to universality. The wrong done to phrases by capital would then be a universal one. Even if the wrong is not universal . . . , the silent feeling that signals a differend remains to be listened to. Responsibility to thought requires it. This is the way in which Marxism has not come to an end, as the feeling of the differend.[67]

There are two ways in which the suffering of the proletarians can be universalized. The first one is that, because the wrong stems from a discourse (capital) that is itself universal in its aspirations, such wrong concerns all groups and discourses. The second and more fundamental one is that, even if capitalism had no claim to universality, "responsibility to thought" requires that we listen to the differend. This responsibility is signaled by a "silent feeling," a "feeling of the differend," which as we know by now, is the sublime feeling. But what is this "responsibility to thought" that the sublime feeling signals to?

We find a hint of an answer in Lyotard's essay "Tomb of the Intellectual," where he addresses the role of the intellectual in a context of postmodernity, in which there are no universal ideas that guide thinking. Addressing the question of whether there is such thing as a responsibility to thought that transcends the particular responsibilities assigned by particular discourses, Lyotard claims,

> The decline, perhaps the ruin, of the universal idea can free thought and life from totalizing obsessions. The multiplicity of responsibilities, and their independence (their incompatibility), oblige and will oblige those who take on those responsibilities, small or great, to be flexible tolerant, and svelte. These qualities will cease to be the contrary to rigor, honesty, and force; they will be their signs. Intelligences do

not fall silent, they do not withdraw into their beloved work, they try to live up to this new responsibility, which renders the "intellectuals" troublesome, impossible.[68]

Postmodernity, which is characterized by the ruin of totalizing systems of thought, does not render thought as such useless, as if intellectuals had no other responsibility than withdrawing into one specific discourse. The "multiplicity of responsibilities" contained in multiple discourses, which are often incompatible to one another, produces a "new responsibility," which compels intelligences not to remain silent. In postmodern conditions, thought consists in listening to the differend, that is, to the silence and suffering that is felt by virtue of the impossibility of phrasing a wrong. As we have seen, this is what "critical thought" exemplary does. Critical thought does not look for the rules by which to regulate the differend, as if one or both parties ignored them and needed to be enlightened by a third discourse. Rather, it acknowledges the heterogeneity of discourses and the wrong that emerges from it. Responsibility to thought is therefore responsibility to that which summons critical thinking, namely, the differend.

Now we can understand how the sublime links the differend to a universal judgment. The enthusiasm that the spectators feel when they contemplate the French Revolution or the suffering of the proletarian signals that there is a wrong, namely, a damage that does not find a discourse by which it can be phrased. The wrong summons thinking precisely because this is what it means to think: to witness the heterogeneity of phrases, and to invent passages by which to communicate them with one another. The transcendental illusion consists in mistaking the feeling of the differend with a universal subject that could be the referent of a phrase. If the suffering of one of the parties summons all thinking, it is not because it is the representative of a common being, but rather because we think by virtue of being confronted with an irreducible heterogeneity—just like the feeling of the sublime arouses a "way of thinking" stemming from the tension between two incommensurable faculties. If the capacity to think is universal, it is because we are all capable of witnessing differends, which announce themselves thought the sublime feeling. This feeling is prior to any regulation, which necessarily creates new wrongs and therefore no longer is universal. The feeling as such, however, demands to be communicated to everyone, insofar as everyone can witness differends.

It should be clear by now that Lyotard's conception of politics in postmodernity has nothing to do with a sort of political nihilism or skepticism. James Williams misunderstands the role of ideas in Lyotard's conception of politics when he claims that "the principal desire in the politics of the differend is a negative one: to negate Ideas of reason as ways of bridging differends."[69] As we have seen, however, political judgments do not simply "resist ideas," as Williams believes, in order to protect heterogeneity from the threat of universal claims. Rather, they resist the transcendental illusion that ideas can be represented by a subject that can be located in history. Following Kant, ideas are not the referents of judgments—they are rather what announces itself in the sublime feeling, which is the feeling of the differend. If this feeling demands to be communicated, it is because we expect everyone else to partake in a universal community. Although the community cannot be represented, it is presupposed by every attempt to make communicable what remains incommunicable, namely, the wrong. The feeling that one must judge when there are no existing shared standards for judgment signals the idea of humanity, namely, the idea of a world community in which all judgments are communicable. It is by virtue of this idea that we are capable of uttering universal judgments, even when there is no rule that explains this universality. As Kant shows, it is not in any describable procedure, but rather in the feeling that the judgment arouses in the spectators, that the idea of humanity announces itself.

Conclusion

Let us go back to the opening question of this chapter: is it possible to talk about good and evil in a context of postmodernity? The answer, as we have seen, is yes, on condition that we understand that postmodernity entails a reformulation of the very concepts of good and evil. According to Lyotard, there is no absolute rule that allows us to distinguish between good and evil, or justice and injustice. But this absence of a rule does not mean that politics should abandon these concepts altogether. Instead, the acknowledgment that the heterogeneity of discourses is irreducible, that is, that any rule regulating the distinction between good and evil does wrong to other rules, leads to a politics of the "lesser evil." This politics does not seek the absolute good, but rather acknowledges that any regulation of the distinction between good and evil will be evil to some extent, insofar as it wrongs alternative regulations. The "lesser evil" does not consist in eliminating evil, but rather in preserving the indeterminacy of the distinction between good and evil, so that those groups and discourses that are wronged by it may be potentially listened to. This is what "the good" means in a context of postmodernity: to be responsible to the heterogeneity of discourses, that is, to listen to the wrong that is produced when heterogeneous discourses interact with one another, and to invent passages that make it possible to communicate this wrong.

The feeling of uncertainty produced by the heterogeneity of language games characteristic of postmodernity serves as a ground for a new kind of responsibility for judgment. Awareness that our judgment silences other possible judgments demands that we remain attentive to the possibility of new rules for judgment. We take responsibility for judgment not by virtue of following the right rule, but rather by virtue of establishing relations with unexpected rules. Instead of overcoming uncertainty, responsibility demands that we judge in a way that does not preemptively preclude other judgments. To cover uncertainty by means of rules that are posited as uncontestable amounts to an elimination of the ground of responsibility, and to the attempt to suppress the plurality of discourses that is characteristic of totalitarianism.

Conclusion

Extreme Evil as a Response to Political Uncertainty

Over thirty years after the collapse of communism and the apparent victory of the free market and liberal democracy, Western politics is displaying phenomena that resemble aspects of totalitarianism: open lying by first-order political leaders, detention camps, unwillingness to aid refugees, systematic attempts to preserve or even strengthen long-standing hierarchies between races and genders, indifference toward looming environmental catastrophes. These phenomena are perplexing because they cannot be explained in terms of backwardness or irrationality. In technically advanced societies, a growing number of perfectly normal people are becoming indifferent, if not sympathetic, to political projects that seem glaringly at odds with basic moral values. Like totalitarianism, this situation confronts us with difficult questions that may seem irrelevant in normal times: Why do people choose to do either good or evil? What do we mean by good and evil to begin with? Why do people even care or cease to care about moral judgments? And what does it mean to make a moral judgment to begin with? These questions may seem theological or metaphysical, as long as we can take for granted that most people at least care about doing the right thing and have a minimal shared understanding of what this means. When this is not the case, fundamental questions regarding the very capacity for moral action and judgment become politically crucial.

Throughout the chapters of this book, I have examined the conceptions of action and judgment of three authors for whom the problem of why people do evil is central. For Kant, Arendt, and Lyotard, evil is not an issue to be settled once we get some set of fundamental principles right. On the contrary, the three authors put the problem of evil upfront, and develop their conceptions of action and judgment to a large extent in response to it. While political theorists in recent years have repeatedly examined Kant's and Arendt's writings on evil, they have mostly considered it as an independent issue to be dealt with separately, rather than as a constitutive element in the development of their political and moral thought. Against this approach, I have argued that we can better understand some fundamental questions involved in action and judgment if we consider them through the problem of evil. My goal has been to suspend the long-standing and still predominant presupposition that doing good is the standard, natural tendency of human beings, and doing evil an exception or aberration. Through my readings of Kant, Arendt, and Lyotard, I have argued that evil is rather an ever-present possibility stemming from the decision to eliminate the uncertainty that is constitutive of action and judgment.

By putting the problem of evil upfront in the analysis of action and judgment, I have sought to overcome a political and theoretical discomfort that may explain why this problem often plays a marginal role in political theory and social philosophy more generally. Discussing evil in politics is politically uncomfortable because the figure of evil is frequently used to affirm moral dichotomies that suspend critical reflection. As Richard Bernstein claims, "we need to probe the mentality that neatly divides the world into the forces of evil and the forces of good."[1] In order to do so, according to Bernstein, political theorists must not suspend reflections about good and evil altogether, thus leaving such categories open to ideological mobilization. Instead, "questioning the new superficial discourse of good and evil requires digging into the foundations of what is rarely critically examined—the dualistic outlook that underlies this mentality."[2] In agreement with Bernstein's approach on this point, my goal has been to understand evil beyond a fixed rule that determines what constitutes a case of evil. I have rather considered evil as an attitude, a way of acting and judging, instead of a specific kind of action and judgment. As María Pía Lara has argued, judgments about evil are often reflective: first, an object strikes us as evil, and it is on the basis of this experience that we then think about what evil is.[3] Following Bernstein's and Lara's views, it is important to limit accusations of evil in the political realm as much as possible, for illusory moral certainties prevent rather than encourage political debate. However, it is neither desirable nor possible to avoid judgments about evil entirely.

In the face of violence and cruelty of massive proportions, the problem of understanding and responding to evil in politics will be unavoidable for all those concerned with the public realm. Suspending talk about evil in politics will not eliminate its reality. Instead, it will leave it up to ideologies to mobilize the idea of evil in a way that conveys moral certainty.

Addressing the question of evil is also theoretically uncomfortable because it confronts political theory with theological and metaphysical issues that do not easily fit in the postmetaphysical turn that has characterized the field in the past decades. It is certainly difficult to examine the problem of evil without addressing questions of subjectivity, intentionality, and transcendental moral values. Recent studies by Bernstein and Simona Forti have developed an inquiry into the problem of evil in politics through postmetaphysical frameworks such as pragmatism and biopolitics, respectively.[4] Despite the many important insights of their studies, these frameworks fall short of clarifying the fundamental perplexities of political evil in modern societies, especially in connection to what Arendt called "the banality of evil." Pragmatism can help us understand how the meaning of the word *evil* is constituted and transformed through communicative practices, while biopolitics can explain the social conditions that produce the actions and behaviors that we associate with evil. But when we judge that a person or action is evil, we rely on a series of presuppositions regarding freedom, responsibility, and choice that frame our understanding of the concept. Following Arendt's later inquiries into responsibility, judgment, and the will, among other central categories of moral philosophy, one goal of this book has been to show how moral categories that are inherently intertwined with metaphysics and theology are unavoidable in order to understand what we mean by evil in politics.

The Eichmann Problem and Responsibility

I have frequently referred throughout the chapters to what I will now call the "Eichmann problem": in a context where traditional moral values have been radically overturned, on what grounds can we hold people morally responsible for actions that we consider criminal? In part 1, I showed that the fundamental challenge posed by the Eichmann trial is that by claiming he had followed the law of the land against his own self-interest, Eichmann rejected responsibility for action beyond strict compliance with duty. According to Arendt, this self-exculpation was more than a simple lie, in the sense of an attempt to deceive others. As far as the evidence available in the trial showed, Eichmann felt that he bore no responsibility for the death of millions of Jews and, more importantly, his self-exculpatory discourse did correspond with many widespread assumptions regarding the distinction between good and evil and the ground of responsibility for action—most saliently, the equation of self-sacrifice with moral virtue. Therefore, following Arendt, taking Eichmann's trial seriously, that is, facing the problem of adjudicating Eichmann's personal responsibility for his deeds, demanded a thorough examination and reconsideration of some of our fundamental presuppositions about the nature of action and judgment. In her view, the accusers as well as the judges in the trail failed to do just that, for instead of acknowledging the novelty of the crime and therefore of the trial itself, they attempted to make the crime fit into preexisting moral categories. In her writings after the trial, Arendt tried to understand the novelty of the crime by problematizing long-standing assumptions regarding responsibility, judgment, and the will.

The Eichmann problem is connected to a long-standing concern in modern moral and political philosophy: in societies that are increasingly integrated and interconnected, as well as technologically developed, personal responsibility is often displaced by larger processes that no single individual can control. In light of this social transformation, political philosophers in the twentieth century have been repeatedly concerned with developing a notion of responsibility connected to the social implications of one's actions, as opposed to their immediate effects. Max Weber famously distinguished between an ethics of conviction, according to which actions should be oriented by principles, and an ethics of responsibility, according to which actions should be oriented by its anticipated social consequences.[5] Sixty years later, Arendt's friend Hans Jonas argued for a transformation of the notion of responsibility, from the concern with the immediate effects of one's individual actions to a concern with the future of humanity.[6] More recently, Iris Marion Young developed a notion of responsibility linked to structural injustice, that is, to unjust structures in which we participate through our everyday actions, independently of whether such actions are "unjust" when considered in isolation.[7] These are all important reminders that in a world where people and societies are increasingly interconnected, political responsibility cannot rely on individual moral considerations separated from the social context in which action takes place. But the focus on the object of responsibility, that is, on that for which we are responsible, should not conceal the problem of the source of responsibility, that is, of the experiences and conditions that make us feel responsible to begin with. One fundamental problem with responsibility in contemporary societies is that technological development and interconnection transform and sometimes endanger these experiences and conditions.

We have seen throughout the chapters that Arendt, Kant, and Lyotard ground responsibility on experiences of uncertainty. These experiences are: the appearance of the actor to others through action, thus exposing herself to their reactions and interpretations; the inscrutable choice for good and evil that is imperfectly revealed in every action; the feeling of moral ideas that exceed representation; the conflict between different rules for judgment and the unavoidable imposition of one set of rules over others every time a judgment takes place. A point of connection between these perspectives is that we take responsibility for our actions and judgments by accepting and responding to a constitutive experience of uncertainty that they involve. It is by virtue of this experience that our actions and judgments become "ours," that is, that they belong to a person who can take responsibility for them. We judge and we act freely, in the sense that we feel that the action or judgment belongs to our own initiative, because we face situations where the meaning of what we do or say is beyond our knowledge and control. This means that responsible people, which is by no means the same as "good" people, are the ones willing to accept and endure uncertainty. They are people who can accept limitations in their capacity to know why they are acting or judging in a certain way and what will come out of it. They are also people who can accept reproach and ask for forgiveness for what has gone wrong as a result of their actions or judgments. Those who, like Eichmann, subordinate themselves to a rule that secures their virtue, as an external authority that is to blame if things go wrong, are unable to take responsibility. They simply do not care about their actions.

If this is the case, the problem of Eichmann's responsibility cannot be solved by identifying the transcendental law that he transgressed. It is a presupposition of any legal process that an action can be considered criminal only if the individual was aware of the distinction between right and wrong at the moment of acting, and was capable of making a choice on the basis of this distinction. In cases where the law itself becomes criminal, it seems necessary to appeal to a law that is beyond any positive law, which allows us to know the distinction between right and wrong even when the law of the land orders that we commit a crime. One can of course rely on such law to create and enforce international institutions, such as international courts of law. But the problem of whether people acknowledge such law as binding is an entirely different issue. The problem of accepting responsibility for one's own actions and the problem of identifying universally valid rules for action, while connected, are not identical. People who commit crimes not against, but in accordance with the law of the land, are not committing a crime in the same way that a murderer who transgresses the command not to kill out of self-interest or hatred. People like Eichmann have a sense of duty toward the law, yet they lack a sense of responsibility for their actions. Consequently, it is misguided to attempt to arouse this sense of responsibility by insisting on a universal law. As Arendt stresses in her later writings, moralistic individuals, whose sense of responsibility is based on compliance with the law, will be ready to comply with a new law if the world changes overnight. Truly responsible individuals, by contrast, take responsibility for their actions on the basis of the unpredictable, uncertain relations that they generate.

On this point, Shalini Satkunanandan's recent analysis of what she calls "extraordinary responsibility" is illuminating. As mentioned in the introduction, Satkunanandan distinguishes between calculable responsibility, which is based on following a rule, and incalculable responsibility, which is based on the experience of encountering an unpredictable situation that disrupts established rules for action. I claimed in the introduction that this conception of responsibility contains an implicit conception of evil, at which Satkunanandan briefly hints but does not develop.[8] Throughout the chapters, we have seen how an extreme attachment to existing conventions, or what Satkunanandan calls "calculable responsibility," can become a form of evil. Of course, as Satkunanandan claims, calculable responsibility is necessary and unavoidable, for any action or judgment takes place in a context of rules that orient it, and it is often the case that the available rules suffice to determine what to do. However, I believe that calculable responsibility becomes a form of evil when a person uses it to conceal and even eliminate extraordinary responsibility. Strictly speaking, calculable responsibility without extraordinary responsibility, that is, without an awareness that the rule we are following may do harm, exclude others, turn out badly, or conceal bad intentions, among many other unwanted implications, is no responsibility in the true sense of the term, but rather a perverted form of responsibility. People who believe that their responsibility is based purely on rule-following will be unable to interrogate the rules as well as their application to a specific context. Like Eichmann, they will claim that their responsibility ends in executing the law as it is given to them.

To illustrate this point, it is worth considering Arendt's remarks on Karl Jaspers in her "Laudatio." Jaspers, I believe, represents for Arendt a counterexample to Eichmann and to many Nazi functionaries who lacked a sense of responsibility. She claims that Jaspers's responsibility "has nothing whatsoever to do with moral imperatives," but flows rather "out of an innate pleasure in making manifest."[9] Jaspers did not take moral conventions very seriously, for "the conventions are always recognized as such, never taken seriously as standards of conduct."[10] Against the usual idea that we are responsible on the basis of some sort of moral code, Jaspers's sense of responsibility has no other basis than the desire to answer for his thoughts, which requires bringing them to the light of the public. For this, it is necessary to be able to take distance from established standards of conduct, in order to be able to think and to act anew in a way that reveals our uniqueness. This is what Arendt calls "the high-spirited independence in which Jaspers has always been at home, the cheerful unconcern for what people say and think."[11] Jaspers preserved his sense of responsibility against totalitarianism because he remained unconcerned with what people say and think. Of course, given Arendt's insistence that Jaspers was committed to making his thoughts public, we should understand this "unconcern" only in the sense of not following established standards for thinking—not of ignoring others altogether. Jaspers answered for his thoughts because they were "his," not the effect of a code of conduct, and precisely for this reason he was eager to test them against the viewpoints of others. This eagerness to expose one's uniqueness to others was the core of Jaspers's sense of responsibility and, according to my reading of Arendt in chapter 1, of responsibility as such.

The essential link between responsibility and plurality is also stressed by Lyotard. Like Arendt, Lyotard believes that it is in the confrontation with other viewpoints, or what he calls "discourses," that we experience a sense of responsibility. Also like Arendt, Lyotard is concerned with uncovering a sense of responsibility that is not subordinated to a specific code of conduct. But while Arendt emphasizes the need to take distance from codes of conduct so as to act and think out of our own initiative, Lyotard stresses the conflict between codes that generates the need to choose some codes over others. Following Lyotard, we may say that we always have specific responsibilities: as professionals, as workers, as owners, as citizens, as activists, as church members, as family members, as friends. As these responsibilities, which are attached to different social positions with their own specific codes of conduct, multiply and often turn out to be in conflict with one another, it becomes necessary to choose one responsibility over the other. We may call this "metaresponsibility": a responsibility for the choice of the code of conduct to which we are responsible. We cannot avoid acting and judging on the basis of rules, but neither can we remain indifferent to the conflict between rules. It is the choice of a rule and the consequent exclusion of an alternative rule that makes us responsible, in the sense that we answer for this choice. Answering for the choices we make at the moment of action and judgment by no means guarantees that we do the right thing, but it prevents us from becoming utterly indifferent to other viewpoints—which, according to both Lyotard and Arendt, is at the root of extreme evil.

Ideological Extremism

The analysis of evil in politics and the focus on responsibility provides a new perspective on what is usually called "ideological extremism." This term does not have a precise meaning, but it generally designates political stances characterized by an open dismissal of at least some fundamental moral values. Of course, political actors transgress moral values all the time, but this is usually done for strategic considerations that do not challenge (at least not openly) the validity of the values as such. By contrast, ideological extremism involves the open denunciation of widely accepted moral values as hypocritical or dispensable for the sake of some higher purpose. Given that, in normal circumstances, we take the validity of fundamental moral values as self-evident, extremist ideologies are the source of perplexity for those who are not part of them. It would seem like people who had acknowledged the validity of moral values all their lives have suddenly turned their back on them. This creates the difficult problem of developing a political response to ideologies that lack a common ground on the basis of which to engage in a discussion. As long as different political groups recognize the validity of some fundamental values, they may take part in a discussion regarding their development and application. If, however, one of the parties dismisses such values altogether, there seems to be no common ground on the basis of which to hold a discussion. Individuals committed to extremist ideologies seem to be beyond the possibility of political discussion altogether.

The problem of ideological extremism was prominent in the humanities and social sciences after World War II, especially in the Frankfurt School. For authors like Theodor Adorno, Max Horkheimer, and Herbert Marcuse, phenomena like authoritarianism, fascism, and totalitarianism are essentially intertwined with modern capitalism. Despite their differences, one fundamental idea shared by these authors is that the central values of modern societies, such as freedom, autonomy, reason, and justice, are both produced and distorted by social relations under capitalism. Capitalist production depends on individuals orienting their actions on the basis of such values, but it blocks at the same time their further development and realization.[12] Let us take the example of "autonomy" in Adorno's *Minima Moralia*, where he claims that under capitalism "the subject still feels sure of its autonomy, but the nullity demonstrated to subjects by the concentration camp is already overtaking the form of subjectivity itself."[13] Autonomy is a central value of modern capitalist societies. However, as it is integrated into the cycle of production and consumption, autonomy becomes nullity, a mere function of the system. The camps are the realization of such nullity, which under normal circumstances is concealed under the idea of autonomy. The example suggests that extremist ideologies are not an anomaly, but rather an internal tendency of modern capitalism: the camps realize the "nullity" that is implicit in autonomy under capitalism. We could say that, from this perspective, extremist ideologies crystallize and express the distortion of moral values that is always operative, even if often veiled, in modern capitalism. This explains the aura of authenticity that characterizes authoritarian leaders and movements: their disregard for moral values expresses a disregard that is already widespread, yet concealed. Thus Adorno claims that when democracy seeks to oppose human values to fascism, the latter "can effortlessly refute by pointing out that they represent not the whole of humanity but a mere illusory image that Fascism has had the courage to discard."[14] In a way, ideological extremism expresses the hidden truth of modern capitalism, namely, that moral values are not universal principles but mere functions of a system.

The focus on personal responsibility and uncertainty that I have proposed illuminates an aspect of ideological extremism that the kind of structural approach predominant in the Frankfurt School often leaves aside. There is no question that modern capitalism creates some of the conditions that make extremism and totalitarianism possible. But the success of extremist ideologies depends to some extent on political dynamics where moral choices play an essential role. Adorno would probably not deny this, but he is unable to examine this dynamics because his conception of moral action relies on a contrast between objective conditions that block true moral virtue, and a capacity for resistance stemming from feelings of suffering as well as from theoretical reflection.[15] This contrast neglects the subjective dimension of evil actions, whose source Adorno explicitly restricts to objective conditions: "Evil . . . is the world's own unfreedom. Whatever evil is done comes from the world."[16] This claim reproduces the view of evil as deficiency, according to which evil is not caused by the person's freedom to do wrong, but rather by her lack of freedom. If objective conditions make true freedom impossible, it is necessary to identify new sources of freedom that resist such conditions. But what about the freedom of those who actively contribute to reproduce such conditions? Adorno, who never addressed evil or responsibility systematically, provides scarce conceptual resources to respond to this question. By contrast, Kant, Arendt, and Lyotard show that the constitutive uncertainty involved in action and judgment generate two possibilities that are equally free. In the face of uncertainty, individuals may choose to expose themselves to the establishment of uncontrollable relations with others, or they may choose to reject this uncertainty by subordinating their actions and judgments to ritualized forms of virtue.

If evil in politics is not only the effect of social structures, but also of choices, then it is important to consider the political dynamics that influences these choices. In order to understand and respond to evil in politics, we must examine how the web of actions and judgments generate choices that determine political stances. Of course, we cannot "explain" a choice the way we explain a natural or social phenomenon, that is, in terms of its causes. But we can explain the experiences and situations that make political choices possible to begin with. The focus on the problem of evil has shown that actions complicit with extreme evil stem from a choice not to care about moral values, which is in its turn an effect of the unwillingness to face the uncertainty involved in taking responsibility for action and judgment. If this is the case, we can see ideologies that disregard fundamental moral values as stemming from and at the same time reinforcing this elimination of uncertainty and responsibility. As we saw in chapter 1, totalitarianism is the ultimate expression of this desire to eliminate responsibility.

Uncertainty and Totalitarianism

Theorists of democracy have been aware of the connection between totalitarianism and the refusal of uncertainty. In his seminal work on democratic theory, Claude Lefort links modern democracy to the "dissolution of the markers of certainty," as a consequence of which societies experience a fundamental indeterminacy regarding the basis of power, knowledge, and law. Democracy, according to Lefort, is not merely an institutional arrangement, but rather a new symbolic order in which "the locus of power becomes an *empty space*."[17] This means that the space of power is not tied to any individual or group, but rather left indeterminate, so that "the exercise of power is subject to the procedures of periodical redistribution."[18] Importantly, this implies a "disentangling of the sphere of power, the sphere of law and the sphere of knowledge," by which the exercise of power, the generation of truth, and the legitimation of law become independent from one another. Democracy is based on a fundamental indeterminacy that affects all spheres of life, and which is actively protected and preserved by institutions that ensure that the place of power is not occupied. Totalitarianism, Lefort claims, emerges as a reaction to this indeterminacy, which leads to the "quest for a substantial identity, for a social body which is welded to its head, for an embodying power, for a state free from division."[19] The distinction between democracy and totalitarianism thus overlaps with the distinction between uncertainty and (fantasized) certainty.

While my examination of the link between evil and the refusal of uncertainty resonates with Lefort's accounts of totalitarianism, it sheds light on aspects that most theories of democracy do not address directly. While Lefort focuses on the ideology of the totalitarian movement, I have focused on the attitudes of those who, like Eichmann, become complicit with such movement without necessarily partaking in its ideological development. At this level, uncertainty does not stem from a specific political form, but is rather disseminated across everyday actions and judgments. If democracy, following Lefort, is not merely an institutional arrangement but, above all, a symbolic representation of power, then this representation permeates all social relations. Democratic values call individuals to be open to other perspectives and to the unpredictable transformation of social structures. This openness involves a degree of frustration. Different perspectives and the social transformations that follow from their encounters may reveal long-standing standards for action and judgment as morally problematic, that is, as oppressive, exclusionary, violent, and so on. Therefore, in order to be open, that is, in order to accept that we are not certain that we act or judge the right way, it is necessary to accept that our actions and judgments may be the subject of reproach in a future moment. The uncertainty that is inherent to democratic societies demands that actors expose themselves to punishment and forgiveness, in the political sense in which Arendt understands them. Responsible democratic actors will take responsibility for their actions by accepting reproach and asking for forgiveness when the time comes, not because they transgressed a transcendental law, but because their actions led to undesirable consequences, concealed egoistic motivations, or excluded certain perspectives. It is this uncertainty that totalitarian ideologies propose to overcome by offering unquestionable rules for action and judgment.

Although Arendt and Lyotard did not consider themselves specifically democratic thinkers, their visions of political pluralism share many of the central tenets of contemporary theories of democracy, such as the one sustained by Lefort. This pluralism is based on the rejection of the possibility of a metalanguage that would stand above multiple perspectives or discourses—a perspective that they develop on the basis of a reading of Kant. The absence of a metalanguage that regulates the relations between different perspectives generates possibilities for action and judgment, but it is by the same token a source of frustration. Without a metalanguage, it is necessary to permanently invent new ways of linking multiple perspectives to one another through action and judgment. But precisely because there is no preestablished procedure that regulates and legitimates these inventions, it is always possible that the linkage will have unwelcomed, regrettable consequences. Both Arendt and Lyotard stress that any action or judgment will fall into a web of actions and judgments. This web makes action and judgment possible to begin with, for we can only act and judge in response to other actions and judgments. Precisely for this reason, however, we cannot control our actions and judgments, whose outcome and meaning will be determined within this web. Like theories of democracy, Arendt's and Lyotard's visions of pluralism reject the possibility of a law or procedure that stands above all particular perspectives.

The focus on the problem of evil helps clarify the kind of political ethics that is involved in the pluralism affirmed by Arendt and Lyotard. Both authors have been repeatedly criticized for failing to provide universal standards for action and judgment. However, as theorists for whom the experience of totalitarianism is at the center of their thought, their political ethics is not oriented to identifying the good, but rather to preventing radical evil. This approach to political ethics is shared by thinkers such as Adorno and Judith Shklar, for whom moral imperatives in politics are not grounded on the identification of moral foundations but rather on responding to experiences of evil.[20] Both Arendt and Lyotard ask what totalitarianism is and, on the basis of the answer, develop a political vision oriented to preventing it. If totalitarianism represents an attempt to overcome the uncertainty that is inherent to the plurality of perspectives that constitutes the political world, then a political ethics oriented to preventing totalitarianism will consist in affirming and preserving a space of uncertainty in social relations.

Political and Moral Judgments

The analysis of judgment with the focus on the problem of evil in part 2 provides a new insight to consider the relationship between political and moral judgments, which has been at the center of a number of debates in recent years. There are two main perspectives on this relationship. The first perspective, influenced by the work of Jürgen Habermas and John Rawls, holds that political judgments need moral foundations in order to be universally valid, and thus to persuade others without coercion, deception, or manipulation. I examined this position in chapter 3 through an analysis of critiques of Arendt's conception of judgment by Ronald Beiner, Seyla Benhabib, and Robert Dostal. For these authors, political judgments are not essentially different from moral judgments, for both rely on universal standards that determine whether they are valid or invalid. Therefore, in order to make political judgments that everyone could in principle recognize as valid, it is necessary to identify the procedure that allows us to arrive at valid standards to begin with. Without such procedure, judgments have no universal validity, and the recognition of moral values is limited to the contingent agreement of each individual community.

A different perspective builds on Arendt's conception of judgment and stresses the distinction between moral universality, which is based on rules, and political universality, which is based on persuasion. Linda Zerilli has thoroughly developed this view in *A Democratic Theory of Judgment*. Arguing against conceptions of judgment informed by Habermas and Rawls, Zerilli claims that political judgments are not universal by virtue of their moral foundation, but rather of their capacity to take into account and persuade other viewpoints: "My judgment anticipates your agreement, but it cannot compel it with proofs (as objectivism would hold). There simply is no extrapolitical guarantee (e.g., epistemic privilege) that my judgment is valid or that it will be accepted by others or that it ought to be."[21] We do not need shared core values or procedures in order to reach mutual understanding, because we are capable of what Arendt calls "representative thinking," namely, of taking other perspectives into account, which is the necessary condition for the generation of a world in common. Throughout her analysis, Zerilli reconstructs a series of approaches that emphasize our capacity to establish relations and find commonalities with other perspectives, as opposed to identifying a prepolitical rule or procedure that guarantees the validity of certain perspectives. Ultimately, Zerilli believes that the philosophical concern with the universal validity of judgment overlooks the kind of universality that is specific to political judgments, where it is "an achievement that is deeply dependent on practical context and thus fragile."[22] Political judgments, properly understood, are not concerned with principles of validity that are independent of perspectives, but rather with relating perspectives in a creative way around a world in common.

My analysis of judgment in part 2 shares Zerilli's view that political judgments are grounded on the recognition of pluralism, as opposed to the acknowledgment of a universal procedure, but it departs from Zerilli's conception of the universality of judgment and of the role of moral ideas in it. Zerilli is right, in my view, that political judgments cannot be settled by means of identifying a prepolitical rule for judgment. But this does not mean that the universality of judgment is limited to contingent, contextual agreements between a number of viewpoints. On this point, Zerilli confuses universality with generality, and leaves her conception of judgment open to the critique that, without universal principles, we have no ground on which to denounce accepted practices that may be unjust or oppressive. If universal judgments are possible even against all the viewpoints that are familiar to us, it is because we feel the moral vocation to transcend all existing viewpoints. The mistake of proceduralist theories of judgment is that they derive from this vocation for universality the necessity to have access to a universal viewpoint by means of a procedure, and assume that without this procedure the vocation itself would be lost. However, following my reconstruction of Kant's analysis of the sublime in chapter 3, it is possible to conceive this universal viewpoint as the object of an open-ended striving that cannot be fully fulfilled. Moral ideas compel us to consider actions as if we could regard them from an absolute viewpoint. Even though we cannot reach such viewpoint, we can strive for it and demand that others agree with our striving. This is the minimal condition for developing a dialogue between different viewpoints, namely, that they feel the demand to move beyond all established positions. It is this demand that grounds the universality of judgment.

Conceived in this way, moral ideas play a central role in political judgments without working as a substantive foundation. Many political judgments, such as "Auschwitz was evil" or "racial equality is a just cause," involve more than a particular viewpoint that we expect others will agree with. When someone does not agree that Auschwitz was evil, not to mention those who were responsible for or complicit in it, we feel an intuitive conviction that their judgment is morally wrong. To sympathize with racial oppression is not simply a perspective—it is a perspective that is morally wrong. No matter how much we try to disentangle political from moral judgments, we will always confront situations where people make political judgments that arouse a feeling of moral condemnation. Therefore, while I share Zerilli's view that we should not subordinate political judgments to a fixed procedure that determines their validity, I do not believe that it is possible to bracket the feeling that some standpoints are invalid, independently of how many people find them persuasive. My suggestion, following Kant's and Lyotard's views on the judgment of the sublime, is that we think of invalid viewpoints not as transgressing a valid rule, but rather as positing one rule as absolute, thus blocking the possibility of relating to other rules. The difference between valid and invalid judgments is that the former stem from the attempt to transcend established viewpoints, while the latter absolutize one viewpoint.

Following this model, we can think of universal political judgments as inherently intertwined with moral distinctions, but not as grounded on principles or procedures that determine this distinction. In chapters

3 and 4, I proposed that universal judgments stem from a feeling that signals moral ideas, even if it does not allow us to know whether an action corresponds to moral ideas. In chapter 3, we saw that, according to Kant, it is possible to judge actions on the basis of a feeling aroused by moral ideas, namely, the feeling of the sublime. In chapter 4, I followed Lyotard's interpretation of the feeling of the sublime in Kant, and showed that the conflict between different rules for judgment produces a feeling that calls for the invention of new rules. One common idea in both perspectives is that universal judgments are grounded on a feeling for moral ideas, which cannot be presented in experience the way concepts can. We judge some actions as good, just, legitimate, liberational, or otherwise evil, unjust, illegitimate, oppressive, not because we "know" what these concepts mean and then apply them to a specific case, but because certain experiences arouse a feeling for these ideas. Political judgments are universal judgments because they appeal to the moral feelings that underlie any judgment on the basis of moral ideas. But the fact that we have a feeling for moral ideas does not mean that we need to know how to apply these ideas to experience in order to validate our judgments. Like the judgment of the sublime, political judgments appeal to the feeling for moral ideas that we all share, without turning this feeling into an object of knowledge.

Yet the same feeling that makes universal judgments possible opens up the possibility of destroying the capacity to judge, a destruction that is at the core of radical evil. Moral ideas can be felt, but they never present themselves in experience. This means that universal judgments involve a displeasure produced by the necessarily frustrated expectation that the idea will become manifest. As we saw in chapters 2 and 3, Kant called the attempt to overcome this frustration "delusion of the sense," which consists in confusing visible signs of virtue with virtue as such. In chapter 4, we saw that Lyotard links totalitarianism to the attempt to subordinate all judgments to the rules of a single discourse. In both cases, evil stems from a desire to overcome the uncertainty involved in judging without a preestablished set of rules. Following this idea, what Arendt described as an "inability to judge" characteristic of "the banality of evil" consists in a refusal to face the uncertainty of judgment by surrendering judgment to "the law of the land," that is, to the predominant rules for judgment. Despite Arendt's sometimes ambivalent terminology in this regard, we should not understand this "inability" as the absence of a faculty. Instead, we should understand it as a possible response to the uncertainty produced by the unavoidable need to judge. The feeling of moral ideas demands that we judge in a way that can be communicated to others, even if we do not know how to communicate to others and therefore need to invent new rules for communication. To be "unable to judge" is to pretend that a set of rules grounds and exhausts the communicability of judgment, relieving us of the responsibility to invent new ways to communicate.

The Politics of the Lesser Evil

In *Machiavelli: The Politics of the Lesser Evil* (*Machiavel, la politique du moindre mal*), originally a dissertation written under the supervision of Lyotard, Gérald Sfez claims that "the singular potency of Machiavelli's thought, or its *Virtù*, is to think the possibility of living-together, the general well-being of a given State, on the express condition of the radical and irremovable character of general evil."[23] Like Arendt, Sfez notes that Machiavelli's political thought is based on a simple premise: in order to resist evil, one must be ready to be involved in evil. The attempt to do only good cannot but lead to the withdrawal from political relations, or otherwise to the subordination of multiple relations to the image of a single good, thus suppressing conflict and plurality. By acknowledging that political actors are never purely good, but at best fighting evil with another evil, Machiavelli affirms the inherently pluralistic, conflictive nature of politics. As soon as one enters the political realm, one is forced to abandon the comfort of the purely good. Yet the acknowledgment of the irremovable character of evil does not lead to a dismissal of moral considerations from politics altogether. Political action may not attain the good, but it can resist evil. Although resisting evil seems to be the same as the good, it is not so in the sense that the good is an idea that we can know and tendentially realize. Instead, the "lesser evil" is a specific kind of political good that does not precede, but rather emerges out of the conflict between evils.

We can understand the politics of the lesser evil by contrasting it with a politics of the good that uses the idea of the lesser evil as a means to realize the good. This is an idea of the lesser evil that Arendt criticizes in her essay "Personal Responsibility under Dictatorship," where she claims that "politically, the weakness of the argument has always been that those who choose the lesser evil forget very quickly that they chose evil."[24] According to Arendt, choosing the lesser of two evils can easily turn into the justification of any evil whatsoever, even that of totalitarian regimes. This version of the lesser evil is close to the view that "the end justifies the means," or "you can't make an omelet without breaking eggs." Here, the impossibility of doing good is negatively turned into a justification of all sorts of evil, given that "the alternative is worse" or "otherwise the best possible outcome cannot be accomplished." The politics of the lesser evil, following Sfez's and Arendt's readings of Machiavelli, does not consist in choosing the lesser of multiple evils from a neutral position that is exterior to them, but in accepting that one can only fight against one evil by engaging in another evil. As Arendt claims, "Machiavelli assumes that evil will spread wildly if men do not resist it even at the risk of doing evil themselves."[25] So understood, the politics of the lesser evil consists in willingness to be involved in evil in order to resist evil. This necessary involvement in evil implies that one is never "in the good," that is, acting or judging from a higher moral standpoint, but always negotiating the tension between "greater" and "lesser" evils.

Is there then such a thing as "the good" in politics? How are we to understand Lyotard's claim, with which I began chapter 4, that "the lesser evil ought to be the political good"? In chapters 3 and 4, we saw that we can feel moral ideas as the effect of conflicting forces. Kant shows in the analysis of the sublime that all sensible forms are limited, yet some objects disrupt our faculty of representation to the point that we feel the vocation for a pure, infinite idea. Lyotard takes the sublime as a model for how the differend between rules for judgment arouses a feeling that calls for new idioms that make possible the expression of silenced voices. In both cases, there is no third element regulating the conflict between the parties. Taking the sublime as a model for politics, we may say that we can only confront an evil (an injustice, an oppression, an exclusion, a violence) with another evil. Yet in the very attempt to diminish evil, the idea of the good (justice, liberation, inclusion, peace) is aroused. A politics of the good seeks to know and tendentially realize these ideas. But this is misleading, because we have no representation of these ideas in their purity, and therefore we cannot know whether we are either approaching them or turning further away from them. The politics of the lesser evil, by contrast, relies on these ideas as an orientation to detect evils and oppose them with other evils. The idea of justice, for example, is not a theoretical standard that we rely on in order to progressively overcome injustice. It is rather in the resistance to particular injustices by means of other injustices that we feel the vocation for justice. The political good consists in always searching for unacknowledged evils in order to resist them by means of other evils. This way, we become responsible for choosing one evil over another, and remain open to future evils that may counteract the evil we have done.

In a context of pluralism, where we lack clear-cut distinctions between good and evil, the politics of the lesser evil represents the most reliable alternative to the authoritarian, fascist, and totalitarian tendencies of modern politics. To fight evil with evil requires that political actors endure the combination of success and frustration characteristic of the feeling of the sublime. Political actors experience the success of overcoming an evil, of rectifying an injustice, of liberating the oppressed, of including the excluded. But by the same token, they bring about new injustices, new oppressions, and new exclusions. The politics of the lesser evil does not strive for a standpoint beyond these ambivalences, but remains attentive to them. In doing so, it invites responses that may reveal current justices as complicit with yet unacknowledged injustices. This ability to detect and respond to existing political evils by engaging in other evils preserves the capacity of action and judgment to relate to other actions and judgments. While the desire to know and to possess "the good" makes us less tolerant of the uncertainty involved in action and judgment, the politics of the lesser evil thrives in it. The open-ended capacity to respond and relate to others does not lead us to the moral good, but it prevents us from becoming complicit in extreme evil.

Notes

Introduction

1. Hannah Arendt, "Understanding and Politics (The Difficulties of Understanding)," in *Essays in Understanding*, ed. Jerome Kohn (New York: Schocken, 1994), 312.

2. Ibid., 321.

3. Ibid., 323.

4. The interrelation between totalitarianism and the Enlightenment is of course the central concern of Horkheimer and Adorno's *Dialectic of Enlightenment*. On this point, it is worth noting Adorno's words on Auschwitz in *Negative Dialectics*: "That this could happen in the midst of the traditions of philosophy, of art, and of the enlightening sciences says more than that these traditions and their spirit lacked the power to take hold of men and work a change in them. There is untruth in those fields themselves, in the autarky that is emphatically claimed for them" (*Negative Dialectics*, trans. E. B. Ashton [New York: Routledge, 2004], 366–67).

5. Susan Neiman, *Evil in Modern Thought: An Alternative History of Philosophy* (Princeton, NJ: Princeton University Press, 2004).

6. Richard J. Bernstein, *Radical Evil: A Philosophical Interrogation* (Cambridge, UK: Polity, 2008), chapter 1.

7. Hannah Arendt, "Social Science Techniques and the Study of Concentration Camps," in *Essays in Understanding*, ed. Jerome Kohn (New York: Schocken, 1994), 232.

8. Ibid., 233.

9. Ibid.

10. Ibid.

11. Hannah Arendt, *The Origins of Totalitarianism* (New York: Harcourt Brace & Company, 1976), 459.

12. Hannah Arendt, "Thinking and Moral Considerations," in *Responsibility and Judgment*, ed. Jerome Kohn (New York: Schocken, 2003), 179–80.

13. Jean-Luc Nancy, *The Experience of Freedom*, trans. Bridget McDonald (Stanford, CA: Stanford University Press, 1998), 123.

14. Ibid.

15. Ibid. Susan Neiman makes a similar point in *Evil in Modern Thought*, 254.

16. Plato, *The Republic of Plato*, trans. Allan Bloom (New York: Basic Books, 1991), 120; Aristotle, *Ethica Nicomachea*, in *The Basic Works of Aristotle*, ed. Richard McKeon (New York: Random House, 2001), 971; Plotinus, *The Enneads*, ed. John Dillon, trans. Stephan MacKenna (New York: Penguin, 1991), 10; Saint Augustine, *City of God*, ed. Henry Betteson (London: Penguin, 2003), 454; G. W. Leibniz and Samuel Clarke, *Correspondence*, ed. Roger Ariew (Indianapolis, IN: Hackett, 2000), 145; Baruch Spinoza, *The Letters*, ed. Samuel Shirley (New York: Hackett, 1995), 143; G. W. F. Hegel, *Lectures on the Philosophy of World History*, trans. H. B. Nisbet (Cambridge, UK: Cambridge University Press, 1981), 42–43.

17. Charles T. Mathewes, *Evil and the Augustinian Tradition* (Cambridge, UK: Cambridge University Press, 2004), 78.

18. Susan Neiman, *Evil in Modern Thought: An Alternative History of Philosophy* (Princeton, NJ: Princeton University Press, 2004); Richard J. Bernstein, *Radical Evil: A Philosophical Interrogation* (Cambridge, UK: Polity, 2008); Peter Dews, *The Idea of Evil* (Malden, MA: Blackwell, 2008).

19. María Pía Lara, *Narrating Evil: A Post-Metaphysical Theory of Reflective Judgment* (New York: Columbia University Press, 2007); Richard J. Bernstein, *The Abuses of Evil: The Corruption of Politics and Religion since 9/11* (Cambridge, UK: Polity, 2005).

20. William E. Connolly, *The Ethos of Pluralization* (Minneapolis, MN: Minnesota University Press, 2004); Stephen K. White, *The Ethos of a Late-Modern Citizen* (Cambridge, MA: Harvard University Press, 2009); Ella Myers, *Worldly Ethics: Democratic Politics and Care for the World* (Durham, NC: Duke University Press, 2013).

21. Bettina Stangneth, *Eichmann before Jerusalem: The Unexamined Life of a Mass Murderer* (New York: Vintage, 2015), xxiii.

22. Daniel Jonah Goldhagen, *Hitler's Willing Executioners: Ordinary Germans and the Holocaust* (New York: Alfred A. Knopf, 1996), 9.

23. Ibid., 47.

24. Richard Kamber raises this problem in "The Logic of the Goldhagen Debate," *Res Publica* 6 (2000).

25. Christopher R. Browning, *Ordinary Men: Reserve Police Battalion 101 and the Final Solution in Poland* (London: Penguin, 2001), 221.

26. Ibid., 215–16.

27. Simona Forti, *New Demons: Rethinking Evil and Power Today* (Stanford, CA: Stanford University Press, 2015), 142.

28. Hannah Arendt, *Eichmann in Jerusalem: A Report on the Banality of Evil* (New York: Penguin, 2006), 289–290.

29. Jürgen Habermas, *The Philosophical Discourse of Modernity: Twelve Lectures*, trans. Frederick Lawrence (Cambridge, UK: Polity, 1992), 325; John Rawls, *The Law of Peoples* (Cambridge, MA: Harvard University Press, 2000), 126–27.

30. Simon Critchley, *Infinitely Demanding: Ethics of Commitment, Politics of Resistance* (London: Verso, 2008), 23–26.

31. Ibid., 9.

32. Claude Lefort, *The Political Forms of Modern Society: Bureaucracy, Democracy, Totalitarianism*, ed. David Thompson (Cambridge, MA: MIT Press, 1986), Chapter 8; Ernesto Laclau and Chantal Mouffe, *Hegemony and Socialist Strategy: Towards a Radical Democratic Politics* (London: Verso, 2013), 186–87; Slavoj Žižek, *The Sublime Object of Ideology* (London: Verso, 2008), 164–67; Alain Badiou, *Ethics: An Essay on the Understanding of Evil*, trans. Peter Hallward (London: Verso, 2001), 65.

33. Jacques Rancière, *Disagreement: Politics and Philosophy*, trans. Julie Rose (Minneapolis, MN: Minnesota University Press, 1999), 126.

34. Richard J. Bernstein, *The Abuses of Evil*, 10–11.

35. Peter Dews, *The Idea of Evil*, 2.

36. Patchen Markell, *Bound by Recognition* (Princeton, NJ: Princeton University Press, 2003), 21.

37. Ibid.

38. Ibid., 23.

39. Shalini Satkunanandan, *Extraordinary Responsibility: Politics Beyond the Moral Calculus* (Cambridge, UK: Cambridge University Press, 2015), 9–13.

40. Ibid., 188.

41. Lisa Jane Disch, *Hannah Arendt and the Limits of Philosophy* (Ithaca, NY: Cornell University Press, 1994); Michael Mack, "The Holocaust and Hannah Arendt's Philosophical Critique of Philosophy: *Eichmann in Jerusalem*," *New German Critique* 36, no. 1 (2009).

Chapter 1

1. Adi Ophir, "Between Eichmann and Kant: Thinking on Evil after Arendt," *History and Memory* 8, no. 2 (1996), 89–136; Richard J. Bernstein, "Did Hannah Arendt Change Her Mind? From Radical Evil to the Banality of Evil," in *Hannah Arendt: Twenty Years Later*, eds. Larry May and Jerome Kohn

(Cambridge, UK: Cambridge University Press, 1999); Peg Birmingham, "Holes of Oblivion: The Banality of Radical Evil," *Hypatia* 18, no. 1 (2003), 80–103; Sophie Cloutier, "La question du mal chez Hannah Arendt: Rupture ou continuité?," *PhaenEx* 3, no. 1 (2008), 82–111.

2. Dana R. Villa, *Politics, Philosophy, Terror: Essays on the Thought of Hannah Arendt* (Princeton, NJ: Princeton University Press, 1999), chapter 2.

3. Paul Formosa, "Is Radical Evil Banal? Is Banal Evil Radical?," *Philosophy and Social Criticism* 33, no. 6 (2007):], 717–35.

4. Margaret Canovan, *Hannah Arendt: A Reinterpretation of her Political Thought* (Cambridge, UK: Cambridge University Press, 1992), chapter 5; Mary Dietz, "Arendt and the Holocaust," in *The Cambridge Companion to Hannah Arendt*, ed. Dana Villa (New York: Cambridge University Press, 2002).

5. Hannah Arendt, *The Origins of Totalitarianism* (New York: Harcourt Brace & Company, 1976), 10.

6. Hannah Arendt, "Organized Guilt and Universal Responsibility," *Essays in Understanding*, ed. Jerome Kohn (New York: Schocken, 1994), 126–29; "Social Science Techniques and the Study of Concentration Camps," 242; "Understanding and Politics," 315.

7. Ibid., 459.
8. Ibid., 411.
9. Ibid., 459.
10. Ibid.
11. Ibid., 457.
12. Ibid.
13. See references to Pitkin and Canovan further down.
14. Ibid., 374.
15. Ibid.
16. Ibid., 375.
17. Ibid., 423.
18. Ibid., 426–27.
19. Ibid., 433.
20. Hanna Fenichel Pitkin, *The Attack of the Blob: Hannah Arendt's Concept of the Social* (Chicago, IL: University of Chicago Press, 1998), 90.
21. Arendt, *The Origins of Totalitarianism*, 446.
22. Ibid., 447.
23. Ibid., 451.
24. Ibid.
25. Ibid., 469.
26. Ibid., 465.
27. Ibid.
28. Canovan, *Hannah Arendt*, 52.

29. Dana Villa, "Beyond Good and Evil: Arendt, Nietzsche, and the Aestheticization of Political Action," *Political Theory* 20, no. 2 (1992), 281; Bonnie Honig, *Political Theory and the Displacement of Politics* (Ithaca, NY: Cornell University Press, 1993), 78.

30. Immanuel Kant, *Critique of Pure Reason*, eds. Paul Guyer and Allen W. Wood (New York: Cambridge University Press, 1998), 486.

31. Hannah Arendt, "Political Theory of Kant," in Subject File, 1949–1975, n.d., Hannah Arendt Papers, Manuscript Division, Library of Congress, Washington DC.

32. Ibid.

33. Ibid.

34. Ibid.

35. Hannah Arendt, *Vita activa, oder Vom tätigen Leben* (Stuttgart, Germany: R. Piper, 1960), 165. The word *responsibility* does not appear in the earlier, English version of *The Human Condition*, where Arendt claims that by word and deed "we take upon ourselves the naked fact of our original physical appearance" (176–77).

36. Hannah Arendt, "The Crisis in Education," in *Between Past and Future* (New York: Penguin, 2006), 186.

37. Ibid., 189.

38. Hannah Arendt, *The Human Condition* (Chicago, IL: University of Chicago Press, 1998), 179.

39. Ibid., 178.

40. Ibid., 176.

41. Ibid.

42. Ibid., 180.

43. Ibid., 179–80.

44. Ibid., 192.

45. Ibid.

46. Ibid.

47. Ibid., 190.

48. Ibid., 192.

49. Ibid., 193.

50. Ibid., 199.

51. Ibid., 233.

52. Ibid., 239.

53. Ibid., 240.

54. Garrath Williams, "Disclosure and responsibility in Arendt's *The Human Condition*," *European Journal of Political Theory* 14, no. 1 (2014), 42.

55. Arendt, *Vita activa*, 214 (my translation); *The Human Condition*, 220.

56. Arendt, *The Human Condition*, 243.

57. Ibid., 233–34.
58. Ibid., 234.
59. Williams, "Disclosure and responsibility in Arendt's *The Human Condition*," 45.
60. Jeff Love and Michael Meng, "A Troubling Banality," *Constellations* 23, no. 4 (2016).
61. Christoph Menke points out the juridical perspective adopted by Arendt's trial report in "Auf der Grenze des Rechts: Hannah Arendts Revision des Eichmann-Prozesses," *Merkur* 67 (2013). In her essay "Some Questions of Moral Philosophy," Arendt claims that the institution of the courtroom "rests on the assumption of personal responsibility and guilt" (*Responsibility and Judgment*, 57).
62. Hannah Arendt, *Eichmann in Jerusalem: A Report on the Banality of Evil* (New York: Penguin, 2006), 287.
63. Pitkin notes that some of the most polemical remarks in *Eichmann in Jerusalem* stem not from Arendt's attempt to exculpate the criminals or incriminate the victims, but rather from "the multiple incoherences of our ordinary ways of discussing agency, responsibility, and causation in human affairs" (*The Attack of the Blob*, 214).
64. Arendt, *Eichmann in Jerusalem*, 48.
65. Ibid., 49.
66. Ibid., 86.
67. Arendt makes a similar remark in her much earlier writing "Organized Guilt and Universal Responsibility," in *Essays in Understanding* (New York: Schocken, 1994), 129.
68. *Eichmann in Jerusalem*, 106.
69. Ibid., 137.
70. Arendt, "Personal Responsibility under Dictatorship," in *Responsibility and Judgment*, 43.
71. Ibid., 42.
72. Arendt, "Some Questions of Moral Philosophy," in *Responsibility and Judgment*, 107.
73. Ibid., 80.
74. Ibid., 97.
75. Ibid., 97–98.
76. Ibid., 100.
77. Hannah Arendt, *The Life of the Mind* (Orlando, FL: Harcourt, 1978), 188. See also "Some Questions of Moral Philosophy," 90.
78. "Some Questions of Moral Philosophy," 91.
79. Ibid., 94.
80. Ibid., 95.
81. Ibid., 101.

82. Ibid.
83. Ibid.
84. Ibid.
85. Ibid.
86. Ibid., 95.
87. Benjamin A. Schupmann, "Thoughtlessness and Resentment: Determinism and Moral Responsibility in the Case of Adolf Eichmann," *Philosophy and Social Criticism* 40, no. 2 (2014), 139. According to Sophie Cloutier, "by renouncing his personal will, Eichmann believed himself to be above all responsibility" ("La question du mal chez Hannah Arendt: rupture ou continuité?," *PhaenEx* 3, no. 1 [2008], 103; my translation).
88. Édith Fuchs, "La 'banalité du mal' comme absence de pensée selon Hannah Arendt," in *Destins de "la banalité du mal,"* eds. Michelle-Irène Brundy and Jean-Marie Winkler (Paris: Éditions de l'Éclat, 2011), 160; Isabelle Delpla, *Le mal en procès: Eichmann et les théodicées modernes* (Paris: Hermann, 2011), 156; Pitkin, *The Attack of the Blob*, 212.
89. Arendt, *The Life of the Mind*, 191.
90. "Some Questions of Moral Philosophy," 111.
91. Dana R. Villa, *Politics, Philosophy, Terror: Essays on the Thought of Hannah Arendt* (Princeton, NJ: Princeton University Press, 1999), 56.
92. Birmingham, Peg, "Hannah Arendt's Double Account of Evil: Political Superfluousness and Moral Thoughtlessness," in *The Routledge Handbook of the Philosophy of Evil*, eds. Thomas Nys and Stephen de Wijze (London: Routledge, 2019).
93. Rosalyn Diprose, "Arendt and Nietzsche on responsibility and futurity," *Philosophy and Social Criticism* 34, no. 6 (2008), see esp., 625.
94. Arendt, "Some Questions of Moral Philosophy," 105.
95. Ibid., 79. See also *The Life of the Mind*, 192.
96. Arendt, "Collective Responsibility," in *Responsibility and Judgment*, 150.
97. Arendt, *The Origins of Totalitarianism*, 476.
98. Arendt, *The Life of the Mind*, 167.
99. Ibid., 172.
100. Ibid., 175.
101. Ibid., 176.
102. Ibid., 177.
103. Hannah Arendt, *Lectures on Kant's Political Philosophy*, ed. Ronald Beiner (Chicago, IL: University of Chicago Press, 1992), 39.
104. Arendt, *The Life of the Mind*, 40.
105. Arendt, "Truth and Politics," in *Between Past and Future*, 237.
106. Arendt, *Lectures on Kant's Political Philosophy*, 41.
107. Ibid.

Chapter 2

1. William E. Connolly, *Why I Am Not a Secularist* (Minneapolis, MN: Minnesota University Press, 1999), 164–77; Bonnie Honig, *Political Theory and the Displacement of Politics* (Ithaca, NY: Cornell University Press, 1993), chapter 2; Raymond Geuss, *Philosophy and Real Politics* (Princeton, NJ: Princeton University Press, 2008), 7–9.

2. Shalini Satkunanandan, "The Extraordinary Categorical Imperative," *Political Theory* 39, no. 2 (2011).

3. Henry E. Allison, *Kant's Theory of Freedom* (New York: Cambridge University Press, 1990); J. B. Schneewind, *The Invention of Autonomy: A History of Modern Moral Philosophy* (New York: Cambridge University Press, 1998); Susan Meld Shell, *Kant and the Limits of Autonomy* (Cambridge, MA: Harvard University Press, 2009); Peter Fenves, *Late Kant: Towards Another Law of the Earth* (New York: Routledge, 2003); Ian Hunter, *Rival Enlightenments: Civil and Metaphysical Philosophy in Early Modern Germany* (Cambridge, MA: Cambridge University Press, 2003).

4. Judith Butler, "Hanna Arendt's Death Sentences," *Comparative Literature Studies* 48, no. 3 (2011), 282.

5. Hannah Arendt, *Eichmann in Jerusalem: A Report on the Banality of Evil* (New York: Penguin, 2006), 136.

6. Ibid.

7. Ibid.

8. Ibid.

9. Ibid., 137.

10. Hannah Arendt, *On Revolution* (New York: Penguin, 1965), 78.

11. Ibid., 79.

12. Hannah Arendt, *Denktagebuch*, Vol. 1, eds. Ursula Ludz and Ingeborg Nordmann (Munich, Germany: Piper, 2002), 182; my translation.

13. Hannah Arendt, *The Life of the Mind* (Orlando, FL: Harcourt, 1978), 63.

14. Hannah Arendt, *Responsibility and Judgment*, ed. Jerome Kohn (New York: Schocken Books, 2002), 71.

15. Hannah Arendt, *The Origins of Totalitarianism* (New York: Harcourt Brace & Company, 1973), 459.

16. Ibid.

17. Arendt, *Responsibility and Judgment*, 62.

18. Arendt, *The Life of the Mind*, 214–15.

19. Arendt, *Responsibility and Judgment*, 94.

20. Arendt, *The Life of the Mind*, 195.

21. Arendt, *Responsibility and Judgment*, 114.

22. Hannah Arendt, "Basic Moral Propositions," unpublished manuscript from 1966, in the Hannah Arendt Papers, Courses—University of Chicago,

Series: Subject File, 1949–1975, n.d., Manuscript Division, Library of Congress, Washington, DC.

23. Hannah Arendt and Karl Jaspers, *Correspondence: 1926–1969*, eds. Lotte Kohler and Hans Saner (New York: Harcourt Brace Jovanovich, 1992), 62.

24. Ibid., 69.

25. Allen W. Wood, *Kant's Moral Religion* (Ithaca, NY: Cornell University Press, 1970).

26. Immanuel Kant, *Critique of Pure Reason*, eds. Paul Guyer and Allen W. Wood (New York: Cambridge University Press, 1998), 486; A448/B476.

27. Ibid., 533; A533/B561.

28. Ibid., 533; A534/B562.

29. Ibid., 534; A534/B562.

30. Ibid., 541; A548/B576.

31. Ibid.

32. Ibid., 533; A534/B562.

33. Christian Wolff, *Rational Thoughts on God, the World and the Soul of Human Beings, also All Things in General*, in *Kant's Critique of Pure Reason: Background Source Materials*, ed. Eric Watkins (New York: Cambridge University Press, 2009), 35.

34. Alexander Baumgarten, *Metaphysics*, in *Kant's Critique of Pure Reason: Background Source Materials*, 122. An extensive analysis of the multiple influences contributing to Kant's notion of *Willkür* is developed by Katsutoshi Kawamura in *Spontaneität und Willkür: Der Freiheitsbegriff in Kants Antinomienlehre und seine historischen Wurzeln* (Stuttgart, Germany: Frommann Holzboog, 1996), chapters 1 and 2.

35. The first major critique was developed by Carl Leonhard Reinhold in "Erörterung des Begriffs von der Freiheit des Willens," in *Materialen zu Kants "Kritik der praktischen Vernunft,"* eds. Rudiger Bittner and Konrad Cramer (Frankfurt am Main, Germany: Suhrkamp, 1975).

36. On this point, see Lewis White Beck, "Five Concepts of Freedom in Kant," in *Stephan Körner—Philosophical Analysis and Reconstruction*, ed. Jan T. J. Srzednicki (Dordrecht, the Netherlands: Martinus Nijhoff, 1987), 37.

37. Immanuel Kant, *Groundwork of the Metaphysics of Morals*, in *Practical Philosophy*, ed. Mary J. Gregor (New York: Cambridge University Press, 1999), 99; 4:452.

38. Ibid., 103; 4:457.

39. Ibid., 104; 4:458.

40. Immanuel Kant, *Critique of Practical Reason*, in *Practical Philosophy*, 165–66; 5:32.

41. Immanuel Kant, *Lectures on Ethics*, eds. Peter Heath and J. B. Schneewind (New York: Cambridge University Press, 1997), 85.

42. Ibid., 86.

43. Allen W. Wood, *Kant's Moral Religion*, 153–55.
44. Allison, *Kant's Theory of Freedom*, 39–40.
45. Schneewind, *The Invention of Autonomy*, 518.
46. Hunter, *Rival Enlightenments*, 343–54; Shell, *Kant and the Limits of Autonomy*, 8–14.
47. Immanuel Kant, *Religion within the Boundaries of Mere Reason*, in *Religion and Rational Theology*, eds. Allen W. Wood and George di Giovanni (New York: Cambridge University Press, 2001), 73; 6:24.
48. Kant, *Groundwork of the Metaphysics of Morals*, 56; 4:402; 73; 4:422.
49. Kant, *Religion within the Boundaries of Mere Reason* 70–71; 6:21.
50. Ibid., 71; 6:22.
51. Gordon E. Michalson, *Fallen Freedom: Kant on Radical Evil and Moral Regeneration* (Cambridge, UK: Cambridge University Press, 1990), 65; 67. Jean-Luc Nancy, *L'impératif catégorique* (Paris: Flammarion, 1983), 15; Hunter, *Rival Enlightenments*, 347.
52. Ibid., 76; 6:26.
53. Ibid., 77–78; 6:29.
54. Kant, *Religion within the Boundaries of Mere Reason*, 83; 6:36.
55. Ibid., 83; 6:36.
56. Ibid., 83; 6:37.
57. Kant, *Groundwork*, 50; 4:394.
58. Ibid., 59–60; 4:405.
59. Kant, *Religion*, 83; 6:37.
60. Ibid., 84; 6:37.
61. Ibid., 84; 6:38.
62. Ibid., 85; 6:38.
63. Hunter, *Rival Enlightenments*, 123–26.
64. Dieter Henrich, "Der Begriff der sittlichen Einsicht und Kants Lehre vom Faktum der Vernunft," in *Kant: Zur Deutung seiner Theorie von Erkennen und Handeln*, ed. Gerold Prauss (Cologne, Germany: Krepenheuer & Witsch, 1973), 232; my translation. Steven Lestition gives a contextual interpretation of this turn in "Kant and the End of the Enlightenment in Prussia," *Journal of Modern History* 65; no. 1 (1993), 91. Satkunanandan finds elements of this view on ethics in Kant's analysis of the categorical imperative in the *Groundwork* in "The Extraordinary Categorical Imperative."
65. George di Giovanni, Introduction to *Religion*, 42; Hunter, *Rival Enlightenments*, 338; Christopher Clark, *Iron Kingdom: The Rise and Downfall of Prussia, 1600–1947* (Cambridge, MA: Harvard University Press, 2006), 267–74.
66. Shell, *Kant and the Limits of Autonomy*, 187–211; Lestition, "Kant and the End of the Enlightenment in Prussia," 76–83.
67. Manfred Kuehn, *Kant: A Biography* (New York: Cambridge University Press, 2001), 54–55; Ernst Cassirer, *Kant's Life and Thought*, trans. James Haden

(New Haven, CT: Yale University Press, 1981), 16–17. See also Michel Despland, *Kant on History and Religion* (London: McGill–Queen's University Press, 1973), 106–7.

68. Despland, *Kant on History and Religion*, 101.

69. Spener's ideas are condensed in his main and most popular work, *Pia Desideria*. For a brief description of the book, see Lewis White Beck, *Early German Philosophy: Kant and His Predecessors* (Cambridge, UK: Harvard University Press, 1969), 159; Richard Gawthrop, *Pietism and the Making of Eighteenth-Century Prussia* (Cambridge, UK: Cambridge University Press, 1993), 107.

70. Gawthrop, *Pietism and the Making of Eighteenth-Century Prussia*, 205–6.

71. Mary Fulbrook, *Piety and Politics. Religion and the Rise of Absolutism in England, Wüttemberg and Prussia* (Cambridge, UK: Cambridge University Press, 1983), 166–70.

72. Martin Brecht, "August Hermann Francke und der Hallische Pietismus," in *Geschichte des Pietismus*, Vol. 1 (Göttingen, Germany: Vandenhoeck & Ruprecht, 1993), 463.

73. Gawthrop, *Pietism and the Making of Eighteenth-Century Prussia*, 148.

74. Klaus Schaller, "Pietismus und moderne Pädagogik," in *Pietismus und moderne Welt*, ed. Kurt Aland (Witten, Germany: Luther-Verlag, 1974), 173–74.

75. Spener refers to deeds as "signs" [*Kennzeichen*] of inner devotion in *Der neue Mensch*, ed. Hans-Georg Feller (Stuttgart, Germany: J. F. Steinkopf, 1966), 64.

76. Johannes Wallmann, "Was ist Pietismut?," *Pietusmus und Neuzeut* 20 (1994), 11. According to Fulbrook, "the need for Pietist testimonials to obtain positions in church and state led to superficial professions of conversion and regeneration according to the routinized general stages of Pietist experience. Pietism, conceived as a spontaneous religion of the heart, had become rationalized and mechanical as the orthodoxy of the state" (*Piety and Politics*, 170).

77. Kant, *Religion*, 137–38; 6:102–6.

78. Ibid., 142; 6:109.

79. Ibid., 146; 6:115.

80. Ibid., 151; 6:122–23.

81. Ibid., 197; 6:179.

82. Ibid., 190; 6:170.

83. According to Peter Fenves's reading, "concealing from itself the source of its selfhood in the secret of freedom, the 'I' hides from itself its responsibility for the actions it undertakes, and this hiding is itself an action for which it is responsible and from which it hides itself" (*Late Kant*, 85).

84. Kant, *Religion*, 189; 6:169.

85. Ibid., 108; 6:66.

86. Ibid., 109; 6:67.

87. Ibid., 109; 6:68.

88. Ibid., 112; 6:71.

89. According to Gawthrop, "while the 'door for betterment' was open for all, closing the threshold did not mean that the individual was free to pursue his or her spiritual development without restriction. In fact, although Francke and his co-workers did not believe in predestination, they none the less regarded themselves as an elite group with the power to direct and control the souls entrusted to them . . . They claimed to possess, as many modern ideologues have done, a type of knowledge that was simultaneously empirical and absolute" (*Pietism and the Making of Eighteenth-Century Prussia*, 152).

90. See Heidegger's analysis of a primordial "being-Guilty" in *Being and Time*, trans. John Macquarrie and Edward Robinson (Oxford, UK: Basil Blackwell, 1985), 326–35; and Jaspers's analysis of "metaphysical guilt" as the precondition for both moral and political guilt in *The Question of German Guilt*, trans. E. B. Ashton (New York: Fordham University Press, 2000), 25–40.

91. Karl Jaspers, "Das Radikal Böse bei Kant," in *Rechenschaft und Ausblick. Rede und Aufsätze* (Munich, Germany: R. Piper, 1958), 114–15; my translation.

92. Henry E. Allison, *Idealism and Freedom: Essays on Kant's Theoretical and Practical Philosophy* (New York: Cambridge University Press, 1996), 181.

93. Alenka Zupančič, *Ethics of the Real: Kant, Lacan* (London: Verso, 2000), 93.

94. Olivier Reboul, *Kant et le problème du mal* (Montreal, QC: Montreal University Press, 1971), 103; my translation.

Chapter 3

1. Robert J. Dostal, "Judging Human Action: Arendt's Appropriation of Kant," *The Review of Metaphysics* 37, no. 4 (1984); Ronald Beiner, "Rereading Hannah Arendt's Kant Lectures," in *Judgment, Imagination, and Politics: Themes from Kant and Arendt*, eds. Ronald Beiner and Jennifer Nedelsky (Oxford, UK: Rowman & Littlefield, 2001); Seyla Benhabib, "Judgment and the Moral Foundations of Politics in Hannah Arendt's Thought," in *Judgment, Imagination, and Politics: Themes from Kant and Arendt*; Alfredo Ferrarin, "Imagination and Judgment in Kant's Practical Philosophy," *Philosophy and Social Criticism* 34, no. 1–2 (2008). I discuss some of these criticisms in detail farther down. Andrew Norris criticizes Arendt for neglecting the link between the judgment of taste and Kant's theoretical philosophy, which shows that the former is not an adequate model for political judgment, in "Arendt, Kant, and the Politics of Common Sense," *Polity* 29, no. 2 (1996).

2. Jean-François Lyotard, *Lessons on the Analytic of the Sublime*, trans. Elizabeth Rottenberg (Stanford, CA: Stanford University Press, 1994); Paul Crowther, *The Kantian Sublime: From Morality to Art* (Oxford, UK: Clarendon

Press, 1989); John H. Zammito, *The Genesis of Kant's* Critique of Judgment (Chicago, IL: The University of Chicago Press, 1992); Robert R. Clewis, *The Kantian Sublime and the Revelation of Freedom* (Cambridge, UK: Cambridge University Press, 2009).

3. Ronald Beiner, "Interpretative Essay," in Hannah Arendt, *Lectures on Kant's Political Philosophy*, ed. Ronald Beiner (Chicago, IL: University of Chicago Press, 1992), 97–101. Leora Y. Bilsky analyzes both aspects of the problem of judgment in the context of Eichmann's trial in "When Actor and Spectator Meet in the Courtroom: Reflections on Hannah Arendt's Concept of Judgment," in *Judgment, Imagination, and Politics*.

4. Especially relevant in this regard are Arendt's remarks on the difficulty of judging after totalitarianism in "Understanding and Politics," in *Essays in Understanding*, ed. Jerome Kohn (New York: Schocken Books, 1994), 316; and her claim in "The Crisis in Culture" that "inability to judge" is one of the characteristics of the modern "mass man" (in *Between Past and Future: Six Essays in Political Thought* [New York: Viking Press, 1961], 199).

5. Hannah Arendt, "Personal Responsibility under Dictatorship," in *Responsibility and Judgment*, ed. Jerome Kohn (New York: Schocken Books, 2003), 19.

6. Ibid., 114.

7. Ibid., 294–95.

8. Arendt claims that "Kant does not believe that moral judgments are the product of reflection and imagination, hence they are not judgments strictly speaking" (*Lectures on Kant's Political Philosophy*, 72). The idea of "moral propositions" as stemming from reason as opposed to judgment appears on p. 10.

9. Arendt, "Personal Responsibility under Dictatorship," 45.

10. Ibid., 27.

11. Arendt, "Some Questions of Moral Philosophy," in *Responsibility and Judgment*, 141.

12. Ibid., 139.

13. Arendt, *Lectures on Kant's Political Philosophy*, 67.

14. Ibid.

15. Arendt, "Some Questions of Moral Philosophy," 140.

16. Ibid., 140–41.

17. Arendt, *Lectures on Kant's Political Philosophy*, 75.

18. Ronald Beiner, "Rereading Hannah Arendt's Kant Lectures," 98–99.

19. Ibid., 97.

20. Seyla Benhabib, "Judgment and the Moral Foundations of Politics in Hannah Arendt," 200.

21. Ibid., 197.

22. Ibid., 193.

23. Robert J. Dostal, "Judging Human Action: Arendt's Appropriation of Kant," 736.

24. Ibid., 736. Dostal's confusion regarding Kant's conception of practical judgment, as analyzed in "The Typic of Practical Judgment" in the second *Critique*, is evident in his claims that "the typic needs to be supplemented by this development of Kant's thought, for clearly in the typic of the *Critique of Practical Reason* Kant cannot quite make good the analogy with the schematism of the *Critique of Pure Reason* and the judgmental application of the pure concepts to sensibility." The reason why the practical judgment has a typic and not a schematism is precisely that the two are not identical, so it is unclear in what sense the latter does not "make good" the analogy.

25. Andrew Norris neglects Arendt's explicit remarks on this point when he claims that her understanding of "communicability" transforms "a transcendental principle into an empirical criterion" ("Arendt, Kant, and the Politics of Common Sense," 188).

26. Arendt, *Lectures on Kant's Political Philosophy*, 74.

27. Immanuel Kant, *Critique of the Power of Judgment*, ed. Paul Guyer, trans. Paul Guyer and Eric Matthews (Cambridge, UK: Cambridge University Press, 2000), 177; 5:297.

28. Arendt, *Lectures on Kant's Political Philosophy*, 75.

29. Ibid. This reference is surprisingly ignored by Richard Bernstein and Ronald Beiner, who claim that Arendt introduced and unbridgeable gap between the viewpoint of the actor and the viewpoint of the spectator, as well as by David Marshall and Jonathan P. Schwartz, who respond that bridging this gap is precisely the purpose of the judgment of taste (Richard J. Bernstein, *Philosophical Profiles: Essays in Pragmatic Mode* [Philadelphia: University of Pennsylvania Press, 1986], chapter 8; Ronald Beiner, "Rereading Hannah Arendt's Kant Lectures," in *Judgment, Imagination, and Politics*; David Marshall, "The Origin and Character of Hannah Arendt's Theory of Judgment," *Political Theory* 38, no. 3 (2003); Jonathan P. Schwartz, *Arendt's Judgment: Freedom, Responsibility, Citizenship* [Philadelphia: University of Pennsylvania Press, 2016], chapter 5).

30. Given Beiner's reading of the sublime as an attempt to hold an "anthropological narcissism," in which nature is interpreted as having the human being as its end, it is not surprising that he neglects its importance for the problem of judging on the basis on moral ideas ("Kant, the Sublime, and Nature," in *Kant and Political Philosophy: The Contemporary Legacy*, eds. Ronald Beiner and William James Booth[[AU: Should the place of publisher be New Haven, CT?] Yes, it should be New Haven, CT] [Ann Arbor, MI: Yale University Press, 1993]). Beiner simply disregards the fact that human beings are natural objects as well, which is the essential problem of conceiving the possibility of judging on the basis of moral principles, as we will see.

31. Immanuel Kant, *Critique of Pure Reason*, eds. and trans. Paul Guyer and Allen W. Wood (Cambridge, UK: Cambridge University Press, 1998), 535; A538/B566.

32. Ibid., 536; A539/B567.
33. Ibid.
34. Ibid.
35. Ibid., 539; A546/B574.
36. Alexander Baumgarten, *Metaphysics*, in *Kant's Critique of Pure Reason: Background Source Materials*, ed. Eric Watkins (New York: Cambridge University Press, 2009), 164.
37. Kant, *Critique of Pure Reason*, 542; A551/B579.
38. Ibid., 542; A551/B579.
39. Immanuel Kant, *Groundwork of the Metaphysics of Morals*, in *Practical Philosophy*, ed. and trans. Mary J. Gregor (Cambridge, UK: Cambridge University Press, 1999), 62; 4:407.
40. Ibid.
41. Ibid., 4:408.
42. Immanuel Kant, *Critique of Practical Reason*, in *Practical Philosophy*, 196; 5:69.
43. Ibid., 186; 5:57.
44. Ibid., 196; 5:69.
45. Ibid., 196; 5:69.
46. Ibid., 196; 5:69–70.
47. Lewis White Beck's otherwise thorough analysis of the practical judgment says little about the distinction between action and maxim, and assumes that the type bridges the gap between what ought to be and what is (*A Commentary on Kant's* Critique of Practical Reason [Chicago, IL: University of Chicago Press, 1984], 157). This is at least problematic, if we consider that maxims for action do not clearly belong to either of the two realms.
48. G. Felicitas Munzel, *Kant's Conception of Moral Character: The "Critical" Link of Morality, Anthropology, and Reflective Judgment* (Chicago, IL: University of Chicago Press, 1999), 126–32. Given Munzel's reading of the aesthetic judgment as one step in Kant's consistent view of the empirical character as cultivated by and expressive of the intelligible character, it is unsurprising that her analysis gives little room to the sublime.
49. Henry E. Allison, *Kant's Theory of Freedom* (Cambridge, UK: Cambridge University Press, 1990), 90.
50. Immanuel Kant, *Religion within the Boundaries of Mere Reason*, trans. George di Giovanni, in *Religion and Rational Theology*, eds. Allen W. Wood and George di Giovanni (Cambridge, UK: Cambridge University Press, 2001), 70; 6:20.
51. Ibid., 84; 6:38.
52. Ibid., 85; 6:38.
53. Ibid., 93; 6:48.
54. Ibid., 92–93; 6:48.
55. Ibid., 93; 6:49.

56. Ibid., 93–94; 6:50.

57. Paul Crowther, *The Kantian Sublime: From Morality to Art* (Oxford, UK: Clarendon Press, 1989), 131–33.

58. Patricia M. Matthews, "Kant's Sublime: A Form of Pure Aesthetic Reflective Judgment," *Journal of Aesthetics and Art Criticism* 54, no. 2 (1996); Henry E. Allison, *Kant's Theory of Taste: A Reading of the* Critique of Aesthetic Judgment (Cambridge, UK: Cambridge University Press, 2001), Chapter 13; Rodolphe Gasché, *The Idea of Form: Rethinking Kant's Aesthetics* (Stanford, CA: Stanford University Press, 2002), chapter 5.

59. Robert R. Clewis, *The Kantian Sublime and the Revelation of Freedom* (Cambridge, UK: Cambridge University Press, 2009).

60. Milton C. Nahm, "'Sublimity' and the 'Moral Law' in Kant's Philosophy," *Kant-Studien* 48 (1956). Zammito explains that the reason behind Kant's "ethical turn" in the composition of the third *Critique*, which led to the inclusion of the "Analytic of the Sublime," "had to do with his desire to reconcile his phenomena-noumena theory of freedom with the problem of actualizing the moral good. He needed, or felt he needed, to reformulate and strengthen the analogue to schematism which he had developed in the *Second Critique*" (*The Genesis of Kant's* Critique of Judgment, 264).

61. Kant, *Critique of the Power of Judgment*, 26; 20:223–24.

62. Ibid., 102; 5:217.

63. Ibid.

64. Ibid., 216; 5:340.

65. Ibid., 128; 5:244.

66. Ibid., 132; 5:248.

67. Ibid., 134; 5:250.

68. Ibid., 135; 5:252.

69. Ibid., 138; 5:254.

70. Ibid., 140; 5:257.

71. Ibid., 141; 5:257.

72. Ibid.

73. Ibid., 172; 5:292.

74. Patricia Matthews claims that "the feeling of sublimity . . . is a feeling based on the relationship of the faculties of reason and imagination, not a direct response to reason" ("Kant's Sublime: A Form of Pure Aesthetic Reflective Judgment," 172), a definition that makes the feeling of the sublime similar to the feeling of the beautiful, but leaves aside Kant's own description of the former as a feeling for the supersensible vocation of our mind. A similar neglect for this difference between the feeling of the beautiful and the feeling of the sublime is present in Rudolf Makkreel's claims that "reflection on beauty leads us to hope for a greater harmony and systematic order in nature; the sublime points to the possibility of an overall integration of our faculties of mind" (*Imagination*

and Interpretation in Kant: The Hermeneutical Import of the Critique of Judgment [Chicago, IL: University of Chicago Press, 1994], 83).

75. Paul Guyer, "Kant's Distinction between the Beautiful and the Sublime," *Review of Metaphysics* 35, no. 4 (1982), esp. 766. A similar point, with a greater emphasis on the contrast between the beautiful and the sublime, is made by Eva Schaper in "Taste, Sublimity, and Genius: The Aesthetics of Nature and Art," in *The Cambridge Companion to Kant*, ed. Paul Guyer (Cambridge, UK: Cambridge University Press, 2006).

76. The feeling of the sublime, according to Peter Fenves, needs a "supplement," which explains why Kant presents the "Analytic of the Sublime" as a "mere appendix" to the *Critique of the Aesthetic Power of Judgment* ("Taking Stock of the Kantian Sublime," *Eighteenth-Century Studies* 28, no. 1 [1994], 78).

77. Kant, *Critique of the Power of Judgment*, 131; 5:248.
78. Ibid., 133; 5:249.
79. Ibid., 143; 5:260.
80. Ibid., 144; 5:261.
81. Ibid., 144–145; 5:261.
82. Ibid., 143; 5:260.
83. Ibid., 145; 5:261–62.
84. I follow here Kant's definition of humanity in the *Third Critique*, 229; 5:355.
85. Ibid., 145; 5:262.
86. Ibid., 146; 5:262
87. Ibid., 146; 5:263.
88. Crowther, *The Kantian Sublime*, 116. Crowther's misreading of the role of deeds in Kant's analysis of the dynamically sublime in an example of his tendency to quickly assume breaks and inconsistencies both within this analysis and in its relationship with Kant's broader conception of the sublime—which is curious given his claim that "after the labyrinthine intricacies of the mathematical mode, Kant's discussion of the dynamical sublime comes as something of a relief, in so far as it contains one of the clearest progressions of argument in any one section of the third *Critique*" (108).
89. Ibid., 118.
90. Clewis, *The Kantian Sublime and the Revelation of Freedom*, 87.
91. Kant, *Critique of the Power of Judgment*, 147; 5:264.
92. Kant, *Critique of Practical Reason*, 199–200; 5:73.
93. Kant, *Critique of the Power of Judgment*, 149; 5:265.
94. Ibid., 153; 5:271.
95. Lyotard, *Lessons on the Analytic of the Sublime*, 234.
96. Ibid., 154; 5:272.
97. Kant, *Religion within the Boundaries of Mere Reason*, 188; 6:168.
98. Kant, *Critique of the Power of Judgment*, 155; 5:273.

Chapter 4

1. Jacques Derrida, "Lyotard and Us," *Parallax* 6, no. 4 (2000), 32.
2. Jean-François Lyotard, *The Differend: Phrases in Dispute* (Minneapolis, MN: Minnesota University Press, 1989), 140.
3. Some examples of this one-sided reading are: Linda M. G. Zerilli, "'We Feel Our Freedom': Imagination and Judgment in the Thought of Hannah Arendt," *Political Theory* 33, no. 2 (2005), 181–82; Claude Piché, "The Philosopher-Artist: A Note on Lyotard's Reading of Kant," *Research in Phenomenology* 22, no. 1 (1992), 158; James Williams, *Lyotard and the Political* (New York: Routledge, 2000), 120. I discuss these interpretations farther down.
4. Jean-François Lyotard, *The Postmodern Condition: A Report on Knowledge*, trans. Geoffrey Bennington and Brian Massumi (Minneapolis, MN: Minnesota University Press, 1984), xxiv.
5. Ibid., 29.
6. Ibid., 30.
7. Ibid., 65.
8. Ibid.
9. Ibid., 66.
10. Jean-François Lyotard and Jean-Loup Thébaud, *Just Gaming*, trans. Wlad Godzich (Minneapolis, MN: Minnesota University Press, 1985), 96.
11. Ibid., 99.
12. Ibid., 72.
13. Ibid., 23.
14. Ibid., 15.
15. David Ingram, "The Postmodern Kantianism of Arendt and Lyotard," in *Judging Lyotard*, ed. Andrew Benjamin (New York: Routledge, 1992), 136.
16. Samuel Weber, "Afterword," in *Just Gaming*, 105.
17. Jean-Luc Nancy, "Dies irae," in *La faculté de juger*, by Jacques Derrida et al. (Paris: Éditions de Minuit, 1985), 14; my translation.
18. Jean-François Lyotard, *Enthusiasm: The Kantian Critique of History*, trans. Georges Van Den Abbeele (Stanford, CA: Stanford University Press, 2009), xvii.
19. Ibid.
20. Ibid.
21. Jean-François Lyotard, *Lessons on the Analytic of the Sublime*, trans. Elizabeth Rottenberg (Stanford, CA: Stanford University Press, 1994), 8.
22. Ibid., 6.
23. Ibid.
24. Ibid., 13.
25. Ibid., 12.
26. Ibid., 82.
27. Ibid., 88–89.

28. Ibid., 208–9; Immanuel Kant, *Critique of the Power of Judgment*, ed. Paul Guyer, trans. Paul Guyer and Eric Matthews (Cambridge, UK: Cambridge University Press, 2000), 214; 5:338.

29. Lyotard, *Lessons*, 210. Kant, *Critique of the Power of Judgment*, 216; 5:341.

30. Lyotard, *Lessons*, 214.

31. Ibid., 215.

32. Ibid., 216.

33. Ibid., 222.

34. Ibid., 180.

35. Kant, *Critique of the Power of Judgment*, 141; 5:257.

36. Lyotard, *Lessons*, 122.

37. Ibid., 150.

38. Jean-François Lyotard, *The Differend: Phrases in Dispute*, trans. George Van Den Abbeele (Manchester, UK: Manchester University Press, 1988), 13.

39. Ibid., 27.

40. Ibid., 13.

41. Ibid., 56.

42. Ibid., 13.

43. Ibid., 130–31.

44. Ibid., 123.

45. Lyotard, *The Differend*, 13.

46. Kant, *Critique of the Power of Judgment*, 141; 5:258.

47. Lyotard, *The Differend*, 141.

48. Ibid., 133.

49. Geoffrey Bennington, *Lyotard: Writing the Event* (New York: Columbia University Press, 1988), 177.

50. Zerilli, "'We Feel Our Freedom,'" 181.

51. Lyotard, *The Differend*, 140.

52. Ibid.

53. Ibid., 147.

54. Lyotard, *Enthusiasm*, 22.

55. Piché, "The Philosopher-Artist," 158.

56. Immanuel Kant, *The Conflict of the Faculties*, trans. Mary J. Gregor and Robert Anchor, in *Religion and Rational Theology*, eds. Allen W. Wood and George di Giovanni (Cambridge, UK: Cambridge University Press, 2001), 301; 7:84.

57. Ibid.

58. Ibid., 302; 7:85.

59. Kant, *Critique of the Power of Judgment*, 154; 5:272; translation modified by author.

60. Lyotard, *Enthusiasm*, 32.

61. Ibid., 21.

62. Ibid., 34.

63. Ibid.
64. Ibid., 39.
65. Lyotard, *The Differend*, 171.
66. Ibid., 172.
67. Ibid., 171.
68. Jean-François Lyotard, *Political Writings*, trans. Bill Readings and Kevin Paul Geiman (London: University College London Press, 1993), 7.
69. Williams, *Lyotard and the Political*, 120.

Conclusion

1. Richard J. Bernstein, *The Abuses of Evil: The Corruption of Politics and Religion since 9/11* (Cambridge, UK: Polity, 2005), 12.
2. Ibid., 13.
3. María Pía Lara, *Narrating Evil: A Post-metaphysical Theory of Reflective Judgment* (New York: Columbia University Press, 2007).
4. Bernstein, *The Abuses of Evil*; Simona Forti, *New Demons: Rethinking Evil and Power Today*, trans. Zakiya Hanafi (Stanford, CA: Stanford University Press, 2015).
5. Max Weber, "Politics as Vocation," in *The Vocation Lectures*, eds. David Owen and Tracy B. Strong, trans. Rodney Livingstone (Indianapolis, IN: Hackett, 2004).
6. Hans Jonas, *The Imperative of Responsibility: In Search of an Ethics for the Technological Age* (Chicago, IL: University of Chicago Press, 1985).
7. Iris Marion Young, *Responsibility for Injustice* (Oxford, UK: Oxford University Press, 2011).
8. Shalini Satkunanandan, *Extraordinary Responsibility: Politics beyond the Moral Calculus* (Cambridge, UK: Cambridge University Press, 2015), 186–88.
9. Hannah Arendt, "Karl Jaspers: A Laudatio," in *Men in Dark Times* (New York: Harcourt, Brace & World, 1988), 75.
10. Ibid., 77.
11. Ibid.
12. Axel Honneth presents an overview of the critique of reason in the Frankfurt School in *Pathologies of Reason: On the Legacy of Critical Theory*, trans. James Ingram (New York: Columbia University Press, 2009), chapter 2.
13. Theodor W. Adorno, *Minima Moralia: Reflections from Damaged Life*, trans. E. F. N. Jephcott (London: Verso, 2006), 16.
14. Ibid., 108.
15. Theodor W. Adorno, "Education after Auschwitz," in *Critical Models: Interventions and Catchwords*, trans. Henry W. Pickford (New York: Columbia University Press, 2005), 193; *Problems of Moral Philosophy*, trans. Thomas Schröder

(Stanford, CA: Stanford University Press, 2001), 4; *Negative Dialectics*, trans. E. B. Ashton (New York: Routledge, 2004), 216–17.

16. Ibid., 219.

17. Claude Lefort, *Democracy and Political Theory*, trans. David Macey (Cambridge, UK: Polity, 1988), 17.

18. Ibid.

19. Ibid., 20.

20. Adorno, *Negative Dialectics*, 365–68; Judith N. Shklar, "The Liberalism of Fear," in *Liberalism and Moral Life*, ed. Nancy L. Rosenblum (Cambridge, MA: Harvard University Press, 1989).

21. Linda M. G. Zerilli, *A Democratic Theory of Judgment* (Chicago, IL: University of Chicago Press, 2017), 183.

22. Ibid.

23. Gérald Sfez, *Machiavel, la politique du moindre mal* (Paris: Presses Universitaires de France, 1999), 163, my translation.

24. Arendt, "Personal Responsibility under Dictatorship," in *Responsibility and Judgment*, ed. Jerome Kohn (New York: Schocken, 2003), 36.

25. Hannah Arendt, *Lectures on Kant's Political Philosophy*, ed. Ronald Beiner (Chicago, IL: University of Chicago Press, 1992), 51.

Bibliography

Adorno, Theodor W. *Critical Models: Interventions and Catchwords*. Translated by Henry W. Pickford. New York: Columbia University Press, 2005.
———. *Minima Moralia: Reflections from Damaged Life*. Translated by E. F. N. Jephcott. London: Verso, 2006.
———. *Negative Dialectics*. Translated by E. B. Ashton. New York: Routledge, 2004.
———. *Problems of Moral Philosophy*. Translated by Thomas Schröder. Stanford, CA: Stanford University Press, 2001.
Allison, Henry E. *Idealism and Freedom: Essays on Kant's Theoretical and Practical Philosophy*. New York: Cambridge University Press, 1996.
———. *Kant's Theory of Freedom*. New York: Cambridge University Press, 1990.
———. *Kant's Theory of Taste: A Reading of the Critique of Aesthetic Judgment*. Cambridge, UK: Cambridge University Press, 2001.
Arendt, Hannah. "Basic Moral Propositions," 1966. Courses—University of Chicago, Series: Subject File, 1949–1975. The Hannah Arendt Papers, Manuscript Division, Library of Congress, Washington, DC.
———. *Between Past and Future*. New York: Penguin, 2006.
———. *Denktagebuch*. Edited by Ursula Ludz and Ingeborg Nordmann. Munich, Germany: Piper, 2002.
———. *Eichmann in Jerusalem: A Report on the Banality of Evil*. New York: Penguin, 2006.
———. *Essays in Understanding*. Edited by Jerome Kohn. New York: Schocken, 1994.
———. *Lectures on Kant's Political Philosophy*. Edited by Ronald Beiner. Chicago, IL: University of Chicago Press, 1992.
———. *Men in Dark Times*. New York: Harcourt, Brace & World, 1988.
———. *On Revolution*. New York: Penguin, 1965.
———. "Political Theory of Kant," 1953. Subject File, 1949–1975. Hannah Arendt Papers, Manuscript Division, Library of Congress, Washington, DC.

———. *Responsibility and Judgment*. Edited by Jerome Kohn. New York: Schocken, 2003.

———. *The Human Condition*. Chicago, IL: University of Chicago Press, 1998.

———. *The Jewish Writings*. Edited by Jerome Kohn and Ron H. Feldman. New York: Schocken, 2007.

———. *The Life of the Mind*. Orlando, FL: Harcourt, 1978.

———. *The Origins of Totalitarianism*. New York: Harcourt Brace & Company, 1976.

———. *Vita activa, Oder vom tätigen Leben*. Stuttgart, Germany: R. Piper, 1960.

Arendt, Hannah, and Karl Jaspers. *Correspondence: 1926–1969*. Edited by Lotte Kohler and Hans Saner. New York: Harcourt Brace Jovanovich, 1992.

Aristotle. *Ethica Nicomachea*. In *The Basic Works of Aristotle*, edited by Richard McKeon. New York: Random House, 2001.

Badiou, Alain. *Ethics: An Essay on the Understanding of Evil*. Translated by Peter Hallward. London: Verso, 2001.

Beck, Lewis White. *A Commentary on Kant's Critique of Practical Reason*. Chicago, IL: University of Chicago Press, 1984.

———. *Early German Philosophy: Kant and His Predecessors*. Cambridge, MA: Harvard University Press, 1969.

———. "Five Concepts of Freedom in Kant." In *Stephan Körner—Philosophical Analysis and Reconstruction*, edited by Jan T. J. Srzednicki. Dordrecht, the Netherlands: Martinus Nijhoff, 1987.

Beiner, Ronald. "Interpretative Essay." In *Lectures on Kant's Political Philosophy*, by Hannah Arendt, edited by Ronald Beiner. Chicago, IL: University of Chicago Press, 1992.

———. "Kant, the Sublime, and Nature." In *Kant and Political Philosophy*, edited by Ronald Beiner and William James Booth. New Haven, CT: Yale University Press, 1993.

———. "Rereading Hannah Arendt's Kant Lectures." In *Judgment, Imagination, and Politics: Themes from Kant and Arendt*, edited by Ronald Beiner and Jennifer Nedelsky. Oxford, UK: Rowman & Littlefield, 2001.

Benhabib, Seyla. "Judgment and the Moral Foundations of Politics in Hannah Arendt's Thought." In *Judgment, Imagination, and Politics: Themes from Kant and Arendt*, edited by Ronald Beiner and Jennifer Nedelsky. Oxford, UK: Rowman & Littlefield, 2001.

Bennington, Geoffrey. *Lyotard: Writing the Event*. New York: Columbia University Press, 1988.

Bernstein, Richard J. "Did Hannah Arendt Change Her Mind? From Radical Evil to the Banality of Evil." In *Hannah Arendt: Twenty Years Later*, edited by Larry May and Jerome Kohn. Cambridge, UK: Cambridge University Press, 1999.

———. *Philosophical Profiles: Essays in Pragmatic Mode*. Philadelphia: University of Pennsylvania Press, 1986.

———. *Radical Evil: A Philosophical Interrogation*. Cambridge, UK: Polity, 2008.

———. *The Abuses of Evil: The Corruption of Politics and Religion since 9/11*. Cambridge, UK: Polity, 2005.

Bilsky, Leora Y. "When Actor and Spectator Meet in the Courtroom: Reflections on Hannah Arendt's Concept of Judgment." In *Judgment, Imagination, and Politics: Themes from Kant and Arendt*, edited by Ronald Beiner and Jennifer Nedelsky. Oxford, UK: Rowman & Littlefield, 2001.

Birmingham, Peg. "Hannah Arendt's Double Account of Evil: Political Superfluousness and Moral Thoughtlessness." In *The Routledge Handbook of the Philosophy of Evil*, edited by Thomas Nys and Stephen de Wijze. London: Routledge, 2019.

———. "Holes of Oblivion: The Banality of Radical Evil." *Hypatia* 18, no. 1 (2003): 80–103.

Brecht, Martin. "August Hermann Francke und der hallische Pietismus." In *Geschichte des Pietismus*. Göttingen, Germany: Vandenhoeck & Ruprecht, 1993.

Browning, Christopher R. *Ordinary Men: Reserve Police Battalion 101 and the Final Solution in Poland*. London: Penguin, 2001.

Butler, Judith. "Hanna Arendt's Death Sentences." *Comparative Literature Studies* 48, no. 3 (2011): 280–95.

Canovan, Margaret. *Hannah Arendt: A Reinterpretation of Her Political Thought*. Cambridge, UK: Cambridge University Press, 1992.

Cassirer, Ernst. *Kant's Life and Thought*. Translated by James Haden. New Haven, CT: Yale University Press, 1981.

Clark, Christopher. *Iron Kingdom: The Rise and Downfall of Prussia, 1600–1947*. Cambridge, UK: Harvard University Press, 2006.

Clewis, Robert R. *The Kantian Sublime and the Revelation of Freedom*. Cambridge, UK: Cambridge University Press, 2009.

Cloutier, Sophie. "La question du mal chez Hannah Arendt: Rupture ou continuité?" *PhaenEx* 3, no. 1 (2008): 82–111.

Connolly, William E. *The Ethos of Pluralization*. Minneapolis, MN: Minnesota University Press, 2004.

———. *Why I Am Not a Secularist*. Minneapolis, MN: Minnesota University Press, 1999.

Critchley, Simon. *Infinitely Demanding: Ethics of Commitment, Politics of Resistance*. London: Verso, 2008.

Crowther, Paul. *The Kantian Sublime: From Morality to Art*. Oxford, UK: Clarendon Press, 1989.

Delpla, Isabelle. *Le mal en procès: Eichmann et les théodicées modernes*. Paris: Hermann, 2011.

Derrida, Jacques. "Lyotard and Us." *Parallax* 6, no. 4 (2000): 28–48.
Despland, Michel. *Kant on History and Religion*. London: McGill–Queen's University Press, 1973.
Dews, Peter. *The Idea of Evil*. Malden, MA: Blackwell, 2008.
Dietz, Mary. "Arendt and the Holocaust." In *The Cambridge Companion to Hannah Arendt*, edited by Dana Villa. New York: Cambridge University Press, 2002.
Diprose, Rosalyn. "Arendt and Nietzsche on Responsibility and Futurity." *Philosophy and Social Criticism* 34, no. 6 (2008): 300–16.
Disch, Lisa Jane. *Hannah Arendt and the Limits of Philosophy*. Ithaca, NY: Cornell University Press, 1994.
Dostal, Robert J. "Judging Human Action: Arendt's Appropriation of Kant." *Review of Metaphysics* 37, no. 4 (1984): 725–55.
Fenves, Peter. *Late Kant: Towards Another Law of the Earth*. New York: Routledge, 2003.
———. "Taking Stock of the Kantian Sublime." *Eighteenth-Century Studies* 28, no. 1 (1994): 65–82.
Ferrarin, Alfredo. "Imagination and Judgment in Kant's Practical Philosophy." *Philosophy and Social Criticism* 34, no. 1–2 (2008): 101–21.
Formosa, Paul. "Is Radical Evil Banal? Is Banal Evil Radical?" *Philosophy and Social Criticism* 33, no. 6 (2007): 717–35.
Forti, Simona. *New Demons: Rethinking Evil and Power Today*. Translated by Zakiya Hanafi. Stanford, CA: Stanford University Press, 2015.
Fuchs, Édith. "La 'banalité du mal' comme absence de pensée selon Hannah Arendt." In *Destins de "la banalité du mal,"* edited by Michelle-Irène Brundy and Jean-Marie Winkler, 147–62. Paris: Editions de l'Éclat, 2011.
Fulbrook, Mary. *Piety and Politics: Religion and the Rise of Absolutism in England, Wüttemberg and Prussia*. Cambridge, UK: Cambridge University Press, 1983.
Gasché, Rodolphe. *The Idea of Form: Rethinking Kant's Aesthetics*. Stanford, CA: Stanford University Press, 2002.
Gawthrop, Richard. *Pietism and the Making of Eighteenth-Century Prussia*. Cambridge, UK: Cambridge University Press, 1993.
Goldhagen, Daniel Jonah. *Hitler's Willing Executioners: Ordinary Germans and the Holocaust*. New York: Alfred A. Knopf, 1996.
Guyer, Paul. "Kant's Distinction between the Beautiful and the Sublime." *Review of Metaphysics* 35, no. 4 (1982): 753–83.
Habermas, Jürgen. *The Philosophical Discourse of Modernity: Twelve Lectures*. Translated by Frederick Lawrence. Cambridge, UK: Polity, 1992.
Hegel, G. W. F. *Lectures on the Philosophy of World History*. Translated by H. B. Nisbet. Cambridge, UK: Cambridge University Press, 1981.
Heidegger, Martin. *Being and Time*. Translated by John Macquarrie and Edward Robinson. Oxford, UK: Basil Blackwell, 1985.

Henrich, Dieter. "Der Begriff der sittlichen Einsicht und Kants Lehre vom Faktum der Vernunft." In *Kant: Zur Deutung seiner Theorie von Erkennen und Handeln*, edited by Gerold Prauss. Cologne, Germany: Krepenheuer & Witsch, 1973.

Honig, Bonnie. *Political Theory and the Displacement of Politics*. Ithaca, NY: Cornell University Press, 1993.

Honneth, Axel. *Pathologies of Reason: On the Legacy of Critical Theory*. Translated by James Ingram. New York: Columbia University Press, 2009.

Hunter, Ian. *Rival Enlightenments: Civil and Metaphysical Philosophy in Early Modern Germany*. Cambridge, UK: Cambridge University Press, 2003.

Ingram, David. "The Postmodern Kantianism of Arendt and Lyotard." In *Judging Lyotard*, edited by Andrew Benjamin. New York: Routledge, 1992.

Jaspers, Karl. *Rechenschaft und Ausblick. Rede und Aufsätze*. Munich: R. Piper, 1958.

———. *The Question of German Guilt*. Translated by E. B. Ashton. New York: Fordham University Press, 2000.

Kamber, Richard. "The Logic of the Goldhagen Debate." *Res Publica* 6 (2000): 155–77.

Kant, Immanuel. "Critique of Practical Reason." In *Practical Philosophy*, edited by Mary J. Gregor. New York: Cambridge University Press, 1999.

———. *Critique of Pure Reason*. Edited by Paul Guyer and Allen W. Wood. New York: Cambridge University Press, 2000.

———. *Critique of the Power of Judgment*. Edited by Paul Guyer. Translated by Paul Guyer and Eric Matthews. Cambridge, UK: Cambridge University Press, 2000.

———. "Groundwork of the Metaphysics of Morals." In *Practical Philosophy*, edited by Mary J. Gregor. New York: Cambridge University Press, 1999.

———. *Lectures on Ethics*. Edited by Peter Heath and J. B. Schneewind. New York: Cambridge University Press, 1997.

———. "On the Common Saying: That May Be Correct in Theory, but It Is of No Use in Practice." In *Practical Philosophy*, edited by Mary J. Gregor. New York: Cambridge University Press, 1999.

———. "Religion within the Boundaries of Mere Reason." In *Religion and Rational Theology*, edited by Allen W. Wood and George di Giovanni. New York: Cambridge University Press, 2001.

———. "The Conflict of the Faculties." In *Religion and Rational Theology*, edited by Allen W. Wood and George di Giovanni, translated by Mary J. Gregor and Robert Anchor. Cambridge, UK: Cambridge University Press, 2001.

Kawamura, Katsutoshi. *Spontaneität und Willkür: Der Freiheitsbegriff in Kants Antinomienlehre und seine historischen Wurzeln*. Stuttgart, Germany: Frommann Holzboog, 1996.

Kuehn, Manfred. *Kant: A Biography*. New York: Cambridge University Press, 2001.

Laclau, Ernesto, and Chantal Mouffe. *Hegemony and Socialist Strategy: Towards a Radical Democratic Politics*. London: Verso, 2013.

Lara, María Pía. *Narrating Evil: A Post-Metaphysical Theory of Reflective Judgment*. New York: Columbia University Press, 2007.

Lefort, Claude. *Democracy and Political Theory*. Translated by David Macey. Cambridge, UK: Polity, 1988.

———. *The Political Forms of Modern Society: Bureaucracy, Democracy, Totalitarianism*. Edited by David Thompson. Cambridge, MA: MIT Press, 1986.

Leibniz, G. W., and Samuel Clarke. *Correspondence*. Edited by Roger Ariew. Indianapolis, IN: Hackett, 2000.

Lestition, Steven. "Kant and the End of the Enlightenment in Prussia." *Journal of Modern History* 65, no. 1 (1993): 57–112.

Love, Jeff, and Michael Meng. "A Troubling Banality." *Constellations* 23, no. 4 (2016): 585–95.

Lyotard, Jean-François. *Enthusiasm: The Kantian Critique of History*. Translated by Georges Van Den Abbeele. Stanford, CA: Stanford University Press, 2009.

———. *Lessons on the Analytic of the Sublime*. Translated by Elizabeth Rottenberg. Stanford, CA: Stanford University Press, 1994.

———. *Political Writings*. Translated by Bill Readings and Kevin Paul Geiman. London: University College London Press, 1993.

———. *The Differend: Phrases in Dispute*. Translated by Georges Van Den Abbeele. Minneapolis, MN: Minnesota University Press, 1989.

———. *The Postmodern Condition: A Report on Knowledge*. Translated by Geoffrey Bennington and Brian Massumi. Minneapolis, MN: Minnesota University Press, 1984.

Lyotard, Jean-François, and Jean-Loup Thébaud. *Just Gaming*. Translated by Wlad Godzich. Minneapolis, MN: Minnesota University Press, 1985.

Mack, Michael. "The Holocaust and Hannah Arendt's Philosophical Critique of Philosophy: *Eichmann in Jerusalem*." *New German Critique* 36, no. 1 (2009): 35–60.

Makkreel, Rudolf. *Imagination and Interpretation in Kant: The Hermeneutical Import of the Critique of Judgment*. Chicago, IL: University of Chicago Press, 1994.

Markell, Patchen. *Bound by Recognition*. Princeton, NJ: Princeton University Press, 2003.

Marshall, David. "The Origin and Character of Hannah Arendt's Theory of Judgment." *Political Theory* 38, no. 3 (2010): 367–93.

Mathewes, Charles T. *Evil and the Augustinian Tradition*. Cambridge, UK: Cambridge University Press, 2004.

Matthews, Patricia M. "Kant's Sublime: A Form of Pure Aesthetic Reflective Judgment." *Journal of Art and Criticism* 54, no. 2 (1996): 165–80.

Menke, Christoph. "Auf der Grenze des Rechts: Hannah Arendts Revision des Eichmann-Prozesses." *Merkur* 67, no. 7 (2013): 227–56.
Michalson, Gordon E. *Fallen Freedom: Kant on Radical Evil and Moral Regeneration.* Cambridge, UK: Cambridge University Press, 1990.
Munzel, G. Felicitas. *Kant's Conception of Moral Character: The "Critical" Link of Morality, Anthropology, and Reflective Judgment.* Chicago, IL: University of Chicago Press, 1999.
Myers, Ella. *Worldly Ethics: Democratic Politics and Care for the World.* Durham, NC: Duke University Press, 2013.
Nahm, Milton C. "'Sublimity' and the 'Moral Law' in Kant's Philosophy." *Kant-Studien* 48 (1956): 502–24.
Nancy, Jean-Luc. "Dies irae." In *La faculté de juger*, by Jacques Derrida, Vincent Descombes, Garbis Kortian, Philippe Lacoue-Labarthe, Jean-François Lyotard, and Jean-Luc Nancy. Paris: Éditions de Minuit, 1985.
———. *L'impératif catégorique.* Paris: Flammarion, 1983.
———. *The Experience of Freedom.* Translated by Bridget McDonald. Stanford, CA: Stanford University Press, 1988.
Neiman, Susan. *Evil in Modern Thought: An Alternative History of Philosophy.* Princeton, NJ: Princeton University Press, 2004.
Norris, Andrew. "Arendt, Kant, and the Politics of Common Sense." *Polity* 29, no. 2 (1996): 165–91.
Ophir, Adi. "Between Eichmann and Kant: Thinking on Evil after Arendt." *History and Memory* 8, no. 2 (1996): 89–136.
Piché, Claude. "The Philosopher-Artist: A Note on Lyotard's Reading of Kant." *Research in Phenomenology* 22, no. 1 (1992): 152–60.
Pitkin, Hanna Fenichel. *The Attack of the Blob: Hannah Arendt's Concept of the Social.* Chicago, IL: University of Chicago Press, 1998.
Plato. *The Republic of Plato.* Translated by Allan Bloom. New York: Basic Books, 1991.
Plotinus. *The Enneads.* Edited by John Dillon. Translated by Stephan MacKenna. New York: Penguin, 1991.
Rancière, Jacques. *Disagreement: Politics and Philosophy.* Translated by Julie Rose. Minneapolis, MN: Minnesota University Press, 1999.
Rawls, John. *The Law of Peoples.* Cambridge, MA: Harvard University Press, 2000.
Reboul, Olivier. *Kant et le problème du mal.* Montreal, QC: Montreal University Press, 1971.
Reinhold, Carl Leonhard. "Erörterung des Begriffs von der Freiheit des Willens." In *Materialen zu Kants "Kritik der praktischen Vernunft,"* edited by Rudiger Bittner and Konrad Cramer. Frankfurt am Main, Germany: Suhrkampf, 1975.
Saint Augustine. *City of God.* Translated by Henry Bettenson. London: Penguin, 2003.

Satkunanandan, Shalini. *Extraordinary Responsibility: Politics beyond the Moral Calculus.* Cambridge, UK: Cambridge University Press, 2015.

———. "The Extraordinary Categorical Imperative." *Political Theory* 39, no. 2 (2011): 234–60.

Schaller, Klaus. "Pietismus und moderne Pädagogik." In *Pietismus und moderne Welt*, edited by Kurt Aland. Witten, Germany: Luther-Verlag, 1974.

Schaper, Eva. "Taste, Sublimity, and Genius: The Aesthetics of Nature and Art." In *The Cambridge Companion to Kant*, edited by Paul Guyer. Cambridge, UK: Cambridge University Press, 2006.

Schneewind, J. B. *The Invention of Autonomy: A History of Modern Moral Philosophy.* New York: Cambridge University Press, 1998.

Schupmann, Benjamin A. "Thoughtlessness and Resentment: Determinism and Moral Responsibility in the Case of Adolf Eichmann." *Philosophy and Social Criticism* 40, no. 2 (2014).

Schwartz, Jonathan P. *Arendt's Judgment: Freedom, Responsibility, Citizenship.* Philadelphia: University of Pennsylvania Press, 2016.

Sfez, Gérald. *Machiavel, la politique du moindre mal.* Paris: Presses Universitaires de France, 1999.

Shell, Susan Meld. *Kant and the Limits of Autonomy.* Cambridge, MA: Harvard University Press, 2009.

Shklar, Judith N. "The Liberalism of Fear." In *Liberalism and Moral Life*, edited by Nancy L. Rosenblum. Cambridge, MA: Harvard University Press, 1989.

Spener, Philipp Jackob. *Der neue Mensch.* Edited by Hans-Georg Feller. Stuttgart, Germany: J. F. Steinkopf, 1966.

Spinoza, Baruch. *The Letters.* Translated by Samuel Shirley. New York: Hackett, 1995.

Stangneth, Bettina. *Eichmann before Jerusalem: The Unexamined Life of a Mass Murderer.* New York: Vintage, 2015.

Villa, Dana R. "Beyond Good and Evil: Arendt, Nietzsche, and the Aestheticization of Political Action." *Political Theory* 20, no. 2 (1992): 274–308.

———. *Politics, Philosophy, Terror: Essays on the Thought of Hannah Arendt.* Princeton, NJ: Princeton University Press, 1999.

Wallmann, Johannes. "Was ist Pietismut?" *Pietusmus und Neuzeut* 20 (1994): 11–27.

Watkins, Eric, ed. *Kant's Critique of Pure Reason: Background Source Materials.* New York: Cambridge University Press, 2009.

Weber, Max. *The Vocation Lectures.* Edited by David Owen and Tracy B. Strong. Translated by Rodney Livingstone. Indianapolis, IN: Hackett, 2004.

White, Stephen K. *The Ethos of a Late-Modern Citizen.* Cambridge, MA: Harvard University Press, 2009.

Williams, Garrath. "Disclosure and Responsibility in Arendt's *The Human Condition*." *European Journal of Political Theory* 14, no. 1 (2014): 37–45.

Williams, James. *Lyotard and the Political*. New York: Routledge, 2000.
Wood, Allen W. *Kant's Moral Religion*. Ithaca, NY: Cornell University Press, 1970.
Young, Iris Marion. *Responsibility for Injustice*. Oxford, UK: Oxford University Press, 2011.
Zammito, John. *The Genesis of Kant's Critique of Judgment*. Chicago, IL: University of Chicago Press, 1992.
Zerilli, Linda M. G. *A Democratic Theory of Judgment*. Chicago, IL: University of Chicago Press, 2017.
———. "'We Feel Our Freedom': Imagination and Judgment in the Thought of Hannah Arendt." *Political Theory* 33, no. 2 (2005): 158–88.
Žižek, Slavoj. *The Sublime Object of Ideology*. London: Verso, 2008.
Zupančič, Alenka. *Ethics of the Real: Kant, Lacan*. London: Verso, 2000.

Index

Adorno, Theodor W., 2n4, 161–62, 165
Allison, Henry, 65, 76, 88, 106, 109
Aristotle, 7
Augustine of Hippo, 7
Auschwitz, 2n4, 167
Authoritarianism, 2, 161
Autonomy, 65, 68, 74–76, 98, 161

Badiou, Allain, 21
Baumgarten, Alexander, 72, 103
Beginning, 42–45, 49, 60, 71
Beautiful, the, 111–12, 114–15, 115n74, 115n75, 130, 136–37, 147
Benhabib, Seyla, 98–101, 165
Bernstein, Richard, 3, 7–8, 22–23, 101n29, 154–55
Biopolitics, 17, 155
Browning, Christopher, 15–16
Bureaucracy, 19, 50, 82

Camps, 2, 4, 6–7, 33, 35–36, 39, 44, 51, 66, 139, 153, 161
Categorical imperative, 66, 81n64, 96, 140
Causality, 42–43, 70–76, 102, 105, 117–18, 140, 147
Choice [Willkür], 28, 64–65, 69–80, 86, 108
Common sense, 97–99, 124

Conscience, 51–53, 58, 96
Crime, 5–6, 8, 13–16, 35, 38, 50–52, 54, 56, 60, 68, 70, 139, 156, 158

Democracy, 153, 161, 163; theory of, 21–22, 163–64
Derrida, Jacques, 127
Differend, 19, 29, 120, 127, 137–39, 141–144, 148–51, 170
Disclosure, 27, 34, 41, 44–45, 49, 60–61
Domination, 11, 37, 132; total, 36–37
Duty, 16–17, 51–52, 62, 65–67, 79–80, 83–86, 89, 96, 103–04, 106–08, 118, 120, 124, 156, 158

Eichmann, Adolf, 13, 15–19, 27–28, 33, 49–52, 54–56, 60–63, 65–70, 85–86, 88–90, 95–96, 123–24, 155–59, 163; trial of, 14, 33, 50, 61, 96, 155–56
Egoism, 33, 55
Enlightenment, 2, 65, 80–81, 129
Enthusiasm, 29, 109, 120–124, 133, 146, 148, 150
Extremism, 160–62

Fetish, 84, 86–87
Final Solution, 14, 51, 66, 96

206 | Index

Forgiveness, 40, 46–48, 61, 157, 164
Francke, August Hermann, 82, 87n89
Freedom, 6, 28, 39, 42, 48, 64, 67–77, 80–81, 101–2, 105, 111, 120, 145, 155, 161–62

Goldhagen, Daniel, 15
Good, the, 4, 6–7, 11, 20–21, 81, 83, 85, 104, 121–22, 127, 143, 152, 165, 169–71
Guilt, 39–40, 48, 52, 56, 87, 103, 50n61, 87n90
Guyer, Paul, 115

Habermas, Jürgen, 20, 165–66
Hatred, 8, 16, 33, 55, 63, 158
Hegel, Georg Wilhelm Friedrich, 7
Heidegger, Martin, 64, 87, 87n90
Hitler, Adolf, 15, 70
Horkheimer, Max, 161

Identity, 14, 27, 34, 44–46, 48–49, 53, 57, 60–61, 69, 141, 163
Ideology, 17, 19, 21, 23, 35, 40, 89, 163
Ignorance, 7–8
Imagination, 28, 96n8, 97, 99, 100–1, 105–6, 109–14, 115n74, 117–24, 135, 137–38, 140, 146–47
Imputability, 42, 45, 70–73, 76, 78, 80, 83, 86, 107
Inclinations, 51, 73–80, 84, 111, 117–18, 122–23
Injustice, 7, 11, 23–24, 131, 151, 156, 170–71

Jaspers, Karl, 64, 69–70, 87–90, 87–88, 159
Jesus of Nazareth, 47
Jonas, Hans, 156
Justice, 11, 99, 103, 129–33, 142, 151, 161, 170–71

Laclau, Ernesto, 21
Law, 4, 29, 37, 39–40, 52, 66–68, 71–76, 79–80, 84–86, 89, 102, 105–7, 114, 116–18, 122, 131–32, 136, 138–42, 155, 157–59, 163–65; moral, 28, 64, 70, 74–75, 79, 103, 105–6, 109–10, 117–22, 124, 140; of the land, 60, 66, 86, 89, 155, 158, 168
Leader, 8, 37–38, 63, 153, 161
Lefort, Claude, 21, 163–64
Leibniz, Gottfried Wilhelm, 7, 72, 80

Machiavelli, Niccolò, 169–70
Mass murder, 2, 5, 13, 15, 17, 36, 63, 96
Motivation, 5, 7–8, 13, 16–18, 20, 28, 33, 35–36, 38, 49–51, 55, 63, 67–68, 75, 89, 90, 164
Mouffe, Chantal, 21

Nancy, Jean-Luc, 6–7, 78, 132
National-Socialism, 14–15
Nietzsche, Friedrich, 17

Personality, 38, 53–54, 59–60, 63, 69
Phrase, 51, 128, 133–34, 139–42, 144, 147–50
Pietism, 82, 83n76
Plato, 7, 59, 129
Plotinus, 7
Pluralism, 12, 127, 164–65, 171; value, 12, 127
Plurality, 47–48, 127–28, 132–33, 152
Prussia, 82
Postmodernity, 29, 127–29, 143, 149–52
Punishment, 39–40, 61, 164

Rancière, Jacques, 22–23

Rawls, John, 20, 98–100, 165–66
Reason, 2, 7, 21, 26, 28–29, 63, 66–69, 71–77, 79–83, 96n8, 101–5, 109–16, 115n74, 117, 119–24, 134–35, 137–38, 140, 148, 161; idea of, 100, 105, 112, 114–15, 119–20, 137–38, 146, 151
Recognition, 23, 166
Rousseau, Jean-Jacques, 67

Sacrifice, 67, 84, 86, 89–90, 96, 108, 118–20, 122–24, 156
Shklar, Judith, 165
Sin, 47
Spener, Philipp, 82, 83n75
Spinoza, Baruch, 7
Spontaneity, 27, 36, 40, 42–43, 45, 68, 71–74, 76–77
Sublime, the, 28–29, 93–95, 101, 101n30, 106n48, 109–25, 115n74–76, 118n88, 129, 133, 136–39, 141–44, 146–151, 167–68, 170–71

Terror, 1–2, 40, 67, 130–31, 143–44
Theodicy, 6
Thinking, 14, 22, 26–27, 37, 52–62, 69, 80, 99, 102, 114, 134–35, 138, 146, 148–50, 159; representative, 58, 60, 99, 166
Trespassing, 47

Uncertainty, 4, 8–14, 17, 19, 21–22, 26–27, 33–34, 44–46, 49, 55–56, 59, 61–65, 76, 80, 83–84, 86, 89–90, 93, 125, 128, 152–54, 157, 161–65, 168–69, 171
Universality, 11, 29, 84, 100, 125, 127–29, 144, 147–49, 151, 166–67
Unpredictability, 9–10, 21, 44–47, 62

Virtue, 9, 11, 16, 20, 42–43, 45–48, 52, 60, 62, 64, 67, 79–80, 84–90, 97, 100, 104, 111, 115–118, 120–21, 123–24, 138, 148, 150–52, 156–57, 162, 166, 168

War, 2, 5, 14, 16, 35, 118; World War II, 1, 161
Weber, Max, 156
Weber, Samuel, 132, 156
Web of human relationships, 48, 60
Wilhelm I, Frederick, 82–83
Wilhelm II, Frederick, 81, 87
Will, the, 38, 66–69, 73–75, 86, 155–56
Wolff, Christian, 72
Wöllner, Johann Christoph, 81

Young, Iris Marion, 156

Žižek, Slavoj, 21

www.ingramcontent.com/pod-product-compliance
Lightning Source LLC
Chambersburg PA
CBHW030651230426
43665CB00011B/1048